PERSPECTIVES ON MARRIAGE AND THE FAMILY
Bert N. Adams and Reuben Hill, Editors

COMMUTER MARRIAGE:
A STUDY OF WORK AND FAMILY
Naomi Gerstel and Harriet Gross

WIFE BATTERING:
A SYSTEMS THEORY APPROACH
Jean Giles-Sims

COMMUTER MARRIAGE

A Study of Work and Family

NAOMI GERSTEL
University of Massachusetts, Amherst

HARRIET GROSS
Governors State University

FOREWORD BY BERT N. ADAMS

THE GUILFORD PRESS
New York   London

© 1984 The Guilford Press
A Division of Guilford Publications, Inc.
200 Park Avenue South, New York, N.Y. 10003

Printed in the United States of America

LIBRARY OF CONGRESS CATALOGING IN PUBLICATION DATA

Gerstel, Naomi.
    Commuter marriage.

    (Perspectives on marriage and the family)
    Bibliography: p.
    Includes index.
    1. Marriage—United States.   2. Married people—
Employment—United States.   3. Married people—United
States—Social conditions.   I. Gross, Harriet.
II. Title.   III. Series.
HQ734.G425   1984   306.8'1'0973   84-12829
ISBN 0-89862-076-7

Acknowledgments

Among the many who helped make this work possible, special thanks and appreciation must first go to the commuter and Merchant Marine women and men who found the time in their busy schedules to talk to us. Without their cooperation — which often went beyond what we expected — this book would not have been possible.

We both wish to thank those who helped us when we began to work together. Bert Adams, Reuben Hill, and Marvin Sussman provided enthusiasm, support, and useful advice. Dixie Butz at Governors State University and Jeanne Reinle and Cindy Coffman at the University of Massachusetts typed, with skill and good humor, seemingly endless drafts of the manuscript. At The Guilford Press, Jody Falco and Judith Grauman were excellent editors.

Given our "commuter colleagueship," we need to thank independently friends, colleagues, and support staff. Harriet gives special thanks to the graduate students at Governors State University: Lynn Strauss who helped with the commuter study and Christine Thomas and Marie Van Gemert who worked on the Merchant Marine study. Indispensable to the success of these projects were faculty grants as well as telephone and secretarial support from Governors State University. To faculty colleagues at Governors State, especially Linda Steiner, go heartfelt thanks for consultations which moved the project through its many stages. Finally, Harriet thanks the members of her family who sustained her throughout the project.

Naomi owes much to Jonathan Cole for his intellectual guidance and careful editing during the early stages of the research. Special thanks go to colleagues and friends — Janet Berkeley, Toby Ditz, Hope Leichter, Eugene Litwak, Mary Clare Lennon, Sarah Rosenfield, Alice Rossi, Pete Rossi, and Elmer Struening — who provided useful reactions and support at various stages of this work. Naomi's part of the research was financially supported by a Lena Lake Forrest Fellowship from the Business and Professional Women's Foundation and an additional grant from Columbia University. A National Institute of Mental Health Traineeship in the Psychiatric Training Program at Columbia University provided a stipend. Naomi owes her parents an enormous debt of gratitude for both their moral and emotional support and their comments on countless drafts. Finally, combining a refusal to accept the accepted with sociological acumen, Robert Zussman helped in the formulation and reformulation of this study. Robert helped Naomi understand all too well the personal pains and professional costs of commuting.

While this book owes so much to so many, we must at the end take full responsibility for its limitations.

Foreword

Shared or coresidence is part of the traditional definition of marriage. However, there have always been exceptions. In polygynous societies, the husband may live in a separate dwelling, with his wives and their children having their own households close by. Or in an African society the man may have gone to the city or the mines temporarily, leaving his family "at home" while he earns money for taxes or for consumer goods. Or a man may leave Appalachia for Cincinnati or Roanoke, living there alone until he can find work and send for his family. Or a husband and wife may have marital problems and decide to live apart for a while, to see if they can resolve the difficulties, or if divorce is the solution.

So what is new about the phenomenon Gerstel and Gross are writing about? What is new is the combination of four factors: equal career commitment, distance, permanence, and preference for living together. It is not a man pursuing opportunities until he can rejoin or send for his family. It is two equally career-oriented individuals, who have chosen not to let their marriage force them to sacrifice individual advancement and success. Second, they live at a distance great enough to require the establishment of two separate households. Third, this is seen as a permanent arrangement in the sense that they have no specific goal or length of time after which they will be back together. The fourth point is equally important, however. They prefer to be together — the separation is not for the purpose of working through marital problems. And, despite the permanence of the situation, they talk hopefully of the day when career options will make shared residence possible again.

In the United States at present two values are strong. One, held by many moral leaders and embodied in much of the legal system, holds the family to be the basic unit of society, with the individual serving the family. The other says that the individual is the unit of economic productivity and society, and nothing — including the family

—must stand in the way of individual potentialities. Commuter marriage is a compromise between the two, so that the woman does not sacrifice career for home and children, nor does the family simply get out of the way. But it is a compromise that clearly favors the individuals' careers. Thus, readers will find that most of the following pages are given to the attempts of married partners to keep their marriages alive and make them "work" in a situation where the career option seems primary. Are these really divorced couples who just haven't gone through the legal process? Not according to Gerstel and Gross's respondents. In fact, they struggle continuously against the centrifugal forces that pull at all marriages, but especially at those in which the couple members are career-oriented and living apart.

There are, of course, commuter marriages at different stages of the marriage cycle. The young married without children face the fact that they may not have been married long enough to build the kind of commitment that can withstand long-term separation. Couples with children face many of the adjustment problems of the divorced, with a great burden of care placed on the parent with the children, and a sense of loss for the parent who is alone. The postparental couples seem to do best as commuters, but they are likely to have strong desires to be together.

Women in some ways find commuter marriage freeing and exciting, for, after all, the new opportunities are theirs. Men, however, no longer have a wife at home to work for them, and while this may increase their sense of domestic competence, they also feel a certain deprivation. Problems of friendship and loneliness, of self-sufficiency and dependence, of togetherness and separateness—all these are dealt with by the authors. In fact, the value of this book is out of proportion to the prevalence of the phenomenon. The reason is that much of what is said is really about traditional marriage, calling into question or confirming that which we have always taken for granted. But I will leave readers to make their own discoveries in the pages ahead.

Bert N. Adams
University of Wisconsin, Madison

Contents

COMMUTER MARRIAGE

CHAPTER 1

Introducing Couples Who Live Apart: Theoretical Issues and Empirical Trends

In the early 1960s, poised at the beginning of a tumultuous decade, few of us could imagine what was in store for "The American Family." To the extent they considered the family at all, scientists, therapists, and journalists alike idealized it — producing an image as conceptually bland as it was ideologically narrow. Then, with amazing speed, what we lived in and what we called "family" began to change — some say irrevocably. As changes unfolded, a cultural tropism toward family life emerged, and it has not yet abated. "Pluralism" and "alternative lifestyle" were terms that entered our working vocabularies, attesting to the weakening, statistically if not yet normatively, of the conventional pattern: "intact–husband/breadwinner–wife/homemaker–2 .2 children." While the idealized version of family life was unraveling, the public and the scientists celebrated the personal options that changes in family life implied. The "Me Decade" (Wolfe, 1976) fostered a solipsistic, inward turn predicated on the presumption that these changes in what we called "family" released members from previous obligations and constraints (Bird, 1979).

However, this celebration of alternatives misread the significance of one family form which was increasing in prevalence — a family form which was more a response to forced options than to voluntarily chosen ones. Commuter marriage, the subject of this book, looked like yet another example of the widely heralded pluralism. But it is, in fact, quite different.

Commuter marriage, as we define it, refers to employed spouses who spend at least three nights per week in separate residences and

1

yet are still married and intend to remain so. The separation is a result of participation by both husband and wife in careers that involve commitments to different geographic locations. Unlike those "alternatives," which seemed to reject or attack the nuclear family, spouses in these marriages choose to live apart, preserving their families, while at the same time meeting professional and career goals. Such concern for the career goals of *both* spouses distinguishes these couples from the older, husband-dominant version of the middle-class families they otherwise resemble. But the rest of their characteristics — the maintenance of bonds between husband and wife and parents and children, as well as the striving for success in the work world — keep commuters in the mainstream of American values.

In fact, it was the tenacity of these couples' commitment to such values, their resolute determination to serve family and career goals simultaneously that journalists featured in the numerous articles about commuters which appeared from the mid-1970s on.[1] The very terms these writers used to describe these couples created the impression that what they were doing was totally unprecedented. Avoiding the term "marital separation," long associated with the period preliminary to divorce, observers favored substitutes such as "two-location," "long-distance," and "weekend" marriages, reinforcing the notion that something new was going on. However, as we shall see, though there are some ways in which commuters are novel, this novelty does not arise from the fact that they are married couples who live apart. There are, and have been, many other circumstances which require couples to set

---

1. Commuter marriage has received quite a bit of recent coverage in mass media publications. Newspapers in various parts of the country have published articles on these couples — for example: *The Times Union* (Rochester), January 14, 1974; *The News and Observer* (Raleigh), August 15, 1974; *San Francisco Examiner*, November 30, 1975; *Los Angeles Times*, December 7, 1975; *The Daily News* (New York), October 2, 1977; and March 11, 1979; *The New York Times*, October 31, 1977; *Boston Globe*, September 8, 1978; *The Wall Street Journal*, August 18, 1981; *The Providence Journal Bulletin*, June 27, 1982; *USA Today*, March 10, 1983. National weekly and monthly magazines have also carried such articles — for example: "Plane Sailing," *Holiday*, June 1974, p. 38; Bernard Carragher, "Long Distance Marriage," *Cosmopolitan*, September 1976, p. 202; Virginia Drachman *et al.*, "Weekend Marriage," *Vogue*, November 1976, p. 235; "Commuter Marriage," *U.S. News & World Report*, October 24, 1977, p. 109; "Commuting: A Solution for Two-Career Couples," *Business Week*, April 3, 1978, p. 65; J. Winn Rousuck, "Commuter Marriage: Apart but Together," *Sun Magazine*, December 10, 1978, p. 18; Suzanne Seixas, "Marriage as a Fortnightly Affair," *Money*, May 1981, p. 78; "Marital Tale of Two Cities," *Time*, January 25, 1982, p. 83; "Relationships: The Loneliness of the Long Distance Marriage," *Working Woman*, October 1983. The free magazines provided by air lines have given prominent coverage to these couples; see, for example, "A Marriage of Inconvenience," in TWA's *Ambassador*, August 1980, p. 31.

up two homes. We must be careful to specify how commuter marriage is both similar to and different from these other marital forms.

Yet the conventional acceptance of the connection between marital viability and continuous coresidence does underscore the strength of the cultural ideal linking "intact" marriages with both spouses' occupancy of a single household. For social scientists, common residence is a defining characteristic of the family (Murdock, 1949; Skolnick, 1978). Even more important, the acceptance of a common residence as a defining characteristic coincides with the view that individuals within the family, particularly spouses, constitute a single entity. Ignoring the individuality of members within the family unit extends beyond definitional issues. For example, until recently, most research methods contained an implicit view that partners in marriage form a single entity and that, consequently, either the wife or the husband was able to act as an informant for the experiences of both. Such a methodology overlooks important distinctions between the views, behaviors, and interests of wives and husbands (Ferber, 1982; Thomson & Williams, 1982). Moreover, recent critics of stratification theory (Acker, 1980; Allen, 1982) suggest that these theories assume the unity of husbands and wives and, in so doing, obscure ways in which their different class backgrounds prevent unanimity in childrearing values or in class-based values for the marital relationship itself.

A similar bias, stemming from the view of family members as a single unit, permeates most sociological models of the relationship between labor force participation and the family. No matter how much they differ in other respects, the presumption that the presence of both husband and wife in a single household is the irreducible minimum of a viable marriage characterizes theories in this area from Parsons (1955) to Mincer (1977) and Laslett (1979). In treating the conjugal unit as such a minimum, theorists neglect the possibility that labor market demands may be at cross purposes for husbands and wives who are both employed. Although highly sensitive to the strains that national labor markets place on the maintenance of multigenerational households, such macrosociological thinking about the economy and the family reveals a remarkable insensitivity to the possibility that labor markets may also strain the ability of the conjugal unit to maintain a single household.[2]

2. Unfortunately, many empirical studies of geographic mobility remain in this tradition. They assume that husbands and wives necessarily move as a single unit, that they share an unnegotiated agreement to do so, and consequently that either spouse can act as an informant about the family's mobility decisions. Such studies do not

The existence of marriages in which spouses live separately in the service of divergent career demands suggests, then, a need to question two presuppositions: first, that coresidence is necessary for marital viability and, second, that husbands and wives totally share their economic interests and fates. More generally, the existence of such marriages calls our attention to the relationship between work life and family life, a subject so long neglected under the mythology that these constitute two "separate spheres" (Kanter, 1977, p. 8; Renshaw, 1976). Most studies of change in family structure have not only neglected the link between work and family life (Kahn, 1981), but also often have concerned themselves exclusively with internal family dynamics, rather than with the wider social structure in which the family exists. In part, this narrow focus is a result of the restrictive nature of sociological specialties, which are organized around specific institutions (Rapoport & Rapoport, 1976).

In the sociology of the family in particular, the tendency to view the worlds of work and family as separate spheres has been especially strong.[3] While efforts are being made to link these two spheres, construct formation is still in its rudimentary stages. "Work" and "family," to the extent they are connected at all, are conceptualized monolithically (for exceptions, see Berheide & Chow, 1983; Oppenheimer, 1982; Piotrkowski, 1979; Pleck, Staines, & Long, 1980). Particularly within an industrial context, there has been very little systematic attention to connections between types of occupational settings and diverse family structures. The study of commuter marriage highlights the necessity of moving beyond gross conceptualizations of "family" and "work" to a refinement of each of these concepts. To analyze the connection between the two, we must ask what type of work at what stage in each spouse's career makes a difference for what type of family at what point in the family's life course?

This book is an effort to specify the relationship between work and family life, frequently called to our attention by events during the

---

recognize that family mobility involves a decision-making process in which spouses may negotiate and even disagree about a particular move and its consequences. In his Introduction, Rossi (1979) recognizes these assumptions and refers to them as a "defect" in the first edition of *Why Families Move*. Nonetheless, recent research on geographic mobility still contains these same "defects" (e.g., see McAuley & Nutty, 1982; Lichter, 1982).

3. As strong as these tendencies toward conceptual isolation have been in sociology in general, they are even stronger in most analyses of alternative family forms which rarely extend beyond discussions of internal dynamics.

last decade. At the same time, it is an attempt to rethink prevailing views about the internal dynamics of families. Our study of commuter marriages speaks to the larger issue of connections between the family and economy on the one hand, and connections between family structure and consequent internal relationships on the other. Commuter marriage is a laboratory for analyzing enduring issues in family theory corresponding to fundamental concerns about family life. How does the way the economy is organized affect the way we arrange our family life? How does the way the family is structured affect the way members act and feel toward one another?

In this chapter, we introduce several issues that provide the framework for our analysis. First, we offer a fuller definition of commuter marriage—contrasting it with superficially similar structures in which spouses do not always share a single residence and with traditional definitions of the family. Second, this chapter considers formulations of the relationship between the family and the industrial economy and questions the adequacy of previous approaches in explaining contemporary developments. Third, theories concerning the structures and functions of various primary groups are discussed, extended, and modified to identify some expected consequences for internal family dynamics when changes occur in family structure.

WHAT IS COMMUTER MARRIAGE?

No doubt journalistic, popular, and even scientific interest in commuter marriage comes primarily from its break with the traditional norms which require coresidence of family members. But married couples live apart in a variety of circumstances. Separation can be imposed on families during times of crisis, as in war, illness, or imprisonment.[4] In many contemporary families, formally voluntary separations result from labor demands placed on couples who presumably consider their marriages intact. Merchant Marines, construction workers, politicians, professional athletes, and entertainers all practice occupations that call for regular periods of separation. Traveling salesmen, and even most business executives, regularly leave their

4. See Hill (1949), Stolz (1954), Price-Bonham (1972), McCubbin, Hunter, and Dahl (1975), McCubbin, Dahl, Lester, Benson, and Robertson (1976), and McCubbin (1979) for studies of couples (and their children) separated during times of war. See Morris (1965) for a study of family separation resulting from imprisonment, and Murray (1981) for separation resulting from migrant labor.

families for their work.[5] Finally, in many societies, men migrate to a distant country for an extended period of time, hoping eventually to bring their families to join them.[6] While all these examples appear structurally similar, they differ in a number of essential ways from the kind of separation we are examining.

First, in most of these other cases, only one spouse's occupation — typically the husband's — occasions the separation. Traditionally, wives have been expected to remain in the family home and usually have been excluded from tasks involving geographic mobility, especially over long distances (Murdock, 1949). In contrast, among commuters — by definition dual-career families — it is the presence of two careers pursued simultaneously rather than the nature of any single job which requires that couples live apart. In this group, the wife chooses to work in a separate location rather than stay home to wait for her husband or follow him wherever his career may lead. Indeed, it is the *wife's* participation in, and commitment to, a career which has led to an interest in this marital structure and has generated the label "alternative lifestyle."

Second, in some of the examples above, the separation is involuntary and obligatory. For instance, if a country calls a man to war, he must go or suffer severe retribution, which often also involves separation from his family. For the commuting couples in this study, separation is voluntary.[7]

Third, for some couples who live apart the primary motivation for separation is increased earning ability. For example, the immigrant often has to leave his family because economic structures are collapsing; the Merchant Marine sails away from his family to garner the high salary such work can command. However, for the dual-career families in this study, commuting actually may have a net financial *cost*. Their primary motivation tends to be the personal satisfaction provided by increased career involvement.

5. See Young and Willmott (1973), Seidenberg (1975), Boss, McCubbin, and Lester (1978), and Margolis (1979) for analyses of managers' and corporate executives' travel and its effect on their marital relationships.

6. See Castles and Kosack (1973) for exemplary research on separated immigrant families, which includes a lengthy bibliography.

7. The commuters may subjectively define separation as necessary, believing the lowered job aspirations required of one mate in a shared residence would be socially and psychologically damaging. Generally, however, they do not need to live separately in order to survive. They could live on one salary, or one spouse could lower his or her job aspirations and take a job not demanding separation.

Fourth, in some cases a separate home is not established. For instance, traveling salesmen and corporate executives tend to live out of hotels. Among the dual-career couples in this study, a second home is established and regularly returned to by one spouse.

Finally, those couples who live apart in order to obtain the legal separation which precedes a divorce are excluded from this study. This study is an examination of a new and, possibly viable, marital structure in which separation is used as a mechanism to fulfill a commitment to both work and marriage.

In sum, commuters are men and women in dual-career marriages who desire to remain married, but also voluntarily choose to pursue careers to which they feel a strong commitment. They establish separate homes so that they can do so. Commuter marriage, then, is a genuinely distinct phenomenon, though analysis of it may also help to understand these other, structurally similar, family types.

Implications of Commuter Marriage for a Definition of the Nuclear Family

Social scientists in diverse sources have defined the family as a unit which necessarily occupies a single residence. Murdock (1949), in his classical formulation, defines the nuclear family as a "social group characterized by common residence, economic cooperation, and reproduction" (p. 1). Berelson and Steiner (1964) state: "A normal family is considered to be the immediate group of father, mother, and children living together" (p. 287). Schneider (1968) notes "a condition which is part of the definition of American kinship: the family, to be a family, must live together" (p. 33).[8] In his recent definition, historian Carl

---

8. Schneider is careful in his definition to specify the American family. He recognizes that anthropologists have written a great deal on the importance of physical proximity as a characteristic that, in fact, differentiates family structures not only in different periods in history but also in different societies today. Anthropologists suggest the need to separate the concepts of household and family, stating their combination leads to unnecessary problems. First, they argue, a household and family are logically distinct categories: a household is a group of people living in the same house, while a family is a kinship or relational concept (Bohannan, 1968; Bender, 1967; Verdon, 1980). Second, they argue that perhaps more importantly, they are empirically distinct. As Bender remarks: "There are numerous societies in which families do not form households and even more instances in which households are not composed of families" (p. 493). However, these anthropologists' discussions are primarily descriptive and confined to the structural level. The resultant differences or consequences for family life are not considered.

Degler (1980) writes that an "essential element" of the family is "that husband, wife and children live in a common place" (p. 3).[9] And according to the U.S. Bureau of the Census (1980), "The term family refers to a group of two or more persons related by blood, marriage or adoption residing together in a household." But this issue is not simply a definitional one.

Many sociologists have elevated these definitions from an empirically-grounded description of the typical, modern, Western family to a theoretical assessment of the *appropriate* family. This assessment has three major ramifications for theory about family life. First, sociologists propose that the intact nuclear family "fits" with the demands of an industrialized economy — a proposition elevated to nearly axiomatic status in contemporary sociology. Second, they suggest that traditional family structure simultaneously fulfills essential functions no other contemporary group can. Though heavily criticized in recent years as an overly sanguine view of the nuclear family, sociological theory of the emotional indispensibility of nuclear family bonds within a single residence remains largely intact. Third, the sociologically sanctioned definition of the family and its concomitant cultural ideal solidified an ideological position which continues to restrict family relationships. In the following sections, we examine these assumptions and, in so doing, provide a framework for the analysis of commuter marriage.

Family Structure and the Economic System: The "Fit" Thesis

Commuter marriage deserves attention because it is an attempt by *both* spouses to juggle work and family commitments in order to serve goals in each arena simultaneously. In this sense, commuter marriage represents a "new" family form — significant in and of itself for whatever consequences it generates. Yet from a theoretical standpoint, it is something more: Commuter marriage is an extension of historical trends in family structure. Unlike some other "alternatives" that represent a "return" to communalism, commuter marriage is a continuation of an historical process that transformed the middle-class family into a small and private conjugal unit.

9. Degler (1980) does note, however, that the shared household is not a universal feature of family life (p. 4).

An extension of the individuating tendencies in an advanced industrial economy, the very existence of commuter marriage highlights a theoretical blindspot common to two otherwise quite divergent (if not antagonistic) views of the relationship between the family and the economy. The two major macrosociological theories about the relationship between the family and the economy — functionalism and Marxism — share the presumption of a common economic fate for husbands and wives, however much they may differ in other ideas about family life. Both treat the married couple as a unit in terms of its ability to meet the needs of the economy. Also, these theories share a broad consensus that the small family unit where the husband, wife, and children share a residence, best meets the economic and occupational demands of an industrialized society. However, the existence of couples who independently pursue individual economic fortune suggests that this presumption of common economic fate and a common household can no longer meet the realities of an economy and a family which increasingly contains two earners. Instead, both the functionalists and Marxists describe an outdated relationship between the family and economy, based on outmoded concepts of the empirical realities within each sphere.

Let us briefly recapitulate each of these theories. Students of the family are familiar with the functionalist view, best articulated in the works of Parsons (1955, 1965) and Goode (1964, 1970) that the nuclear family, in which husband, wife, and children live together, "fits" the economic demands of an industrialized economy. At the very core of the functionalist conception is the argument that the intact nuclear family succeeds the extended family because of its capacity for geographic mobility. They argue that where there are national labor markets, an extended family structure is incompatible with either the rational allocation of labor or the maximization of occupational achievement. They write of the need for mobility, of the need to match individuals with jobs; they assume the nuclear family is best suited to these needs. In this well-worn view, the national labor market "needs" a family structure which frees the individual worker to move in response to the market's requirements. That individual worker is the husband with dependents whose economic contributions, if any, are subordinate to his.

Although Parsons and Goode differently elaborate the "fit" thesis, each concentrates on the need to match individuals with jobs and each shares the presumption that the family's "individual" will be the husband. Parsons's rationale for treating the family as one individual is simple and concrete. He argues that the nuclear family can be treated as a unit because a sex-segregated division of labor is necessary for both the family's survival (where a division of labor reduces the potential for corrosive competition between spouses) and for the economy's survival (which relies on geographically mobile workers who receive emotional sustenance from "naturally" expressive wives at home). Parsons suggests that all employable individuals are allocated to the appropriate jobs because wives are simply not counted as possible full participants in the labor force.

Though Goode's version of the "fit" thesis does not disregard the personal strains wives experience in a traditional division of labor, he does share Parsons's basic premise: the unity of spouses' economic interests, fates, and residence. Goode recognized the potential for weakened ties between parents and children in an industrialized economy, but not between spouses. By assuming the unity of spouses, he too fails to recognize the possiblity that in advanced industrial societies the occupational demands on husbands and wives may force their separation. Because both he and Parsons assumed that the woman's primary role involves commitment to a portable domestic sphere, both suggest the small family can move without apparent strain for its members or for the economy as a whole.

Marxists would probably not welcome the commonality, but their view of the family in a capitalist society shares a conception which presupposes the couple's common residence and, derivatively, their common economic interests (see Barrett, 1980, p. 131). To be sure, Marxists do not argue that the nuclear family serves the needs of society as a whole (indeed Marxists would question the assumption that the society as a whole may be characterized as having needs), and by no means do they assume that it meets the needs of all its members. But Marxists and neo-Marxists alike have argued that the residentially intact nuclear family — with its sex-segregated division of labor — is not only compatible with, but essential to, the stability of the capitalistic economic order. Eli Zaretsky (1976), a major spokesman for this view, argues that the unpaid labor of wives in the shared home sustains the wage labor system, making the family "an integral part of the economy under capitalism" (p. 35; see also Seecombe, 1973; Smith, 1978). He argues that wives in the home insure the reproduction of the relations of production — generationally by socializing their children and daily by providing sustenance for their wage-earning husbands. In their delineation of wives' economic roles Marxists include their important consumer work which is necessary to the vitality of the capitalist economy (Weinbaum & Bridges, 1979). Some Marxists also suggest that wives, whose mobility is limited, serve as a reserve labor force in the locale of the husbands' work to be called upon in times of economic expansion and dismissed in times of economic recession (e.g., Benston, 1969; Gardiner, 1975).

Thus, though the economic value of wives' physical and emotional contribution within the home is no longer invisible, Marxists do preserve the functionalist presumptions about the necessary fusion of interest for husband and wife which is, in turn, based on a division of labor between them. Throughout the Marxist interpretation of how the family serves the capitalist economy runs the presumption that husbands and wives share a material base. Such a view leaves little room for the possibility that husbands and wives may each independently pursue producer roles necessitating their residential separation or that this residential separation may, in fact, best serve the interest of capitalist expansion (if not the interests of family members themselves).

Though criticized on many other grounds, this bias, common to both functionalists and Marxists, remains largely unchallenged. For example, historians have questioned the view common to both that the nuclear family is a product rather than a precursor of industrial capitalism (Laslett, 1974; Modell & Hareven, 1978; Stone, 1977).[10] Feminists have contrasted the empirical reality of widespread domestic violence, marital rape, and child abuse with the theories' portrayal of the family as a personal retreat (Dobash & Dobash, 1979; Dworkin, 1974). Other social scientists have questioned the assumption, underlying both functionalist and Marxist analyses, that a sex-segregated division of labor is necessary to the stability of the family, to the emotional adjustment of its members, or to the family's efficiency as an economic unit (Laws, 1976; Oppenheimer, 1977; Weitzman, 1981). But none criticizes the contention contained in the "fit" thesis about the rational allocation of human resources. Though some researchers have shown that the immobility of wives constrains their careers (Heckman, Bryson, & Bryson, 1977; Long, 1974), no theorist to date has focused on the more general assumption, which functionalists and Marxists make, concerning the geographic unity and transferability of the family. The view that the economy (if not the individual family member) is best

10. A recent critique attacks the notion that kin are not useful for job placement in professional careers even in advanced industrial society (Greico, 1982). However, even this critique of the fit thesis does not allow for the possibility of different geographic constraints operating within the nuclear family.

served by the intact nuclear family structure—that this form allows a rational (if not necessarily humane) allocation of labor—remains very much with us.

Yet commuter marriage throws the inadequacy of such assumptions into relief. This marital arrangement points up the strains produced by the coincidence of an economic system that requires geographic mobility for the allocation of labor and a family system which entails a shared residence for spouses. Our call to recognize the possible independence of spouses' economic interests and fates acknowledges that most couples, even most dual-career couples, do reside in a single home. Studies do find that when spouses share a home—even when both are professionals—the husband's job opportunities carry greater weight than the wife's in determining the location of their joint residence (Duncan & Perucci, 1976; Ferber & Huber, 1979; Linn, 1971; Long, 1974; Poloma, Pendleton, & Garland, 1982). However, the prevalence of such a pattern does not mean that it is cost-free or exists without strain. On the contrary, as more and more women become full participants in the labor force, the disjunction—rather than "fit"—between the mobility demands of the industrial economy and the single residence home becomes increasingly clear. The very appearance of commuter marriage may be looked at as a response to the mounting structural strains imposed on "normal" families, increasing numbers of which are dual-career.

We are suggesting that the structural strains imposed by the single home, nuclear family affect more than the fates of its individual members. The economy suffers when skills of a high value to society are not used to maximum potential. If we assume that women are at least potentially as valuable workers as men—given equal training and motivation—contemporary society is losing much of its human resources in promoting the intact nuclear family structure. Such losses may appear, at least superficially, consistent with Marxist assertions about women's roles in the economy. As captive workers, women who remain in a shared home, when leaving it might improve their career options, do constitute a "reserve labor force" which is available to move in and out of poorly paid jobs located near the husband's place of employment. However, a reserve labor force consisting even in part of highly trained and specialized women professionals is a far cry from the successful utilization of labor. Seen this way, a commitment to the intact nuclear family represents a structural constraint on the allocation of labor in the marketplace. Indeed, commuting—the geographic separation of spouses each of whom is mobile—can be understood as a response to the increasing penetration of the market into the family.

Commuter Marriage: An Extension
of Individualism and the Home–Work Split

Ironically, then, neither the functionalists, Marxists, nor their critics have gone far enough. In the last decade, changes in the labor market, changes in gender-based roles in the home, as well as in ideology, have rendered obsolete these older models of the relationship between the family and the economy. More and more married women are employed and more are becoming professionals. A growing number of married women, committed to careers that bring them income and status, are likely to face the costs — both occupational and psychological — of subordinating their individual interests. Moreover, two earners per family are increasingly necessary as inflationary pressures mount. A reduced job market and high unemployment rate, characteristic of many fields in the United States today, reduce the ease of finding two jobs in a single locale. So, too, these tightening job markets are occurring in an ideological context that supports alternative marital structures like commuter marriage. The women's movement has, in some measure, legitimated women's demands for independence within and outside the home. Furthermore, while the marital ideology of the 1950s was that of "togetherness," today's ideology emphasizes the personal development and ambitions of each spouse. Commuter marriage is a structure spawned by this ideology of individualism which emphasizes that each spouse's worth depends on individual achievements rather than on family membership. This American ideology has a long history of application to husbands; what's new is its application to wives.

Finally, commuter marriage represents one extreme of a strong tendency in advanced industrial society: the territorial separation of home and work. Today, members of most social classes travel between work and home. Commuter marriage extends this separation of work and family with neither spouse available to the other on workdays, reuniting at most, on "social weekends."

Commuter marriage, then, may be thought of as a further expression of the individuating tendencies that began to disperse family members several centuries ago. Thus commuter marriage does not become just another alternative in a pluralistic potpourri, but instead becomes an embodiment of the tensions — or lack of "fit" — between the economy and the family in contemporary society.

DOES COMMUTER MARRIAGE WORK?

We have suggested that commuter marriage is an adaptation to the disjunction between the single residence nuclear family and the modern economy. There is, however, another equally important perspective from which to view the adequacy of a particular family structure: How well does it fulfill the needs of individuals, couples, and families? In the previous section, we asked what problems commuter marriage is a response to; here we examine the consequences of commuter marriage. The question now focuses on the structural bases necessary for satisfactory relationships among the family members.

The major structural difference between the nuclear family and a commuter marriage is the degree of physical proximity among family members. The question commuter marriage raises becomes: Is daily face-to-face interaction necessary for the viability of the family unit? Or, as we are often asked: Does commuter marriage work?

Family Functions and the Single Home

Not only does Talcott Parsons argue that the nuclear family "fits" industrial society's need for geographic mobility, but he states that a shared residence is necessary for the provision of the family's "irreducible functions." His argument that the family is the only group able to provide satisfactorily the dual functions of "tension management" — the emotional support of adults — as well as the adequate socialization of children has been widely discussed and disputed. But what has been less widely cited is his insistence that the daily face-to-face interaction of family members in the shared home makes these specialized family functions possible:

> The sharing of the common household as the place to live — with all its implications — is the fundamental phenomenon. It is this sharing which makes the normal nuclear family a distinctive unit which cannot be confused with any other based either on kinship or on any other criteria. The home, its furnishings, and the rest contribute the logistic base for the performance of family functions. (Parsons, 1965, p. 199)

For Parsons and others like him, the functions that only the family can provide hinge on the daily face-to-face interaction that a shared home allows. Given this argument, one would expect the complete disintegration of the family (and hence society) when its members reside in separate households.

Survival of Primary Groups
Despite Members' Geographic Dispersion

Prior to the 1960s, it was assumed that all primary groups, of which the family is only one example, require daily face-to-face interaction in order to survive.[11] Theorists from Toennies (1887) to Wirth (1938) to Simmel (1950) argued that such groups were doomed because industrial societies required geographic and social mobility of its members. However, research conducted since the 1950s challenged the assumption that all primary groups require daily face-to-face interaction in order to function. Though researchers recognized that contemporary primary groups are certainly different from classical ones — individuals no longer live together from birth to death — they contend that in these groups change was not equivalent to breakdown. Geographic distance does not destroy individuals' relationships nor obliterate their ability to help each other in practical ways.

Significant data have accumulated to show that primary groups persist despite the separation of their members. First, friendships survive across geographic distance, especially in the middle class (Babchuk & Bates, 1963; Bell, 1981; Hess, 1976). Second, studies of neighborhoods show that transience does not necessitate breakdown; even though neighbors are faced with continual turnover, they form cohesive groups (Cohen, 1977; Fischer, 1982). Finally, it is now widely known that relatives, living in different cities or states, often maintain strong attachments, providing one another with financial assistance, joint recreation, care in times of emergency, as well as im-

11. Much of this thinking was based on Cooley's (1909) classical definition of the primary group: "By primary groups, I mean those characterized by intimate, face to face association and cooperation. . . . Primary groups are primary in the sense that they give the individual his earliest and most complete experience of social unity, and also in the sense that they do not change in the same degree as more elaborate relations, but form a comparatively permanent source out of which the latter are ever springing" (pp. 24–25).

portant emotional support (Adams, 1966; Lee, 1980; Sussman, 1965).

The persistence of these primary groups, Eugene Litwak proposes, may be explained by a "shared functions" approach. Primary groups, linked to formal organizations, perform "nonuniform tasks."[12] Kinship groups are based on permanent relationships, but not face-to-face interaction. Neighboring involves face-to-face interaction, but not a permanent relationship. Friends have voluntary affective ties, but usually not daily face-to-face interaction nor permanent legal or biological ties. Because each of these groups has different, though viable, structures, each performs different, though necessary, nonuniform tasks.[13]

Furthermore, Litwak suggests that industrial societies provide the mechanisms which allow dispersed primary groups to survive. Long distance communication by telephone, rapid reunions via planes and trains, a monetary economy (allowing the exchange of financial aid across distances), group norms oriented to "orderly change" (allowing rapid group reintegration) — all sustain primary groups in an occupational system that requires geographic dispersion.

Survival of the Nuclear Family
Despite Members' Geographic Dispersion

The logic that Litwak and others have applied to primary groups can be extended to the nuclear family. That is, we ask if kin, friends, and neighborhood ties can survive despite geographic dispersion, can the nuclear family function despite the geographic separation of its members? No one has questioned whether or not the nuclear family does depend, as Parsons would have it, on the shared residence. Rather,

12. Litwak and Figueira (1970) define "nonuniform" tasks as those which include: "1)problems for which there is no knowledge; 2)problems for which knowledge is so simple that the average person can do it as well as the experts, and 3)problems which are so idiosyncratic that it would be costly to maintain experts for or to get them to the place where they might make use of their training" (p. 360). They go on to argue that the tasks performed by primary groups are not static. For example, the simplification of tasks with new technological developments allows primary groups to perform those tasks previously performed by experts. (See also Litwak & Meyer, 1966.)

13. Kin, distinguished by their biological or legal permanent ties, "do best where the tasks involve long-term ties." Neighbors, who are face to face, are able to provide "time emergencies, services based on territoriality and activities which require every day observation." And, finally, friends with voluntary affective attachments, are "especially well-suited to dealing with explicit reference orientations (i.e., fashion, political values, etc.)" (Litwak & Figueira, 1970, pp.370–372).

many researchers assume that since most families share a single home, they must continue to do so. But given the proposition and supporting evidence that other primary groups cohere despite dispersion, we might expect the same to be true of the small family unit. Or, more precisely, we might expect that while the physical separation of spouses would certainly bring about changes in their relationship, these changes are not necessarily equivalent to breakdown. In a general way, we are asking to what extent the physical separation of family members threatens their intimacy with and attachment to one another. More specifically — can spouses who reside in two separate households continue to provide one another and their children with the emotional sustenance and practical aid expected from family members?

We can extend the questions raised by Litwak and others still further. He suggests that there are mechanisms in modern society that help prevent the dissolution of relationships separated by distance. Are there, then, mechanisms to help separated spouses cope with their lack of daily interaction? The previous work on primary groups suggests that, for individuals, different groups serve different needs. Thus, we might expect that these other primary groups, so different from the nuclear unit itself, could not substitute for it. But this question remains an empirical one. Thus, we ask: To what extent can spouses separated from one another turn to others — kin, neighbors, friends, and lovers — as substitutes for one another?

Family Strains and the Shared Residence

Extending these earlier arguments to the nuclear unit could, however, obscure another equally important issue: *Strains* may occur because family members *do* engage in daily interactions over long periods of time. That is, by focusing on the links between a shared residence and the functions of the family, earlier theorists did not consider that this very characteristic — the daily sharing of a single home — also produces strains.

However, sociologists have recently begun to suggest that the nuclear family, with its present structure and expectations, may actually prevent couples from achieving satisfaction and intimacy. In fact, the formulations that focused on family integration and functions are now being construed as sentimental models of family life. According to this view, values promoting personal growth, self-actualization, and independence have become more widespread while traditional marriage seems to spell the end of self-development. Neither spouse feels satisfied individually. Thus, we find that the women, limited to a marginal position in the labor force, identify themselves (and are seen by others) as their husbands' wives rather than as unique individuals (Papanek, 1973), resulting in, not a sense of vicarious achievement, but a frustrating denial of identity (Macke, Bohrnstedt, & Berstein, 1979). If they take a career while remaining in the home, wives retain primary responsibility for the care of the family residence (Hartmann, 1981; Vanek, 1980) and, as a result, often experience stress (Oakley, 1981). At the same time, men's lives are dominated by the competition and aggression central to the occupational system (Kohen & Feldberg, 1977; Margolis, 1979; Rubin, 1976). Though accorded both status and respect in the family, men experience inequitable amounts of work-related tension that they carry home nightly (Aldous, Osmond, & Hicks, 1979; Piotrkowski, 1979). Because the wife and husband each feels dissatisfied, the couple's relationship suffers. Seeing one another every day, both spouses may learn to take the other for granted (Cuber & Harroff, 1966). At the same time, the increased privatization of the family results in spouses exercising inordinate control over one another. Since the family is a small, though sheltered group, their relationships all too often become explosive (Martin, 1976; Straus, Gelles, & Steinmetz, 1981).

A central theme running through these critiques of the nuclear family is that the marital dyad is a form of social control, imposing unnecessary and excessive constraints on each spouse. They may seem to be extreme indictments of marriage, but they are heard often. These critiques suggest that it is not fruitful to pose the question of the relationship between family structure and family goals in terms of either positive consequences attributed to sharing a home or strains found among those who live apart. Instead, neither the overly roseate view of family life nor the subsequent exposure of its dark side allows a full picture of the costs and benefits.

Commuter marriage, we suggest, offers a site where we can examine the limits of these contradictory assessments of family life. Commuters' reactions tell us just what costs *and* benefits derive from daily face-to-face interaction. Thus, we ask not only what couples lose by living apart, but also what positive outcomes accrue to commuters as a result of their separations. Or, how does the structure of the "normal" American family obstruct individual and family functioning?

The Course of Family Life

One additional set of questions should be included in an analysis of family viability. Previous theorizing about primary group functioning not only focused on positive consequences, rather than strains, but also tended to state propositions in an either/or fashion. The possibility that the physical proximity of primary group members may only be essential under certain conditions, or at certain times, is not considered. In fact, the functions and strains can best be understood when the relationship among the family structure, family life course, and occupational structure and career are considered concomitantly.

Rodgers (1973) and Aldous (1978) have formulated a developmental approach to the family which suggests that any given family undergoes a series of predictable changes. Rodgers (1973) suggests that the "institutional theories," emphasizing the functions of the family, "satisfactorily handle broad patterns of family structure and major sweeps of time" (p. 9). However, he also points to two disadvantages inherent in the use of these approaches:

> Only partial explanations can be given to the phenomenon of differing behavioral patterns in specific subgroups of the society at any given point in time and little can be found to explain how families change during their own history. (p. 10)

When one does take account of these "individual family histories," the need to maximize family unity may be great at one stage and not so great at another. For example, while a major function of the family is the socialization of children, face-to-face interaction between parents and children, of course, decreases steadily as children mature, until it reaches its lowest point when they finally leave home. Or, looking at the spouses themselves, they often provide one another with daily care during times of illness. However, the likelihood of incapacitating illness requiring daily interactions is high typically only when couples are elderly. These are just two examples that suggest that the requirement of face-to-face interaction during the family life course is variable rather than static. Thus, we might expect that the advantages of any given family structure will also vary in different periods.

Career conditions may also affect the amount of face-to-face interaction that family members can provide. Careers typically involve a series of stages—training, apprenticeship or trial stage, establishment (which itself can be broken into stages), and disengagement. At any given point in this career, an individual may desire or need more or less involvement in his or her work. For example, individuals may feel the greatest need to invest themselves in the early stages of their jobs to establish a reputation (Clausen, 1976). Such career involvement may mean less family involvement during that time. And the required amount of occupational involvement, as well as the timing of it, may differ for the husband and wife. Furthermore, jobs may vary in the degree of individual control they allow over location, timing, and involvement. In sum, if we look at each spouse's occupational cycle and job conditions as well as the course of family life, we may find that a particular family structure may cause varying degrees of strain.

COMMUTERS AS A TEST CASE

Our assertion that the analysis of commuter marriage enables us to draw conclusions about the consequences of different family structures rests on the validity of our claim that what happens to commuters results from the fact that they live apart. The experience of commuters does not add to our understanding of what shared residence promotes or undermines, if what we see among commuters is not a result of separation. For example, commuters tell us they are more egalitarian in their domestic division of labor after they set up two homes. However, this fact alone tells us little about the costs and benefits associated with living together or apart. We must also show that this equality is a consequence of separation itself rather than other factors associated with commuting. In fact, it is both, as we shall see. However, this example makes clear that the utility of commuter marriage as a test case for considering the relationship between the structure of family life and its viability is grounded on the strength of our argument that we have located effects of separation per se.

The need to specify the effects of separation led us to compare commuter families with another kind of family which lives apart. This comparison, allows us to consider how much of what we found among commuters was a response to living apart and how much was a response to other characteristics of these dual-career couples. Many types of separated couples exist; many predate the advent of commuter marriage. We chose to study Merchant Marine families. These couples are quite different from commuters: They come from working-class backgrounds, they do not establish a second home, and they separate solely because of the husband's career. In the final chapter, then, we compare these couples to commuters to specify how separation itself determines the costs and benefits to family life and how other characteristics play a part.

CONCLUSION

In this chapter, we discussed commuter marriage in the context of other types of marriages which require that couples live apart. We then presented a two-part framework for the analysis of commuter marriage. First, we examined ideas about the relationship between the nuclear family and the economic system, arguing that commuter marriage is an alternative family structure responsive to the apparent disjunction, rather than previously proposed "fit," between these two spheres. In Chapter 2, we will explore the implications of this relationship by examining:

     1. the costs of the traditional patterns where wives follow their husbands;

     2. why some wives and husbands are particularly sensitive to these costs and, as a consequence, set up two homes;

     3. the current social conditions that act as precipitants in the decision to commute.

Second, we traced the development of general approaches concerning the relationship between daily face-to-face interaction and primary group functioning. We suggested that commuter marriage provides an ideal context for applying conclusions from those theories to the nuclear family. However, instead of looking at the positive consequences attributed to sharing a home or the negative ones of commuter marriage, we have suggested an analysis that includes an examination of:

     1. the links between ongoing face-to-face interaction and the family's ability to support and aid its members;

     2. the links between ongoing face-to-face interaction and family strains;

     3. the availability of other primary groups that may serve as supplementary sources of support in the absence of the spouse;

4. the conditions under which these strains are experienced to a greater or lesser degree.

Chapters 3 through 7 address these issues.

Finally, we suggested that comparing commuter, dual-career families with single-career, Merchant Marine families who live apart could help us specify the effects of separation. Thus, our final question is: To what extent do the experiences of other families living apart parallel or diverge from those of commuters? Chapter 8 addresses this question.

The Appendix provides a description of the commuters we interviewed, the interviewing techniques we used, and a comparison of the characteristics of commuters with those of Merchant Marine couples.

CHAPTER 2

Deciding to Commute

Because it is still a relatively rare choice, we might expect that a couple's decision to set up two homes would be a long and agonizing one. We might imagine them making lists, talking long into the night, consulting with friends and relatives. But this is not the case. Surprisingly, the commuters seem neither to have agonized over nor even to have seen their decisions as a matter of choice:

It was not a decision. It was not one spot where one pulls oneself together and says "let's face up to it."

We fell into it. Not a conscious thing to do it.

No real discussion. It was the only logical thing to do.

The decision just grew on its own.

We talked about it very little before it began. I don't have a good deal of imagination and we didn't talk about it a great deal. It happened.

It was not really a decision. It was an evolution. There was nothing to talk about.

There is no reason to disbelieve these comments or even question how typical they are. Yet, they tell only a small part of the story. If the decision to commute is not itself difficult, it is only because it emerges out of a long series of earlier decisions, commitments, and experiences. To understand the choice of commuter marriage, we must look at the couples' lives preceding that choice.

THE BACKGROUNDS

The Women's Early Ambitions and Professional Goals

During our interviews, we were often impressed by high levels of ambition, intelligence, and training of the women in our sample. These women, who became commuter wives, had all completed college, many at prestigious schools. Nearly 90% had gone on to graduate school, some immediately after college, others as re-entry students of the 1970s. Over half received the highest degree available in their fields, including PhDs, JDs, and MDs. When they married, they married highly trained men who supported their ambitions.

Describing childhood and adolescence, many of these women remarked that they had "always been independent," or "career oriented," or "different from my other girl friends who were just interested in dolls and then boys," or just "smart." The younger ones stated they pursued professional goals as a matter of course. Some of the older women had put aside career goals to raise children, but returned to school or the labor force after children reached school age, suggesting they had always known they would do so.

Family backgrounds varied enormously, including a high proportion of fathers in professional fields and a larger proportion of working mothers than would be expected for their generation. For those women whose mothers worked, this experience became an important model:

My mother was an attorney. She was my image, my model of a wife and mother.

Among those whose mothers did not work, their mothers also often became models, but of a negative sort:

I always wanted a career because I thought my mother, who was always a housewife, didn't have any options. She was a frustrated housewife–martyr and I always knew that I didn't want, couldn't be, that.

Thus, most of the women in our sample could trace their own ambitions back from graduate school, to college, even to childhood. But what was to become of these ambitions when combined with marriage?

History of Professional Commitment

While both spouses had early ambitions and high level skills, most couples did not set up the commuter arrangement at the beginning of their marriages. Instead, the wives' ambitions were frustrated. Wives were expected to follow their husbands — that was the way families lived. Initially, these couples never even considered rejecting these norms.[1]

In most families, particularly in the middle class where relocation is frequent, the husband's job opportunities almost always carry more weight than the wife's in determining where they live (Deitch & Sanderson, 1983; Long, 1974; Neimi, 1975). But few women hold jobs as well paying, demanding, or prestigious as their husbands, and many are in occupations that allow easy relocation. For these women, the choice to follow their husbands is often a simple, economically rational decision: He makes more money, so I should follow his career. However, we might expect that the smaller group of women who are in better-paying, more prestigious positions would have greater influence on where their families live. But some research suggests that even these women, often highly trained and highly skilled, tend to follow their husbands (Duncan & Perucci, 1976; Ferber & Huber, 1979; Gillard, 1979; Heckman et al., 1977; Yohalem, 1979). Thus, in her study of dual-career families in which all the wives had PhDs, Holmstrom (1973) found: "If someone takes a risk in deciding where to live, it is almost always the wife who does so" (p. 37).

For this group, the decision for a wife to follow her husband is not a simple economic choice. Instead, the decision seems to be a matter of cultural values and norms attached to gender roles. Nurturing the husband's career is simply perceived as more important, outweighing any economic costs to the family that may result from the decreased (or discontinued) earnings of the wife.

Most commuter couples in our study had, earlier in their married lives, abided by these rules. We asked them about their mobility decisions before they began to commute: their decision to remain in one place when job possibilities existed elsewhere, as well as their relocations in response to job offers. Even in this vanguard population, the husband's career was the determining factor in 80% of the

1. Only three couples began commuting when they first married. All three cases were second marriages in which both husband and wife were already deeply involved in professional positions.

joint-mobility decisions; both spouse's careers were given equal weight in only 8% of these decisions. And in only another 8% of the cases was the wife's career the determining factor. (The other 4% of the mobility decisions were not determined by careers; e.g., couples moved to be near kin or for styles of life associated with particular cities.) These figures suggest that almost all the wives, just as most married women professionals, had previously followed their husbands when they received job offers which required moving. The figures also suggest that these wives were unable (or unwilling) to move for their own employment opportunities.

Let us examine in some detail one couple's mobility history since it exemplifies, in broad outline, most of the couples in this study. After college, the couple married and the husband entered law school in the same area where he and his wife had attended college. Before marrying, she had intended to go into the foreign service. But, as she said:

That would have required too much traveling. I had to decide between the foreign service and marriage. I chose marriage.

Like other women in the study, she had given up an occupational aspiration even before she had a chance to pursue it. Here we see the initial stages of the process whereby family structure contributes to the sex-typing of jobs: the family's migration pattern helps insure sex-segregation in the marketplace.

Having rejected the foreign service, the woman decided that she wanted to get a PhD in political science and entered graduate school near her husband's law school. But when he finished law school, it was time to make the first of many career moves:

When I finished law school, I went to the Department of Justice for a year and liked it very much. The military interrupted it. After that I decided to try practicing in another part of the country. So we went to California for three years. And then U of P offered me a visiting teaching position. I thought I'd like to try that and we came for a year.

Note his easy slippage between "I" for personal desire in terms of career gains and "we" when referring to consequent relocations for his family. While the husband pursued his career, the wife's was interrupted; she worked on her PhD at four different universities.

This pattern of mobility contains many elements common to other couples. Many families relocated so that the husband could go to a different law firm, regional office, or university to move up the rungs of a career ladder. In some cases, the move involved only very minor career gains for the husband. Some couples moved across the country or abroad so the husband could take a year's sabbatical. Others moved to pursue marginally better training in the husband's particular field.

By contrast, none of the wives took sabbaticals away from the family home. None moved, with a husband to support them, to go to a particular school known to be outstanding in her particular specialty. Only a few women relocated, with families in tow, when offered a better position. And these few went only when their husbands were offered a position nearby.

The women said they followed this mobility pattern because they believed it was "natural" for a wife to follow her husband and/or because they felt social pressures to do so. Typical comments from women of all ages were:

He was offered a job in Ohio and as far as I was concerned it was the far end of nowhere. But his job was the main family commitment. The last thing that ever occurred to me was that I should take a job in some other town than the one where my husband lived or that he should follow me. I just didn't even consider it then.

It never occurred to me not to follow him. I always went along and we both looked at a place that he wanted to go and decided what to do. But, I must say, I never vetoed anything. I wasn't even aware of any other options.

It seemed only natural to follow him. I mean that is just what I had always learned you were supposed to do.

In a few cases, though the wives had more advanced degrees, they followed their husbands. But they felt cheated by this pattern. For example, one woman first completed her PhD, then married and moved to where her husband was working. When asked about this decision, her husband simply reported the facts:

I re-entered school after the research ended. I decided to finish my PhD in Tennessee where I'd been working instead of going back to Wisconsin. Polly came down during the summer. She'd finished her PhD. That's it I guess.

But his wife, giving the same information, told the story differently:

When I finished my PhD, we got married. His research project was almost over and I went to join him just for the summer. Then, we were going to go back to Wisconsin where I had a nice Post-Doc lined up in a lab where I wanted

to work while he finished his PhD. Then he decided he wanted to stay in Ten-
nessee to work there with a man he'd been working with. He didn't ask me. He
just decided. I was so mad at him. But, you know, then he talked me into it.
I was a pushover.

From such remarks it is clear that these women followed their husbands
because they had been persuaded to live by norms prescribing the
priority of their husbands' careers, even when these norms were inconsistent with economically rational decisions.

When spouses were considering becoming parents, the norms to
follow the husband were further reinforced. Some spouses agreed, often
without discussing it, that parenting was to be primarily the wife's
responsibility. Concomitantly, this meant the husband would assume
the primary, if not the only, breadwinning role. For them, it "made
sense" to invest in his, rather than her, career. There was no question, then, that his work would determine the family's migration. But
in a few other cases, it was the wife herself who felt she wanted to be
a "good" mother and, as a result, made her family her major commitment. These husbands either left this decision solely to their wives or
disapproved, but went along with it. For example, one woman said:

When we were married, my husband was willing to have me stay at my job.
He said he would change his job so that we wouldn't have to move. I disagreed.
I was just thinking that it was time for me to have children and that I had to
make a choice between being a mother and being a career woman. So I became
the mother and he had the career.

This woman's husband, who was not typical, was willing to give up
his career gains to support her career. But she, like many others, had
internalized norms of "good mothering" which dictate against such a
pattern.

For most of the couples, the plan to have children, or the actual
birth of a child, solidified the traditional pattern. Motherhood implied
a primary commitment to family, while fatherhood implied a primary
commitment to breadwinning. Such a pattern is not based on purely
economic factors, which might lead to other choices—both spouses
could maintain careers and hire help to provide child care. However,
this was not thought to be a viable alternative as the spouses believed
only a parent could provide adequate child care, which, in turn, meant
a diminished commitment to that parent's career, especially in the early
childrearing years. Perhaps more importantly, *either* spouse could have
assumed the major parenting role. Couples could then "invest" in the
other spouse's career by migrating wherever it required. But these

couples, in earlier years together, had not even considered such a reversal. Therefore, during the childbearing and early rearing years, most of these families move as a unit to a locale determined by the husband's career.

Many of the couples made several moves for the husband's career. Some couples felt they may have been unfair in these early relocation decisions, but that the choice was made because, at the time, it seemed the only way to live. One woman's comments exemplify internal, as well as external, pressures:

I was working on my law degree in Michigan. Then my husband got his first job offer in Boston. Then we made, let me see, three moves for his work. I didn't even consider staying where we were at the time or looking elsewhere. A lot of things have changed I think. Everyone — family, friends — put pressure on me not even to get too involved in my career. They thought I was crazy.

With each move, the wife's career became increasingly secondary. With a widening gap between the spouses, it did seem more and more rational, for economic as well as normative reasons, to invest in the husband's, instead of the wife's, career. In sum, even these highly career-oriented women subordinated their work to their family in pursuing the husband's career.

These women did so for several reasons. First, some had simply internalized that it was natural for a married woman to follow her husband. At the time, no other pattern fit their idea of marriage. Second, a decision to have children reinforced the asymmetry the marriage had created. Third, external social pressures solidified this pattern of geographic mobility that the spouses themselves had accepted. Typically the husbands had not pressured their wives to follow them. They did not have to. Rather, both usually agreed and had their feelings reinforced by others around them. That these women were willing (for some period of time) to give up their intense commitment to work speaks to the strength of norms in American society. But it does not tell us their consequences.

Costs of the Normative System

OCCUPATIONAL COSTS

Though these norms may have guided commuters' lives, they, nonetheless, imposed serious costs. It is exactly these costs which eventually serve as major factors in the decision to set up two separate homes. These decisions had serious occupational consequences. On the one hand, these decisions allowed the men to follow orderly career plans as they moved to maintain or advance employment opportunities. The work histories these husbands gave sounded like well-ordered resumes, indicating advances up some career ladder. On the other hand, the women faced grave barriers as they formulated career goals and attempted to achieve them. As a result of their geographic mobility, some of the women had significant periods of unemployment:

I graduated from a prestigious school with distinction and had no problem getting jobs when I first finished. I accepted the first one I did because my husband was also going to be there. That worked out beautifully. Well, then my husband found he was in a job he didn't care much about. So we moved. The new one turned out to be a fine situation for him. But I was told that there was an antinepotism clause that husbands and wives could not both be employed. I had always thought I'd find something there. But I didn't.

This woman's story is not uncommon: good credentials, prestigious employment, followed by a family move that limited job possibilities. In her particular case, antinepotism rules were barriers to employment. Other women mentioned the same barrier. These rules were (and in their informal application, still are) particularly constraining for women as they coexist with family and job structures which encourage both spouses to be present in the community where the husband works.

Most of the women did not remain unemployed while they shared a single family home. But all they could find were part-time jobs or jobs below the rank they could have gotten in another area. Some spoke angrily of the "exploitation" they were subject to as members of a captive labor force:

When we went to the college where Jeffrey was going to teach, I took a temporary instructor's job while Jeffrey had the full-time job. We had the same credentials. I didn't get to vote. I got a crummy salary. And some people said I was lucky to get work near Jeffrey. But let me tell you, it was a rotten experience.

Moreover, a few tried changing fields entirely, taking "sex-labeled jobs" which, as Oppenheimer (1970) points out, are easily transferable from location to location:

Jim was offered a job in North Carolina. I wanted to be a journalist, had my degree in journalism, but nothing was available, so the other choice was to teach in elementary school. I didn't like that but it was the only available alternative if I was going to work at all. Professionally, it was great for him. Professionally, it was nowhere for me.

In sum, the women who had followed their husbands experienced negative consequences—from the worst possibility, unemployment, to a somewhat better situation, part-time work or "sex-labeled jobs" outside their chosen field. *Not one of these women was able to obtain a position that she felt made full use of her skills.*

PSYCHOLOGICAL COSTS

For women, the costs of this mobility pattern were not only practical: They suffered severe psychological costs as well. The women professionals in this study experienced identity dilemmas, not because they refused to abide by norms for appropriate feminine behavior, but because they adhered to them too well. Many found that when they followed the husband, they felt like his extension, not like an independent person.

This unsatisfying dependency occurred in many different marital situations. Wives who began their marriages on an equal footing with their husbands, but who then saw their own career ambitions stifled, felt frustrated. As one woman put it:

It was very difficult for me because for the first time, I didn't really have a separate life and I became, in a way, like a leech. He was my only lifeline to what was going on in the world.

Another remarked:

I didn't want to move to Boston, and I said to him: "You've already made the decision." And he said, "No." But, in fact, he had and it was important for his career that he do so. But it was a very hard move for me. I was really miserable. The only thing I could find was a part time job in a local clinic. I didn't know anybody except Leonard. And the people I met were all through him. I almost felt invisible.

One woman's husband felt burdened by her pain:

I got a job in Boston that I really wanted. But it was really hard on her. I'd come home at night and she'd be in tears. I felt like a real villain.

Other women married men who were older and higher up the career ladder. Following their husbands, they, too, were unprepared for the psychological distress they experienced. For example, one woman married a man who was a full professor while she was just finishing graduate school. It seemed exciting to move to where he was well-known and established. But, after actually going to live there,

she discovered that no one was particularly interested in what she was
doing:

*All of a sudden, I lost my identity. And I had a real fit. A lot of crying. It was
the kind of thing where before they asked what you were doing and what your
plans were and so forth, all of a sudden, the same people would ask me what
my husband was doing. It was an incredibly frustrating experience.*

Some of the women forced themselves to adjust to this situation for
a period of time. They had so fully accepted a subordinate role that
they found themselves helping to assure their compliance with it by
blaming themselves for their feelings of dissatisfaction and being angry
at themselves for having such negative responses. Others were more
critical of their predicament and described the period as the worst time
in their lives. They knew they had to change it. A few women even
recalled these periods as suicidal ones:

*I was just climbing the walls. I considered murder. I considered divorce. I con-
sidered suicide. I am not kidding. It was just awful.*

*After we got settled, I started feeling depressed staying home, and I think the closest
I ever came to committing suicide. My husband would leave for work. And I
was left out in the community with nothing to keep me going.*

Internalized norms, continued social pressure from friends and
kin, nonresponsive employers as well as the legal system dictated, for
the large majority, the conventional pattern in which the family
migrated as a unit for the husband's work.[2] The result was that wives
experienced serious setbacks in their careers—from unemployment
to "sex-labeled jobs" to part-time professional positions. It was they
who suffered psychological distress in the process. The experience of
these losses became motivating factors in the decision to establish a
commuter marriage.

THE DOMINANCE OF WORK

Early in their marriages, the commuter wives had abandoned a total
pursuit of their careers, and they suffered for it. But this type of suffering is not unique to commuters. Indeed, the fact that even wives

2. In the laws of many states, the domicile of the husband—as legal head of the household—is the legal domicile of the family (see Weitzman, 1981).

who later became commuters suffered from the abandonment of careers shows just how extensive the pattern of career subordination is among middle-class women. Still, commuters, both men and women, are distinctive in at least two ways: both spouses' continuing and intense commitment to professional work and the husbands' support of their wives' professional involvement.

One common characteristic of professionals is the dominance of work, the "intense personal involvement" (Gross, 1958) they feel with their careers. Commuters, most of whom work in or are at least trained for professional positions, are no different. What differentiates commuters from other professionals is the salience of work for *both* spouses and their willingness to live in separate residences to maximize their career satisfactions.

When both had jobs, work seemed to pervade the entire lives of these commuter spouses. Many of these women, as well as their husbands, describe themselves with words like "workaholic" and "obsessive–compulsive." They speak of long work weeks, about guilt when they are not working, and about their pleasure in work. As one woman said:

I go to pieces when I don't work. I get bored when I am not working. We probably work too hard and occasionally feel guilty about it. But we're not the kind of people who can just relax. We think we have to do something.

And her husband commented:

I am an obsessive worker. I don't take vacations. Uh, you know what I mean. Occasionally at Christmas time, we go away for ten days. I read mystery stories for a week and I go out of my mind. I can't do it. The major exception to work in my life is sleep.

Another woman said:

I want to feel I am accomplishing something. It's important to work. And I suppose I do it because I want to do it. I think it is FUN! And if it is that much fun, why not do it seven days a week?

Her husband commented:

I am obsessive–compulsive about my work. I can't not work.

And another woman remarked:

I think God winds people up differently and I was wound up to work. I almost think of people like little wind-up toys in that I think I got wound up more tightly than most people. When I was just at home, I was compulsively neat. I got upset if people messed things up because I spent so much time cleaning it up. But my own sense of self worth is very much tied up with intellectual achievement. So I just fall apart when I don't have work.

Her husband said:

I don't think I really know how to stop without some purpose to the whole thing. I've never made sharp distinctions between my work and the rest of my life.

For others, their dedication to work is a consequence of the dynamics of their marital history. For example, one woman described the importance of her husband's intense work commitment for her own career concerns:

I enjoy my work. But the other thing is that I think my husband plays a major role. Because his image of me is that he expects me to be just as successful as he is. And he is very successful in his own career. So, actually, he pushes me to be productive, to work. Our life is work, work, work.

Her husband spoke of their work as mutually involving:

We always end up making sacrifices for our work. I have brothers and sisters who can spend the evening bullshitting and so on. I just can't do that. I prefer to be working and mostly I have to be working.

His deep involvement in work clearly served as an impetus for hers. But, in other cases, the wife was the one who promoted the work involvement. We can easily imagine the consequences for the husband of the wife who explained:

I don't think he thinks I should work quite as much as I do. I pursue things in a kind of Kamikaze fashion. I run experiments that run on Christmas, on New Year's Eve; he's gone to parties and I've gone off to the lab in a blue chiffon dress and silver shoes and then washed my hands and joined the party at 11:30.

The commuters give many reasons for their devotion to work, including its rewards and the costs of not working. The former includes the joys experienced in working with ideas and the interpersonal gains of colleague companionship. One woman favorably compared the colleagueship of professional employment with the interactions of housewives or volunteer workers (both were situations she had experienced):

I like to experience growth and that comes from interchange with other people, people who have something valuable for me to learn. I don't know how you get that in the house or through volunteer activities. I couldn't. Because most people in volunteer activities have not worked and about all I can learn from them is how to keep a neat and pretty house, new recipes, and how to take care of the kids. None of which I am interested in. And the same goes for a crummy job.

For her, as others, work provides a means to avoid isolation. But it is not simply that she wants to be with other people. Rather, she wants to be with a certain type of people — stimulating colleagues or people with whom she shares work-related interests, she respects, and she can "learn from." For these women, the negative consequences of not working included the boredom or lack of structure that occurred without a job:

I need an organization telling me what I am supposed to be doing, pressuring me to perform.

Underlying many of the commuters' responses to the meaning of work is the sense that work is their primary source of personal identity: Their work is who they are. One woman gave an emotionally charged response to the thought of living without work:

It's like denying myself to give up some part of me. It's like being permanently crippled in some respect. Like some sort of physical handicap.

Another explained:

I identify myself as a chemist. I don't think of myself as a mommy or a housewife. And when I am not able to practice being a chemist, I suffer a severe identity crisis.

Taken singly, none of these comments seems particularly exceptional. But their cumulative effect, in their pervasiveness and their intensity, among wives as well as husbands, marks commuters as a special group.

Such intense commitment to professional work by both spouses provides the framework in which the choice of a commuter marriage is likely to occur. Precisely because both think of work as a central life interest, these husbands and wives have made the decision to pursue their careers even if it meant living apart for a time. Other couples — for whom employment for either spouse is a necessary, though unpleasant, circumstance, for whom a job is solely a means of financial support, or even for whom employment figures less prominently in a sense of self — would be less likely to make the same choice.

HUSBANDS' ATTITUDES TOWARD WIVES' CAREERS

While most of these wives, as well as their husbands, are deeply committed to their careers, they are, most emphatically, married and want to remain so. A husband's commitment to his own career is not equivalent to his willingness to support his wife's career. Yet, just such support on the part of the husband may be necessary for the maintenance of the wife's career and even their marriage. Research shows that the attitude of a woman's husband is a major factor in her willingness and even ability to work (Birnbaum, 1975; Weil, 1971). An examination of the attitudes of the commuter husbands suggests that they typically provide support for their wives' career involvements and often they even pressed for it. Thus, we should understand these men's attitudes as a factor in the decision to live apart.

Almost all of these husbands strongly supported their wives' professional activities. Only a very few opposed them, while the large majority (about 90%) were, or became over time, either "laissez-faire" or "demanding." The largest group of commuter husbands are "laissez-faire": They want a wife who does whatever she feels is appropriate. These "laissez-faire" husbands typically respond to questions concerning their current attitudes toward their wives working by saying:

I want her to do it only because she wants to, not because I want her to.

Who am I to tell her to work or not? She works because she wants to. That's okay by me. If she didn't want to, I suppose it would be okay by me as well.

These men do not assume that their wives will live through them or for them. Rather, these husbands believe their wives are individuals who can be expected to pursue their own interests.

Although we know of no national data that speak directly to this issue, we suspect that if these "laissez-faire" husbands are not a majority, they are at least not rare, especially among highly-educated men (see Lopata, 1980). They are not opposed to having a working wife, but neither do they exert pressure on their wives to continue their careers. Thus, they presumably have different expectations for men and women. For a wife, work is a choice. The choice happens to be paid professional employment. For a husband, there is no alternative; it is still not considered legitimate in our society for men to drop out of the labor force.

It is in the second group, those whom we call "demanding," where we find husbands who seem exceptional. These husbands clearly expect their wives to be professionals and exert pressure on them to develop careers. They will accept no alternative. These men provide the clearest support, even impetus, for the commuter arrangement. Statements like the following were made by men in this group:

I like her to work. I've always encouraged her to work. It makes her more interesting to me. I couldn't even imagine not being with a professional woman. There is just no way the woman who is my wife could be a housewife. For me, that kind of marriage just wouldn't work.

I should tell you frankly, I don't think I'd ever be interested in a woman who wasn't a professional. I couldn't be.

These men, unlike the "laissez-faire" group, expect their wives to pursue careers. For them, an interesting wife is one who is professionally engaged. To this extent, these ideas of marriage presume an orientation more typically found among wives toward husbands, rather than the reverse. To both of them, then, employment is not a matter open to question; it is an essential element of an attractive identity.

The attitudes of the men in this "demanding" group can be seen even more clearly among those couples where the wife, at some point, expressed ambivalence toward her career. During periods of work-related frustration, the wives might veer toward the housewife role. If they did, they found little support from their husbands. For example, one woman felt some attraction to the traditional housewife image. She, herself, felt frustrated when she was not employed, but it was her own discontent coupled with her husband's demands that fully motivated her. She spoke of a period when she felt she should stay home and raise children. But her husband only became irritated with those wishes:

He would come home at dinner and I would mention something about the children and he was very resentful of the fact that all I had to talk about was the children. He kept after me and finally I decided he was right and I'd go back to work.

Her husband recounted the experience of her staying at home in much the same way:

The tensions in our marriage got very great and I eventually laid down the law. Maybe that's a little strong, but it was in that direction that she had to do something; either she had to go out to work or she had to go back to school. She had to get out of the house.

In this case, "getting out of the house" meant the wife had to set up a residence in a separate locale, commuting home on weekends.

These "demanding" husbands have identical expectations for both sexes. What makes a woman interesting is the same thing that makes any human interesting. "Demanding" husbands may feel as they do, in part, as a way of rationalizing their own high commitment to work. They want to put a great deal of time and energy into their own careers. If the wife became "only" a housewife, she might place greater demands on her husband. By contrast, the wife's deep involvement in her own career reduces the pressure on her husband. A wife's equal professional commitment legitimates the husband's extensive work involvement: She will understand, through her own experience, the pressure on her husband.

It may be that some of those in the "laissez-faire" group would have been more demanding if their wives had expressed a desire to remain housewives. But as they did not, the husbands understood the situation to be one in which their wives should do what they wanted to do, and this happened to be professional work. Eventually that professional work came to prescribe the establishment of a commuter marriage.

PRECIPITATING CONDITIONS: WHY NOW?

These personal histories set the stage for the decision to commute. Those who finally set up two homes are typically ambitious, highly skilled women, most of whom are married to supportive or even "demanding" husbands. Their ambitions had been frustrated, often at no small cost. But their decisions to commute are not simply a matter of personal ambitions or personal frustrations alone. Structural and ideological conditions currently existing in American society interact with personal experiences to produce this voluntary decision to commute. These conditions help explain why commuting is a contemporary response and why these particular couples decided to commute. When these couples establish two separate homes, they are acting in the context of contemporary social conditions which both facilitate and force that choice.

Ideological Conditions: The Effect of Feminism

A major factor facilitating the decision to commute is an ideological commitment to equality between the sexes, especially in the occupational sphere. Only if a woman believes her aspirations are as legitimate as her husband's will she consider searching for a job in a separate location. If there is a supportive climate for this belief, such as the feminist movement presently provides, then a woman is more likely to engage in an open job search unbound by her husband's locale. The feminist movement has, in some measure, legitimated women's demand for individual freedom and personal growth. Commuters, who are already committed to equalizing their job opportunities, may well be the ideological vanguard of women professionals. What is the commuting women's understanding of and relationship to the women's movement? Do they perceive it as causing changes in their behavior?

All of the women commuters expressed a positive orientation toward the women's movement. Some are active members of feminist organizations. Others are less active, though still supportive of many feminist goals. Even those who express some criticism do so in the context of a basic sympathy with the women's movement.

Perhaps more important than their general sympathy toward feminism, these women feel that the women's movement eased their own personal adjustment. Typical comments were:

It helped me stand up more and more.

It made me feel better about myself. It's like a rebirth having all these women say all those things. I do still feel some guilt, but less and less because there are so many people out there saying what you're doing is okay.

It helped me assert myself and be treated like an individual.

It made me realize my options are much broader. Made things easier for me.

It's had a tremendous effect. Instead of being like 10 or 15 years ago, I would have been a weird, strange person and now I am not a weird, strange person anymore. There's an acceptance of what I am doing. So it's easier to feel good about myself.

It has given credence to me in that it makes it easier to be who I am.

Commuting women are likely to support the women's movement and to feel its effects in their own lives, since it provides visions of justifiable alternatives, makes legitimate their freedom of choice, and upholds their self-esteem when they decide to choose a different marital structure. With this comes a new self-understanding that they can express more openly.

A few women even suggested that feminism not only legitimatized their desire to pursue careers, it simultaneously put pressure on them to do so. For example, one woman was offered the presidency of a university almost 400 miles away from her family home. Yet, she felt she had no choice but to accept: to do otherwise would be to damage women's claim to equality. As she put it:

I'm kind of doing it in a sense, not for myself, but because of a commitment. Once I though of giving it up, resigning, right away before it got too far, so they could find somebody else. And that really shocked them, women, women friends. They felt that it was a cop out. I think it is very important, it's symbolic, you know. If I can do this job, I have had the chance to prove that a woman can. And I think that is really what is at stake here. You've got more than yourself on your shoulders. And this is really what's keeping me from giving it up. If I had my way, I'd just go back to my husband.

Feminism, then, not only supported these women's personal drives for equality, but also furthered behavior consistent with accomplishing those goals.

In past decades, professional women rejected their identification with other females (Epstein, 1970). In contrast, women commuters identify themselves as having specific needs and problems resulting from their positions as professionals. They support the women's movement because it deals with these issues and contributes to their own development as well as that of other women. The feminist perspective is not a cause of commuting. Rather there is an affinity between the lifestyle these women adopt and the ideology which supports it. As discussed earlier, most of the women in this study had previously followed their husbands and assumed, in the past, that this was required of them as wives. Only recently had they come to see that relocation pattern as an illegitimate subordination of their lives. Feminism, then, provided an ideological climate for new combinations of family and work that reduced strain and encouraged innovation. In other words, the women's movement helped transform "ideas of marriage." Though they are still a minority, women commuters no longer feel that they are viewed as selfish, sexless deviants. In fact, some of them suggested that others envy their independence. If they are still deviants, that "deviance" itself has become a source of admiration. Changed objective conditions may have preceded these changes in ide-

ology, but the new equality between the sexes facilitates such new social
forms as commuter marriage.

Conditions of the Job Market

For many couples, the newly supportive ideological climate coincides
with crises in their careers. These crises are not simply personal, but
are linked, more generally, to tight job markets which reduce the opportunity to chose positions in specific locations. In this situation, when
both spouses have high commitments to their careers, they may see
no choice but to commute between a work residence and a home residence, spending some nights apart.

The specific market conditions that pressured a spouse into a decision to commute vary with the career stage of that spouse. One group
consisted of younger spouses, both in the early stages of their careers,
who had trouble finding any job in their fields. A second group consisted of older couples in which the wife was in an early stage of her
career — having put aside earlier career interests to raise children. In
both these groups, individuals did not commute to find better jobs,
but to avoid unemployment or severe underemployment. There was
a third group, consisting of older spouses both in advanced stages of
their careers, who faced crises of a different sort. For them, the issue
was not avoiding unemployment, but maximizing career goals by accepting a better position, which was a logical career opportunity they
preferred not to miss.

NO JOB OPPORTUNITIES

There were several different situations in which jobs were not available
for both spouses. In some cases, one spouse could only find work away
from the area where the other was attending professional or graduate
school. In other cases, both spouses were beginning careers at the same
time and could only find acceptable employment at some distance from
each other. Two journalists, for example, found themselves in such
a situation. The wife tried working as a freelance reporter for a small,
local newspaper. But they finally decided they both needed full-time
work. Emphasizing the lack of personal choice in their decision to commute between jobs 300 miles apart, the wife said:

*We tried to get full-time jobs near each other. Oh, did we try! Letters everyplace
and phone calls to everyone. We sent applications all over the country together.
Finally, we had to take these two jobs. It wasn't easy. We can't even talk about*

it now. Every now and then we try and one of us ends up crying and we give up and decide to keep on and see what happens.

As she went on to describe their move, she remarked, defensively but with much insight:

I think that when people focus on the internal dynamics of this, they miss the point. It's the economic climate not some quirk in our psyches or in our relationship.

As journalists sharing the same field, their situation was more difficult than most. However, other spouses in different fields also faced the same situation and tried "applying all over the place" so they might stay together in a single home. But they, too, could find nothing.

Finally, there were couples in which one spouse had a job, while the other, just beginning or renewing a career, could find no employment in the same location. In one such couple, the husband finished his degree before his wife finished hers. While writing her dissertation, they moved, with some excitement, near his new job. Upon finishing, she applied to every school in the area around their home. At first, finding nothing, she tried staying home. Finally, she "decided" they had to commute:

There was never any real discussion about it. It was the only logical thing to do. I mean, I had applied to over 100 schools in the area — from community colleges on up — and there just weren't any jobs. Graduate school is just not so much fun that you just go to it to do it. And I couldn't stay home any longer without a job. We both knew I had been wretchedly unhappy sitting at home.

All of these couples who were beginning careers had to commute to find any acceptable employment. Though in some cases they received more than one job offer, the choices did not include jobs in the same place for both spouses. As their comments illustrate, the situation then *demands* that they look elsewhere. As they put it, it was only "natural" or "logical" to do so. Most did not even think of themselves as having chosen to live apart; they could not sit down, discuss the possibilities, and chose between an intact nuclear structure or a commuter structure. Rather, these couples saw no choice but to commute. Most saw it as a temporary adaptation. They hoped, by continuing to look for other positions and by establishing themselves in careers, that their situations would change and they would be able to share, once again, a single residence.

However, not all of the couples who did commute were unable to find two jobs in the same locale. In the second situation, where the couples were at a later stage in their careers, the spouses had been working for a period of time — most for many years — in the same location. They were both established and could have remained together in one home. Then, one of them was offered a "better" job — a job more attractive in terms of prestige, interest, security, or intellectual growth, as well as income — in a different location. In some cases, the new position involved a move within an organization; in other cases, a move from one employer to another. For this group as compared with both of the others (where at least one spouse was still in the initial stage of a career) how they got the job offer represented a crucial difference determining the choice to commute. Almost all of the spouses in this more-established group were sought out by employers.

For some, the job offer was a consequence of changes in the structure of the job market. Here, instead of a tightening job market which cut off options, affirmative action policies led to a widening job market as employers reached out for highly skilled women. Before the offer, these commuters had not actively pursued a position. But, since the offers were appealing career opportunities, they felt they could not turn them down.

The following case illustrates this situation. The husband was a therapist with an established practice. His wife had a job, but one dependent on periodic state funding. A prestigious organization approached her and offered her a stable, high level position. In explaining their approach, she said:

I was very fortunate to be a woman. I have to admit that. I will have to admit that they were hiring my potential and hiring a woman, but it was a situation I could grow into.

Because she had always followed her husband and minimized her own career, this potential "growth," the ability, finally, to maximize her career chances, led her to accept:

No other position offered such an attractive package. I really wanted something I could focus on, grow with, expand with. This offered prestige and a national orientation, a great deal of possible leverage, a great deal of challenge. If I hadn't accepted, I would never have had the opportunity to develop.

Her husband was not quite so excited about the change but, nonetheless, agreed that she should take the job:

She had worked her whole life. This is not a new thing, a commuter marriage that came out of nothing, or some kind of middle-aged doldrum from being chained to the stove. It was never a "sit down, think it out" decision. We talked about it, of course, but it just runs its natural flow. We both understood what it meant, that it wouldn't be easy. But it was just something she had to do.

Like other commuters, he felt that the establishment of two homes did not constitute a "decision" as we generally understand that term. Instead, the commuter arrangement grew from the way they had lived their lives and occurred at a time that did not speak so much to newly developed preferences as to a changing national climate.

However, it was not always women who responded to an employer's pursuits. In another, far less typical, case both the husband and wife had jobs in one location. Their situation was the reverse of most: She had tenure at a prestigious university, he was at a nearby community college where he felt frustrated. Having established a national reputation through his publications, he was approached by a much better university with an offer of tenure. Though accepting meant that he had to move far from their shared home, he could see no other choice:

I was very dissatisfied with my position and I had never intended it to be a permanent kind of thing. I was kind of dilly-dallying and didn't really know what to do. A tenure offer at such a good school was really hard to turn down. It was a very painful kind of thing. I felt deep down that I should get out of the other situation or I never would. So, I finally decided I had to move.

At the same time, his wife felt that she could not abandon her tenured position with no job in sight to replace it. But she fully supported her husband's need to move ahead in his career.

For all of these couples who could have remained in a single home work is clearly a dominant status. But, they, like commuters in the earlier stages of their careers, would have preferred to remain together. Not only are they willing to travel to their jobs, but back to their marital partners as well, investing a good deal of time, energy, and money in the process. Because they were in the latter stages of their careers, they have to commute if they are ever to attain the professional stature consistent with their aspirations and abilities. Both groups of commuters attempt to deal with the disjunction between the occupational and familial systems. Both groups respond to external pressures that, in concert with their personal predispositions, lead them to "choose" a commuter marriage.

WHAT THE DECISION INDICATES

As we have seen, by the time a particular position appears, commuting may well be a foregone conclusion. Commuters have developed a shared history in which professional involvement is important for both husband and wife. One spouse — typically the wife — is frustrated in this ambition. An egalitarian ideology legitimates the resolution of this frustration through a commuter marriage. At the same time, a bleak job market or changing job opportunities undermines the possibility of a wife remaining in the same locale as her husband. Thus, the job market, either the lack of any job or of the best job, pressures couples into the choice of a commuter marriage. In concert, these personal and societal factors promote the decision to commute and, at the same time, make the decision appear as though it were not a choice at all.

It is in this context that we can examine a number of factors that one might expect, at least at first glance, to promote the decision to live apart. First, we might expect couples, especially in an inflationary economy, to live apart for financial gain or even survival. This is not the case. Second, we might expect couples who set up two homes, while committed to their careers, are not deeply committed to their marriages. This, too, is an erroneous assumption. Let us look at each of these assumptions.

Work Is Not for a Wage

Commuters did not primarily accept job offers for financial gain. This fact can be demonstrated in two ways: Almost all commuters said that they would continue working even if it were not financially necessary; their actual behavior, as indicated by a cost–benefit analysis of commuting, supported this assertion.

To determine whether the separation of residences was undertaken for increases in revenue, we computed a financial cost–benefit analysis in the following manner. First, we subtracted each individual's salary before commuting from his or her salary while commuting. Second, we computed the yearly cost of commuting for each individual by adding the yearly cost of (1) the second residence, (2) phone calls to spouse, and (3) travel between homes. Third, we obtained the total cost or benefit of commuting by subtracting the yearly cost of commuting from the yearly change in income.

To analyze the data, we had to separate two groups of commuters.

First, some commuters did not have any job before they established two residences. Of course, these individuals did make substantial gains in income by moving away from their spouses. However, their increases were far less than they would have been had they obtained the same salaries without commuting. If one subtracts each individual's yearly cost of commuting from his or her increase in salary (as described) the median income is at least $6110 below what it would have been if that job was in the same location as the spouse's.

It is among the second and larger group of commuters, who moved from one job to another, where the data show most clearly that commuting (and employment) is not undertaken for financial reasons. In this group, there were more reductions in individual income than increases (after commuting costs are subtracted from change in salary). Here commuting resulted in a median loss in family income of $1830. (The range of gains and losses was from + $6620 to − $9840.) Pursuing a particular job cost couples money.[3]

These figures would not surprise commuters. Most of the respondents in this study point to the financial drain of commuting as one of its greatest burdens. In many cases, expenditures they could previously support had to be foregone:

Some of the things we used to do, we can't do anymore, like taking expensive vacations. Everything we do is just to be together.

All kinds of money is just going down the drain that we might be using to travel together or enjoy ourselves. It's just a very expensive arrangement.

One man commented on the disadvantageous tax laws that are not even included in the above cost–benefit analysis:

I will say one of the real disadvantages of this is purely a financial one. On top of travel and living up here, are the very adverse tax laws whereby my two states of residence don't have reciprocal tax arrangements, so I end up paying taxes twice. So, I am paying for the privilege of commuting.

We see from this analysis that most couples launch a commuter mar-

---

3. Of course, these figures only indicate that commuters were not working for a wage in the short-term. It might be argued that by commuting, they were investing in careers and consequently were likely to be increasing long-term returns. But, these figures were also computed without considering the higher rates of taxation that accompanied commuting: The costs of travel and a second home are rarely deductible. Some couples even paid taxes in two areas.

riage to participate in careers which usually do not raise their standard of living. Though there may be gains in prestige, interest, "identity," and colleagueship, generally there is no gain in family income.

Marriage Retains Its Importance

We have suggested that work is a central life interest for both spouses in a commuter marriage. However, this does not mean they do not value their marriages. Rather, for individuals who are committed to their careers, the choice to commute in no sense means that they are not highly committed to their marriages. Because individuals value *BOTH career and marriage*, they may be forced to live apart from their spouses for some of the time.

Family and work are not independent of one another. Rather, satisfaction in one affects satisfaction in the other. Much research (Piotrkowski, 1979; Aldous *et al.*, 1979) documents the negative marital consequences when a husband does not perform adequately in his job. The interdependence of the husband–worker roles partially explains such findings: if a man's performance in his job is adequate, he has, in some measure, fulfilled his family obligations. However, this fact alone does not explain the interdependence of family and work. Put simply, an individual's self-esteem or happiness is the sum of performance and satisfaction in his or her various endeavors. Though some areas of life may be weighted more heavily than others, especially at different stages of family life and career, throughout life frustrations and gratifications in one affect behavior and sentiments in the other.

If the commuters had not chosen to live apart, and thereby gain satisfaction in their work, their marriages would have suffered. Throughout the interviews, their comments indicated awareness of the connections between these two spheres. Interestingly, their comments revealed two different perspectives. Some said that if they *themselves* were not satisfied with their careers, their marriages would suffer:

It was not just a career that led us to do this [commute]. A great deal has to do with how you see yourself and so on. It was very demoralizing for me to be there. And obviously, if I was going to be demoralized, in some way or the other, it was going to affect our relationship. I see a connection between the two and it is very hard to separate them.

It is important to realize that if I am unhappy in my job that I'll be unhappy in my marriage.

Simultaneously, they also suggested that if their *spouses* were happier in their work, they themselves would be happier in their marriages:

I want her to be successful. And I don't think there's any insincerity in my saying that. I think that she'll be a lot happier and I think she'll like me more as a result.

When he's feeling good about his work, he likes himself better and he likes everything better. That includes me. So it's just plain good sense to set up this arrangement [commuting].

Both sets of comments reflect a relatively new notion of marriage, a transformed "idea" of what marriage is and should be. That is, there is an unwillingness or inability to sacrifice oneself for the happiness of the marital unit. These spouses do not abide by the old image that supports models of marital "togetherness." Instead, marital satisfaction is predicated on individual work satisfaction.

The complementarity of work and family suggests that individuals need to perform well in both to be satisfied in either. However, the demands imposed by family and occupation are unequal. An individual who wants both a career and a marriage has more control over the latter. The employment system is relatively inflexible. Many employers still can, and do, require that employees follow prescribed patterns for output or amount of time on the job. In most cases, those hired are expected to spend much, if not all, of their time in the area near their jobs. In contrast, the structure of family is more susceptible to individual manipulation. Because family attachments are diffuse and emotional, they can be changed to allow concessions for work roles over which spouses have less control. If both spouses want careers as well as a marriage, adjustments have to be made in the more flexible — family — sphere rather than in the work sphere. Consequently, some couples are forced to set up two separate homes.

For commuters, such a choice does not imply that their marriages are unimportant or even that their careers are more important than their marriages. Instead, their willingness to expend a great deal of time, energy, and money commuting to their families (as well as to their jobs) highlights the value they place on their marriages.

In fact, most of these couples exhibit an intense commitment to maintaining the quality of their emotional relationships. They want to preserve this quality and are mindful of the threats that commuting imposes on it. One husband made this especially clear in discussing how annoyed he gets at imputations that there may be something wrong with his marriage if he is willing to endure separation. On the contrary, he argued:

Our relationship is like a potlatch. We're going through all this just because we want to keep what we have together.[4]

In general, these spouses provide descriptions of their marriages as emotionally valuable or significant to them. The premium they put on the relationship makes it worth their efforts to maintain it. They understand very well the significance of the relationship to their own individual well being and this recognition helps them choose and endure the challenges of commuting.

Clearly then, the choice to commute does not signal an unstable marriage or unstable individuals, unless commitment to a career itself is taken as a sign of instability. Rather, commuting is a response to an endemic condition of occupational life rooted in the social structure. As wives' lives change because of new values and behaviors, so, too, must the lives of their husbands change. Commuter marriage is better understood as a rational response to a societal disjunction than as a rejection of marriage.

CONCLUSION

Our examination of individuals' simultaneous commitments to both their occupations and their families has partially answered the question of who engages in a commuter marriage. More generally, our analysis would suggest that couples may choose between two contrasting patterns of commitment: an asymmetrical one, in which couples' priorities are the reverse of one another, and a symmetrical one, in which they are the same.

In the first pattern, which is still most common, the husband's work is dominant and, as a result, determines his entire family's geographic mobility. His wife follows him to the location of his job. Her dominant status, wife–mother, is not tied to a specific locale. If she

4. The term "potlatch" refers to the North American Indian custom which involves the purposeful destruction of property to express status and thereby "earn" leadership in the community by such conspicuous consumption (see Mauss, 1954).

desires or needs a job, her occupational commitment is secondary. This is the predominant mode even in those families where both spouses are professionals.

Sociologists like Goode and Parsons have argued that this pattern is most efficient for an industrial society. However, as we have shown, society loses full utilization of much of its work force in this supposed "fit." Women, following their husbands, suffer stunted careers, income losses, and may even be forced into unemployment. As a result, they are likely to experience psychological strains.

A minority of couples choose to shift their priorities, making the husband's and the wife's career and family priorities symmetrical. If equality between the spouses is desired, there are several symmetrical patterns from which the partners may choose. In some fortunate families, both spouses may be able to find the best positions in the same locale. No data are available on how large a group this is, but it is very likely small. Since professionals typically have to switch jobs more than once, there is little chance that both spouses in a dual-career family will continually be able to find optimal positions in the same area. However, if they cannot, they can still choose between two other egalitarian modes of dealing with conflicts over where to live.

First, both spouses may make compromises in their careers to stay in one home. In contrast to the predominant pattern, this represents an increased commitment to the wife's career and a decreased commitment to the husband's. Both spouses can lower their job aspirations to remain in one area where each can find a position though neither takes his or her first choice. Or each spouse can make a compromise in his or her career at different points in time. One choice may favor one mate; a second, the other. Such "compromise" options may eventually affect the structure of the labor market. To get the employees they want, employers may need to begin hiring couples, overcoming remaining prejudices against nepotism. Employers could hire a couple for one job, or even for a position and a half, getting the person they want while saving themselves money. If compromise options should become more prevalent among couples, notions about "orderly careers" may need revamping. Gaps in work history may need to be reinterpreted as a result of commitment to both work and family, rather than as a lack of commitment to work.

However, since those who compromise are still in the minority, this pattern may result in career costs for both spouses rather than simply the wife. Alone, each could be more successful. And just as the wives in the conventional pattern suffer psychological pains as a result of career limitations, both spouses in this compromise pattern may also. Because, as we have seen, work and family satisfactions are so highly related for these couples, such occupational costs may strain their marriages. In addition, each spouse may experience pressures, both internal and external, because they are still somewhat different from the norm.

As a second alternative, commuters exhibit an increased commitment to the wife's career while retaining a high commitment to the husband's career. Commuters, then, are couples in which both spouses perceive their work as a dominant status and act to maximize it. This choice may be increasingly common if societal conditions, such as the feminist movement and a tight job market, continue. And there is no reason to suspect they will not.

To understand commuter marriage as an attempt at equality is not to evaluate it as the best solution. Rather, given present social conditions, it is, for many, the only solution. Only in a commuter marriage can both spouses participate fully in careers. This is precisely what commuters understand when they decide to set up two homes.

CHAPTER 3

Emotional Support at a Distance

The household is the basic intimate environment in every society and the process of living together rather than facts of kinship or marriage produces intimacy. — *Skolnick (1978, p. 119)*

In the new families . . . the couple and their children are very much centered on the home. . . . They can be so much together and share so much together because they spend so much time in the same space. — *Young and Willmott (1973, p. 29)*

As discussed in the previous chapter, commuters view the decision to set up two homes as a logical, even necessary, one. Yet, once apart, these couples become outsiders looking in, acutely aware of what they once had and now miss. Simultaneously, they discover what many couples forget or suppress: the day to day constraints that "normal" households impose. These commuters, married yet single for much of the time, are in a position to tell us what marriage — with its members' daily proximity — both provides and denies. In the next two chapters, we will examine the positive and negative consequences of living apart for the commuters' marital relationship. In doing so, we find that the experiences of these couples provide an important argument for the irreplaceable character of the stable, single-residence marriage while at the same time they provide a critique of that "normal" relationship.

The epigraphs which introduce this chapter assert the prominent view that it is physical proximity — the couple's shared residence — that enables the modern family to fulfill its major function: the provision of emotional support, or what Parsons called "tension management." Yet assertions of a link between family structure and function do not specify the actual elements that make up the general concept of emotional support, nor do they explain why it requires daily face-to-face interaction.

Commuter marriage provides a particularly sensitive context in which to discover the actual impact of daily proximity on emotional support, as well as to specify its various components. In the first section of this chapter we ask what commuters miss in their emotional relationships as a result of living in two separate homes. Such an analysis allows us to examine what commuters miss by living apart and to ask *how* daily face-to-face interaction helps manage tension. In the second section of this chapter, we shall see that by altering two constituent elements of social relationships — the sharing of time and space — commuter couples render problematic what coresident couples "take for granted" and assume to be inherent elements of married life. We shall see that when the time and space dimensions of relationships vary, the couple's subjective sense of reality responds in kind.

The analysis of the consequences of living apart shows still another side to the relationship between daily face-to-face interaction and emotional support. Changes in the commuters' marriages remind us that the constant presence of both spouses does not always lead to harmonious and relaxed interaction. Instead, it often leads to boredom and an intensification not a reduction of tension. Thus, the very same structural features of the family that allow it to achieve some of its goals inhibit the realization of others. In the final section of this chapter, we will ask how the structure of the "normal" American family stands in the way of a couple functioning as a supportive, caring unit. Or, to what extent does the physical separation of spouses result in emotional gains as well as losses?

LOSSES IN THE ABILITY TO PROVIDE EMOTIONAL SUPPORT

Marital Conversation

In the last decade, social scientists and therapists have written many books and articles about the difficulty spouses have communicating satisfactorily with one another. The capacity and willingness to do so is understood as an essential component of a good marriage and as a prerequisite for emotional support (Miller, Corrales, & Wackman,

1975; Montgomery, 1981). For example, in the best-selling book *Open Marriage*, O'Neil and O'Neil (1975) suggest that a couple's ability to "explore their relationship verbally" is an index of their ability to achieve "individual growth and true commitment to one another" (p. 105). Training courses in effective marital communication are offered throughout the country. These do not simply target the need for spouses to talk to one another, but the need for a certain kind of talk: empathetic, sensitive, and revealing talk.

Such literature distinguishes daily conversation from "real communication"—only the latter is emphasized as the means by which spouses reduce conflict and engender intimacy. The experiences of commuters, however, suggest that it is not solely this intense, personal communication that provides spouses with emotional support. Rather, it is the opportunity to engage in informal conversations and to share daily experiences regularly that distinguishes the shared residence from other personal relationships and allows it to manage tension.

Commuters, because they live in separate locations for much of the time, cannot engage in such daily conversations. Although most do not feel that they are less open (or "communicative") with their spouses, they do experience the reduction in simple talk as a serious loss. One wife spoke explicitly about the distinction between daily conversation and "real communication":

I make every possible effort to stay open and talk about my personal inner life with Phil. I do, especially when we see each other because we have so little time. But, on the other hand, the other levels of intimacy, you know, ordinary household intimacy, I don't think that is there as much. The relaxed conversation while you're cooking dinner. Or the reading something to him I come across in the newspaper while we're both sitting in the living room. That's gone and I find I really miss it.

The conception of the sharing of "trivia" as an essential aspect of the emotional content of marriage appeared in many commuters' accounts:

I miss the opportunity to share the everyday things like "what did you have for lunch today?"

You have a lot of immediate impressions and little jokes and observations that you can't save for a week. You can't reconstruct that kind of trivia in an effective way. I find the loss of that material really annoying.

What commuters call attention to in elaborating this point is not a substantive interest in such minutiae, but rather their sense that such exchanges between spouses cement intimacy and sense of involvement with each other. Small talk confirms, indeed constructs, the familiar web of shared meanings which help produce an ordered (and ordering) world.

These commuters not only spoke of "missing" such talk, but stated explicitly that they experienced more tension because they could not speak with their spouses daily:

Commuting just raises the level of tension in my life and in our marriage. We don't have that time after dinner, or whenever, to sit, relax, and talk. I even miss our battles.

The man's wife spoke in very similar terms:

I think in general the emotional pressure has been raised. Now we both have the tendency to brood over things. Don't have the chance to talk or even yell at each other.

The loss is compounded by the fact that complaining about disagreeable experiences, one way of dealing with the anxiety they produce, becomes more difficult. Living apart made one husband realize:

She keeps me on an even keel. When I get mad at work, and come home, she is steady as a rock. She's like an anchor for me. She stops me from going crazy. Now, I am much more likely to stew about something.

Clearly this "emotionally" supportive role is not simply that of the wife, as some social theorists would have us think. Rather, both spouses need someone to complain to, as the following wife's statement suggests:

Sometimes I just feel like I am fighting the world. When I come home to Harry [her husband], he just levels me out. It takes him ten minutes to make me realize that things aren't that important, that I'm getting overconcerned about little things. When he's not here, I find myself dwelling on things. I try to tell myself that it doesn't matter, but somehow it just doesn't work as well.

In their continuous face-to-face interactions, spouses in the shared home serve as sounding boards for one another, sharing their good and bad experiences, gossiping, and recounting their daily activities. If each spouse is willing to listen and respond, the supportive function of marriage is partially fulfilled. Other studies have found a relationship betweeen the *amount* of talk and marital satisfaction (Miller *et al.*, 1975; Navran, 1967). Such findings are at least an indication that conversation, not just open, revealing communication, is an element of a good marrriage (although, of course, the two may be closely linked and are likely to appear in the same marriage). Certainly some homes enjoy little interaction of either type.[1] But the fact remains that when spouses share a single residence, the *possibility* for both daily conversation and communication exists. Others, who live in separate homes — like neighbors or even intimate friends — are not in the same position to provide daily, ongoing conversation. The single residence family is, then, in a unique position to provide "tension management" for individuals in our society. When marital conversation is not possible, as with the commuters, spouses are likely to experience frustration and increased anxiety.

Telephone Conversations as a Substitute for Face-to-Face Interactions[2]

We might expect that commuters could replace some of their daily conversation by picking up the phone and calling one another. Indeed, sociologists suggest that the telephone makes the maintenance of other geographically dispersed relationships, like those with kin, possible.

Most commuters call each other frequently. Forty-two percent call at least once a day; 30% call every other day; 17%, once a week; only 11%, less than once a week. Many of them noted the phone's important, though circumscribed, use. Typical comments were:

1. As not all conversation is pleasurable, quantity of interaction is not, alone, an adequate measure of marital satisfaction. Yet, it provides some indication. In its absence, satisfaction is clearly difficult to obtain. As Navran (1967) found: "Happy couples differ from others in that they talk to one another more. . . . Couples who are cut off from each other because of the husband working an evening or 'graveyard shift,' or by each spouse working different schedules, are exposed to the danger of impaired communication which could lead to impaired marital adjustment" (p. 182). Commuters are in such a situation, and thus are exposed to some of the same dangers as those in the "graveyard shift" or those "working different schedules."

2. Obviously the telephone is a major mechanism allowing for direct communication across distance. Though commuters also could have written letters, very few did so. The availability of the phone made letter writing obsolete. Also, though letters are cheaper, they do not allow immediate responses and require more time and effort on the part of the sender. Of course, telegrams cannot serve the same purpose as the phone, while they, too, cost money. Two couples did, however, send one another tape recordings of their thoughts, finding it cheaper and more satisfying for long-distance reviews of their weekly events.

We call each other. That's limited but it's something. If there weren't the telephone, this whole thing would be much harder.

If anyone else listened to our calls, they would sound very boring and maybe even impersonal. But just that contact, it's contact, saying I'm still here and you're still important.

If I couldn't just pick up the phone and talk to her, I couldn't live this way. It helps, not like being there, but it helps.

The phone can reduce loneliness, provide a sense of security in the face of geographic separation, and offer some limited emotional support.

However, the phone is far from a complete substitute for face-to-face interaction. The long-distance call is expensive, as commuters are keenly aware. Consequently, their conversations are affected adversely in several ways. First, they tend to summarize their experiences:

We talk every day about what has gone on that day. Sort of "I did this and this," and she says, "I did that and that and that." Just to keep each other up on things. Those long intense personal conversations just aren't possible on the phone. Or even going over in detail like we might have done when we were together. I'm always aware of the minutes and dollars ticking away.

Second, commuters miss the luxury of shared inactivity, or silence, that is impossible over the phone:

Sometimes when you are talking at the table, and its over coffee, something occurs to you, it may occur after a long silence. And a lengthy silence for us can be ten minutes. Well a lengthy silence over the phone is impossible. You can't finesse it in that medium. So I think an awful lot of intrinsic experiences of daily life are lost.

Such silence is unacceptable not only because of its high cost, but because the phone requires constant exchanges.[3] One must keep up one's side of the conversation:

When I'm on the phone, I always think I have to say something. I feel awful when I don't or can't. Phone calls have always seemed to me a very awkward way of communicating.

3. See McLuhan (1964) for his discussion of the need for full participation of individuals when they engage in telephone talk.

The relaxation provided by the informal interactions in the shared home is lost.

Because of the expense and change in conversational form, the content of conversation is changed as well. Many commuters commented that they often used the telephone to talk about primarily practical matters, which needed immediate attention:

We don't usually call just to say, "I miss you." It's for information. Like which plane will you be on or there's an important letter here for you. Sometimes we call just to talk, but not usually.

Even though they may still review events of the day, they do so matter-of-factly, almost impersonally:

We call every night, but as a general rule, we don't talk seriously about personal matters. We talk primarily business. Somehow over the phone, I feel like I am just filling some kind of obligation to stay in touch.

We talk about the children, about what needs to be done, about paying bills. Phone calls are just emotionally neutral.

Another problem of phone conversations is what Ball (1968) calls "insistency": "The telephone induces a sense of obligation and urgency regarding the answer" (p. 63). Commuters, like others, feel they must respond to a ringing phone whether or not they want to talk. Because their respective moods may be different, they sometimes find these interactions disconcerting. Several commuters commented on this:

Sometimes she will call me and I'll be really tired. I just won't have any life in me. And she'll want something more from the call. There's a clashing. Or it happens the other way around. I'll feel good and she'll be focused on something she's doing. It's hard to shift gears to get into someone else's mood when there is no forewarning and the phone call will soon be over.

At any moment the phone intrudes on private space. Moods may be different; tasks may be interrupted. The phone is answered, but little time is available for adjustment to unanticipated responses.

Commuters sometimes stated such differences made them feel lonelier or more separate from one another after they hung up than before the phone call. Having established separate territories, with a pleasant image of the spouse constructed in their minds, the phone conversations leave each alone to brood over their differences. Of course, when couples are together, their moods are not always the same, but they can see each other and wait for the right time to talk. They know their chance to interact will not disappear.

Some commuters attempt to deal with this problem by establishing a particular time for phoning one another. This technique helps ease the sense of interruption, but these spouses find they sometimes need one another at an unplanned time and then they, too, face the same problems, if not exacerbated ones because they have not followed an agreed-upon routine.[4]

A final problem with the phone is that it is unidimensional;[5] the visual cues abundantly available in face-to-face interaction are completely absent:

The phone is bad. I'm adverse to using it for really personal conversations. You can't read each other's faces, you can't read each other's psyche or mental state — whatever you want to call it. And it's very unsatisfying.

The participants are not only unable to see each other, but they cannot touch each other, which is one of the aspects of emotional support commuters miss most.

The inadequacy of the phone, resulting from its expense, insistency, and unidimensionality, becomes especially clear when we examine exchanges that express strong emotions. As one man said:

Phone calls are consciously constructed. There is no emotion on the phone. No saying: "I love you." If you say it, it comes out sounding perfunctory.

Both strong positive and negative emotions are typically repressed on the phone. Many commuters talked about their inability to raise, discuss, and resolve disagreements in long-distance calls:

If the conversation starts not going right, there is no way to resolve it. I remember a few times when the phone got slammed down in anger. What would happen if we were together, it would normally be me — after 15 minutes or half an hour,

---

4. Perhaps this routinization of phone calls is a mechanism of social control. Each spouse has to be home at an appointed time ready to respond to the other's needs. This may be detrimental since one of the benefits of commuting is the freedom it allows for pursuit of individual activities (see Chapter 6).

5. As McLuhan (1964) suggests: "Since all media are fragments of ourselves extended into the public domain, the action upon us tends to bring the other senses into play in new relations. . . . Why can we not visualize while telephoning? . . . When the reader has a chance to try the experiment deliberately, he will find he simply cannot visualize while phoning, though all literate people try to do so" (p. 234).

I'd go over and touch her, put my hand on her shoulder or something and often times not speak. Just a kind of signal of: I hope you're over your tension. And I still like you, love you. That kind of thing you can't do on the phone. A person may be able to respond to your touch, but not to your voice, which is what caused the irritation in the first place.

Because conflict is difficult to deal with over the phone, anger can build.

Phone calls, though valued, cannot substitute for face-to-face interaction, and can even contribute to resentments and frustrations. Despite the phone company's insistence, telephoning may not always be "the next best thing to being there."

Togetherness: The Sharing of Leisure

Marriage, for most middle-class couples, is the major source of steady companionship in leisure activities. Duncan, Schuman, and Duncan (1973) found that "companionship in doing things together with the husband" was chosen by the majority of wives in their sample as the most valued aspect of marriage, outstripping love, understanding, standard of living, and chance to have children.

Commuter couples who are unable to share many planned leisure activities when they live apart, recognize the loss:

If I wanted to go to a movie, I wouldn't go there by myself. Or if I wanted to go out to eat, I wouldn't want to go alone, sit there, and just look at the other people in the restaurant. I don't get out a whole lot these days.

Since these activities are not perceived as enjoyable alone, each spouse does less and the couple, as a unit, suffers from decreased companionship.

In addition to the reduction of planned leisure activities, most commuters experience a loss of impulsive, unplanned recreation:

There was nothing sweeter than coming back from a hard day at the office and suddenly saying: "Let's jump in a cab and go see a film and go to a restaurant." We can't do that as much because we're just not together as much.

Commuters, because they do have such limited time together, tend to be highly organized, often planning in advance how to spend their shared time. Much of the spontaneity characteristic of a single-residence marriage is lost. When both spouses are together regularly, they can count on each other to share a meal at home or they can decide to go out, to discuss problems, or just sit and talk. None of these activities require much planning in advance. In contrast, planning is usually required to meet friends, relatives, or neighbors. As one of the women, who was cited above, speaking of the increased anxiety resulting from limited conversation, said:

When I want to relax and enjoy myself, I don't like the idea of having to call somebody up and saying: "Hey, let's do this," and they say, "I can't today, maybe tomorrow." Everybody's life is so scheduled. You have to sort of plan things. But with Harry [her husband] everything is spontaneous. I miss that. Like all of a sudden, you have an hour, or a couple of hours to do something, and it's very hard to get somebody else to do something in those couple of hours.

Thus, we see that physical proximity provides for "tension management" by allowing the spouses to pursue leisure activities jointly in an easy, spontaneous way.

Finally, marriage typically allows not only for the sharing of activity, but also of inactivity. The commuting couples in this study were keenly aware of this shared quietude and prized it as a unique component of their marriages:

We don't have much time to sit down with a good book now when we're together. That's a real loss. Now we have so much to say to each other and so much to do together that we just don't have long quiet hours at home. That's something I miss. And it's funny, I am not even sure I was aware how much I liked it when we had it. I guess it was just one of those things that you take for granted.

We like to sit in the same room and read, you know, different books. Now we don't have time to do that as well as do things together, you know, talking and going places. You have to give up one, and we've given up the quiet sitting together. Those quiet times, I'd like them back.

Studies that only consider communication and joint activity as aspects of the companionship characteristic of marriage, overlook the importance of such quiet, inactive periods. With friends or others with whom one has a personal tie, such calm noninteraction is unlikely to occur. It is only with persons sharing a home that one has the freedom not to talk, not to do things together. The opportunity to sit quietly in the room with another obviates feelings of loneliness while providing a sense of unity.

Marital Sex

Despite many changes in recent years, marriage remains the primary relationship in which sexual activity is legitimate. Through marital sex, spouses may express emotional involvement and support as well as enjoy physical release. Thus, it is clearly one element of tension management. However, though there is the expectation that marital partners will, and should, satisfy sexual needs with one another, many American couples are sexually incompatible (Hunt, 1974; Masters & Johnson, 1970).

Before separation, commuter couples, like others, differed greatly in their experience of and feelings about their sexual lives. A few speak of a sexual incompatibility that existed before they set up two homes, while others speak in glowing terms about their marital sex lives. But the majority of spouses were neither totally dissatisfied nor continually excited either before or after commuting. Rather, they speak of periodic peaks and lulls in their sexual relations.[6]

Bearing in mind this wide variation in sexual activity before commuting, we looked closely at the effects of separation. In terms of frequency, for a small group whose activity was already slight, commuting has no further limiting effect. For another small group with a high rate of sexual interaction (estimated average of intercourse three to five times a week) the decline is substantial. For most others (estimated average of intercourse twice a month to twice a week), there is some reduction, depending both on previous frequency as well as how long an interval they are separated.

Most of those who do see each other every weekend do not experience a radical decline in sexual interactions; many of these couples confined their sexual activities to weekends anyway. Typical of this group was a wife's comment:

Sex has been sort of confined to weekends for a long time anyway. We're both busily involved in our work during the week when we're together, too. So we relaxed on weekends and that's when we would be likely to make love. We just didn't have time to think of it during the week. So commuting may have lessened the frequency but not by much.

---

6. This lack of consistency may, in fact, be a problem with those sexual surveys that ask: "How often do you have intercourse with your spouse?" As the frequency varies so much from one week to the next, it is difficult for an individual to give an accurate estimate, and the estimate, if given, will have very little meaning.

And those who see one another less than once a week typically do face more of a decline in the number of sexual interactions.

But we still must ask whether there are changes, as a result of commuting, in the intensity or the passion of the couples' sexual relations. It is now well documented that many couples who live together become habituated to one another; their sexual passion declines over the years (Cleveland, 1976; Pietropinto, 1980). Some observers, such as Keller (1982), have suggested that the maintenance of romantic sexual passion is impossible in long-term relationships like marriage. Of the commuters, we might ask: Does distance make the heart grow fonder? Are they able to translate their separation into increased sexual attraction and passion for one another?

On the one hand, most commuters — while alone — do miss their mates' affectionate responses. Typical comments were:

I miss the hugging, the touching, the holding hands.

I walk down the street, seeing couples with their arms around each other, and I go back to my empty apartment really missing Jack. I mean, where is the hug when I come in the door?

The bed feels so empty at night. We usually at least hold each other. I miss her warm body.

Yet, on the other hand, only a minority of commuters translate this longing into an intensification of sexual ardor when they reunite. And, of this minority, only in some cases did both spouses agree that their relationship had, in fact, become more exciting.[7] A more frequent response was that if there had been any change at all in the intensity of their sexual interactions, it was slight. In fact, among the majority of commuters, both spouses agree that the intensity of their sexual relations did not change at all. As one woman put this shared experience:

It's just not the way it was in the beginning of our marriage. I don't know why. It's just not new I guess. That bothers me because it was really great then. I know that's what happens, but you still want it even if you do know intellectually. We both feel less passionate. Commuting just hasn't brought back the old excitement in bed.

---

7. Since sexual passion is, at least in part, a subjective experience, there is no reason to suspect that these husbands and wives were being dishonest in their disagreement.

Several explanations for the lack of change are possible. First, though commuters are apart for periods of time, their sexual relationship is not novel. As Hardy (1964) suggests, it is novelty that promotes sexual passion. Hence, the decline in intensity that typically occurs in the shared home is rarely overcome by separation. Second, the spouses' availability to one another is just delayed, not cut off. There is a time lag, but both spouses know they will reunite on a regular basis. In an "affair," that regularity is not always assumed: It is the insecurity that creates the passion (Neubeck, 1969). Third, some analysts have suggested that the excitement of an extramarital relationship is associated with its illegitimacy (Hunt, 1974). Marriage, whether in one or two residences, remains a legitimate place for sexual activity. Whatever the cause—lack of novelty, ease of access, or legitimacy—the sexual passion associated with a new relationship or an affair is not recouped when a couple sets up two homes.

About one fourth of the commuters actually experience a decline in the intensity of their sexual relations. Here, again, the spouses do not always agree either on the quantity or quality of their sexual experiences or on the reasons for the decreased passion. But, they use essentially three types of explanations for the lowered intensity. First, some suggest that the more hectic life of commuting, requiring travel between two homes, causes tension and fatigue which reduces the desire and energy for passionate sex. As one woman remarked:

There's always the energy and tiredness you get from commuting. I come back exhausted. Not just ready to jump into bed. There's the feeling of more of a need for recuperation and not saying: "Let's go to bed." That takes more energy than we have.

Her husband understood:

She comes home really tired. We're happy to see each other and sit talking about our respective weeks. But, sex, when it happens, which isn't usually on the first day back together, is not particularly passionate, not more than before, maybe even less. Her energy level is just really low.

Second, some commuters report that they feel pressured to have sex when they reunite. Lewis and Brisset (1967) have suggested that many Americans now have an "ethic of work" in sex, feeling that they have to live up to some general standard of "production" during intercourse. In the same way, some commuters feel they are driven to "produce" in their limited shared time, which reduces their pleasure.

The result is action but not passion. For example, a wife indicated that her reduced pleasure in sex was the result of such a demand:

He gets home Friday night and we usually have sex that night. There's the feeling we only have so much time and he always says: "I'm horny already by Wednesday." And I always feel I'm really needed to fill a quotient and that cuts down the spontaneity.

In this case, her husband saw it entirely differently:

Sex has gotten better. It's less frequent, but Friday night, after we've been apart, is our best sex night. I'm tired but I try hard not to be. She's very excited Friday night. But Friday night is our only sex night. But I think one good night is better than three lousy nights. I guess I am more into quality than quantity.

Other spouses agree that the push to have sex lessens the intensity. A husband commented:

I think it is a little more frantic with the commuting. Again we feel we have to fit a week's worth of living in three days. That applies to sex. So, it's just less passionate.

His wife remarked:

Well, it means sex isn't quite as free as it was because you're only together on weekends, and you know there's going to be a separation after the weekend. So we're likely to have it on a particular night even if we are not in the mood. You know, there's the feeling that you've got to have sex, or something is wrong.

Finally, some of the commuting women (though not men) experience a "stranger effect." Apart for a period of time, they first must readjust themselves to their husbands. For example, in one couple both the husband and wife said they were quite satisfied with their sexual relationship before they began to commute. However, living apart made the wife feel a need for readjustment:

I guess it's changed the intensity somewhat in that we've got to get reacquainted each time because we haven't seen each other. It's not instantaneous sex. We find we have to work things through, get into each other's worlds first.

Though she thought this was a shared sentiment, her husband's description is quite different:

It's more exciting after two weeks apart. It is only, in effect, when you look at the fact that you only have a couple of days every couple of weeks. So, from the sex point of view, if one is turned off that night, that sort of takes care of the whole month. That will be a point of conflict sometimes. So, it's a plus and a minus.

In contrast, for another couple, the wife had never been particularly interested in sex — a tense point even before they lived apart. Compounding this problem, the wife reports that she feels the "stranger effect" when they reunite:

The bad thing about commuting is that it has got to be good because you don't have very much time. And he arrives and wants to make love that night. And I don't because every time he goes away and comes back it takes about 24 hours or so to recognize him again.

Her husband, with the greater desire, does not experience the same need for a period of readjustment. But his comments show that they had discussed their different feelings. He is trying to understand:

It takes her a little time to adjust, to readjust, to get to know me again. I happen to readjust faster. I have to admit that has caused a certain amount of tension. But now I've gotten used to it and it doesn't strike me as so strange.

In sum, the experiences of commuters suggest that it is not solely the daily face-to-face interaction of marriage that makes it a "companionate" rather than "romantic" relationship, at least in sexual terms. Only a minority of these separated couples experience increased passion because of their distance from one another. In fact, some even experience a decline while most suggest that their sex lives remain basically the same. This is true for all types of couples: those who had very good sex lives before separation and those who felt deep dissatisfaction in this area. These experiences are true of both men and women; couples who had been married only five years as well as those married 20 years. Again, we see that these separated couples experience costs in the ability to provide one another with emotional support. They face a decrease in the frequency of physical interactions without a compensating increase in passion or intensity.

TIME–PLACE DISJUNCTIONS IN COMMUTER MARRIAGE

This analysis has shown that commuting involves costs in couples' ability to provide one another with emotional support. Without daily face-to-face interaction, they miss daily conversation, shared planned and unplanned activity, as well as physical intimacy—elements of emotional support possible in a shared home. And their absences from each other limit commuters' ability to be intimate and "manage tension."

Something else significant is missing in these commuter couples' lives. Living apart challenges the "taken for granted" quality of their relationship. This experience produces distinct emotional losses beyond those we have thus far discussed. We can explain such losses by the fact that living separately sunders the time and place underpinnings of conventional marriage.

Berger and Kellner (1974) call attention to the order-bestowing quality of marriage—the fact that marriage is a relationship that creates for the individual "the sort of order in which he [sic] can experience his [sic] life as making sense." They further suggest that this sense-making function of marriage derives from the meaning-sustaining conversation between partners that physical proximity permits. Thus, marital conversation, via physical proximity, produces the "taken for granted" quality that signals the ordered (and ordering) world typically provided by a viable marital relationship. If the reality-making force of marriage hinges on the proximity of partners to one another, as these authors suggest, we should expect marriages which separate spouses to experience difficulties with this reality- or sense-making quality.

As predicted, commuter spouses do register responses which indicate that the sense-making function of their relationship is in jeopardy. The stranger effect they allude to in their sexual relationships is, in fact, a more general sense. They talk of feeling "weird," "awkward," and "strange," at least initially, when they reunite. They recognize emotional distance in a relationship they know should be, and they want to be, "close."

I've noticed with my husband now, there's a period of strangeness. It takes several days for that to break down and for us to begin chattering in detail—to really feel comfortable.

It's usually sort of strange. There's a "What do we talk about first?"—a distance. It's weird.

When I get there it takes a day or so to decide that nothing has changed and to feel comfortable about it. There's always that worry when you first get back together.

Our earlier discussion of marital communication suggested that couples who live apart miss the conversation that looms so large in Berger and Kellner's formulation of how marriage orders the worlds of its partners. However, our analysis of responses suggests that it is more than face-to-face communication that creates the base on which marriage's sense-making quality depends. The marriages of couples who live apart lack something beyond the diminution of meaning-sustaining conversation.

In coresidence marriages, couples have a common base (their home) and coordinated schedules around which they create a shared world which, in turn, provides a sense of order to their lives. Such time and place commonalities are constitutive dimensions of marriages that ground the partners in the relationship and set them off from other relationships. By contrast, couples who live apart do not build their daily schedules around each other's time constraints, nor do they have one common base which is their "home." Because commuting alters the time–place dimensions of their relationships it dislocates the partners. The subjective experience of such dislocation is the sense of emotional distance, the inappropriateness one partner feels toward the other, which threatens the important "taken for granted" quality of their relationship.

Time Apart

Coresident couples who separate each working morning and regroup each evening have a daily regimen obviously different from couples who live apart. On the one hand, commuter couples experience a freedom from the need to coordinate schedules. This freedom, to which we will return in Chapter 6, is an advantage — the benefits of which both spouses, but particularly wives, articulate.

I have so much more time, I am able to do what I want, when I want.

Yet, on the other hand, there is a concomitant response, usually subjectively unconnected, that implies a diminished capacity to concentrate as concertedly as they might like. The wife quoted above went on to say:

I tend to waste a lot of time. He does that too. We've been talking about that. We'll daydream, futz around, and we had thought that we sort of interfered with each other's work, living together, but it turns out that I think it's been, overall, more interference being apart, because I'll sit here all night and realize at twelve o'clock that I've read three pages and I'll just drift off.

In a similar vein others said:

I don't get down to business the way I'd like to.

I'm not as focused as I'd like to be all the time.

Such responses occur most often in the context of discussions about how time is spent when normally spouses would be together.

Statements about diminished ability to concentrate may be regarded as evidence for the feeling of being unmoored from a meaning-giving relationship. That fact that partners in such couples are not around to sustain everyday realities for one another results in a kind of unhinging, as if they literally felt detached from the unit that orders their world. Such responses seem to confirm the thesis that intimate relationships provide the moorings that facilitate purposeful action.

Especially for those couples who do not come together on a regular basis, for example, every weekend, an awareness develops that "it is time" to get back together. One husband, whose work depended on what he called creative bursts, said he knew it was time to visit his wife when his creativity seemed to be waning.

After about four weeks of this sort of pagan lifestyle, I get less motivated.

For professionals, whose careers demand heavy intellectual and emotional output, any such threat to their ability to concentrate or work concertedly could become extremely costly. The increased productivity that spouses connect to freedom from the restrictions of their mates' schedules could be counteracted by this diminished capacity to work purposefully.

Time Together

Couples who live apart are very aware of their need to use constructively the time they are together, and in this respect, they are like other dual-career couples. However, time together is even more vital for commuters because they are apart so much of the time. As a result, they develop high expectations for the time they do share. Yet, these expectations often make time together more difficult. Even for those couples who see each other fairly often, the disappointment of unfilled expectations can mar the satisfaction of reunions:

Our expectation level was so high because it was important that every minute count and everything be perfect and it just wasn't. The pressure was always on and it was a real strain and we felt it.

Because time together is so clearly bracketed from "other" time, it becomes more vulnerable to disappointment. These couples are cognizant of "spoiled time" together in ways, we suspect, coresident couples are not. Relating the difficulties she has in "feeling comfortable" when she joins her husband, a wife said:

When you have only a couple of days, there's that strangeness, that letdown — like, "Why aren't I enjoying this more?"

Expectations affect perceptions of "spoiled time" in still another way. Having been apart, these partners anticipate that when they reunite, they will focus on each other. When they do not, the enjoyment of their reunion is clouded. For example, one husband, whose wife is away for three of four days a week during the legislative session (she holds a political office in a state capital), pointed this out when talking about whether he missed her while she was away. He said he did not, but explained that he was bothered by the effect her absence had on their time together. He said when they spent time together, she brought the demands of her job home with her, which kept her psychologically invested — that is, "away":

She's pretty busy when she's home and I guess I find that more trying than her being away partly because since she is away a substantial part of the time — then it seems more important that we be together during the few days that she's here. It seems less understandable sometimes why that's not possible. When a person is away, of course, you're not with them. But when she comes home, "Why is it so important to have that political conversation right now? Why don't you talk to me?" So there is some friction.

In effect, then, their time together was colored by his view of their time apart. Because they do separate, they should, in his view, spend their time together in a more focused manner.

Moreover, the fact that much of their time is not shared makes a spouse's reference to experiences while living apart seem like an intrusion on their relationship together. Still, when couples come together, each needs time to tell his or her "stories," to recount things that happened. But because these events and experiences occurred "away," removed from the other spouse, they cannot feel the connection that they would have felt, had the couple been together when it happened. They literally cannot share the experience; they either do not know the people with whom the event took place, or even if they know their spouse's associates, the time elapsed since the event makes it a part of the mate's "away" life, not the shared one. Contrast this situation with couples sharing a single home telling each other stories every night. Such stories may be the continuation of an earlier phone call, which included the spouse: "Guess what just happened to me? I'll tell you more about it later when I see you." Even if couples only discuss the event that evening, spouses living in the same home will, most likely, know more about each other's daily life and routine: They will feel more a part of the event in question. Consequently, living apart may make it difficult for spouses to "know about" each other's lives.

If we were together daily, "What did you do today?" and that kind of thing, I'd hear more about it. There is a way in which I feel her experience isn't shared by me. It's not like she doesn't ever talk about it, but a crisis on Monday may be over by Friday. I feel very "un" a part of her life.

Because of feelings like these, the period together often suffers from overload. Since time together is limited these couples urgently need to draw sustenance from it, which the urgency undermines. They need more from their relationship at the very time they can draw less from it.

"His," "Her," and "Their" Place: Space Dislocations

Time dislocations, centered on not spending time together on a routine, joint basis, jeopardize the taken-for-granted quality of the relationship. Couples use the terms "artificial," "awkward," and "weird." In similar and connected ways (difficult to distinguish because time and place variations occur simultaneously), the irregularities of not sharing one place contribute to the awareness that something is awry.

In discussing shared and separate space, these spouses report reactions they recognize as inappropriate, reactions they themselves find puzzling. For example, one husband reported that his wife felt as if they were doing something illicit when they stayed together in her dormitory room.

She kind of felt, at least early in the year, kind of immoral when she had a man staying in her room. It was a weird situation.

Despite the fact that her own moral view did not condemn sexual liaisons among others who lived in the dorm, and though it was a coeducational residence, she felt "nervous" with her own husband there. An-

other husband said that he consciously had to avoid the feeling that
he should "play host" when his wife visited him at his apartment. He
knew the response was inappropriate, but it was something he apparently associated with someone "visiting."

A wife of a state legislator discussed the place dislocation quite
explicitly in her response to a question about how she felt when he
was away:

*I wouldn't say I feel lonely as much as disconnected. It could be a redirected form
of loneliness because if he were there everything would just fall back into place.*

Disconcerting reactions like these are evidence of disturbance to an
ordered world, to the "nomos," that marriage produces and commuting
undermines.

Commuters used terms such as "turf" and "re-entry problems" to
express their place-related sense of incongruity. Not unexpectedly, the
place dislocations are most apparent for the partner who sets up a new
residence and for both spouses when they are together in that residence.
As the following comment indicates, "a new place" can add novelty
to their relationship, but it is not "their place":

*Oh yes, it's not nearly so good here because he's not so comfortable here. This
isn't my beat, this isn't my turf. And that's okay, we do things together, we explore. It's fun, it's an adventure, but what I like for total relaxation and happiness is to go home.*

Here, the reference to "total relaxation," which only "home" can produce, attests to the order-sustaining value of that shared familiar space.

The re-entry problems commuters discuss show that they miss
the familiarity, the sense of being "in place," living together provides.
Feeling ill at ease in "his" or "her" place is further indication that the
sense of order provided by relationships comes from sharing a common space. To the extent that they feel "out of place," commuters are
acknowledging that feeling "in place" gives the relationship the order-
constructing quality they expect from it. Feeling like a guest in the
company of the mate, seeming to intrude, are reactions that bespeak
the dislocation they feel. Such feelings of not being a part of a space
that is identified as "his" or "hers" (as distinct from "theirs") are apparent in the following quote:

*She had her own little world here that I was definitely not a part of. I got the
feeling that she kind of — resented is perhaps too strong — but thought, I was intruding into her sphere.*

"Not Having Our Place": Loss of a Shared Base

The place dislocations are especially pronounced when both spouses move into new residences as a result of the decision to live apart. They may want to reduce expenses and, therefore, each takes a less costly apartment, or job changes have moved both of them to new locations. In such instances, neither one of them has a shared base to retreat to and they both have alien "turfs." One husband recognized this, but thought it affected his wife more than it did him.

It's kind of interesting, the fact that I moved out of what had been our apartment gave her a greater sense of being cut off. She didn't have a home to go to, she never really felt at home here.

A wife for whom separation began only five months after marriage felt very strongly this lack of a shared base. When asked what she considered "home," she said:

What's really home is my parents' home still, I always talk about going home and that's Rockford to me. Going to Idaho is going to see Henry [her husband] and that's not really "going home." Part of it is not liking it there. I do feel pretty unsettled in terms of having a place to call home.

Significantly she used several space-related figures of speech when she responded to whether she would ever want to live apart again. Note how the terms "settling down" and "torn apart" in her response suggest the dislocations she feels have resulted from their separation.

I wouldn't do it without awfully good reasons. I'd never want to do it again, if we could avoid it. We went into it pretty naively and sure, we're going to get through it now — we're on the home stretch — but it's been an awful strain. We look forward to settling down and enjoying a relationship instead of having to work at it and being emotionally torn apart all the time.

In sum, what we have termed time–place dissonance presumes implicit comparisons with coresident living. That is, the discrepancies that spouses express reflect the contrast they are making with time and place reactions of intimates who live together. "I have more time" and "I feel like a guest" are comparative statements, made in relation to how one would or should feel if he or she did not live apart. Part of the strain results from diverging from what one senses is "normal," what "should be." Implicit in these statements is recognition that these spouses' idea of what marriage "is" is tarnished by the way they are "doing marriage." But, this analysis suggests that even if commuter relationships should become prevalent enough to eliminate the feeling that they are deviant, intimate relationships could tolerate only limited reductions in shared time and place without breaking down. Such limits influence judgments about commuting's prognosis; perhaps no amount of societal acceptance can completely neutralize its disabling effects.

Beyond this prognosis, we think the study of couples who live apart reaffirms that intimate relationships, like all social arrangements, are quite sensitive to time–place variations. Intimate relationships make sense of experience because partners spend time and share space together, fashioning their sense of order from this common ground. When partners alter time and place, they disturb their sense of order and consequently become disoriented. Marital relationships apparently need time and place constancies which can only be changed so far before these disorientations become disabling. As one wife poignantly put it:

You know the old issue: If a tree falls in the forest, does it make a noise if nobody's there to hear it? Does a relationship exist if you don't spend time in it?

GAINS IN THE ABILITY TO PROVIDE EMOTIONAL SUPPORT

Up to this point, we have discussed the losses in commuters' ability to provide one another with emotional support. Without daily face-to-face interaction, they miss daily conversations, shared leisure, as well as physical closeness. And, without shared time and space, the taken-for-granted nature of their relationship is thrown into question. These losses negatively affect their ability to manage tensions. However, many of these same couples discover—often to their own surprise—there are also gains that result from living apart.

"Rediscovery" and "Heightened Communication"

Some commuters speak of greater "appreciation," "rediscovery," or "less boredom" in their marital relationship during their limited periods together:

It's really kind of exciting to be separated from him, because when we do have contact, it's just the biggest thrill in the world. And we don't get bored. We real-

ly appreciate each other more. I think we've always had a good relationship, but, like the saying goes, we did kind of take each other for granted.

Because separation introduces new stimuli into their shared lives, the marriage is not only "rediscovered," it is, in some ways, transformed. In this respect, a wife said:

Because of the fact that you are in some way leading a much more independent life, you have different things to bring back to the relationship between you. You also, in a sense, stop taking each other for granted.

Similarly her husband remarked:

I think our marriage has, in some ways, been strengthened by the outside new experiences we can bring back to each other. I bring home interesting things and she has a lot to tell me about what happens during her week.

In a similar vein, many commuters speak of heightened communication as a response to having stored up experiences in anticipation of coming together:

We're just almost always talking now when she comes home. There just doesn't seem to be enough time to say all we have to say. Not little things like we used to. But the major things. The highlights. And now our talks are so engaging.

Here, we see that "being taken for granted" is the dismal side of the need to be able to "take for granted" the relationship if it is to offer emotional mooring. This advantage is well understood by these couples. One wife put this feeling very concretely:

The main advantage that I see in commuting is that it resolves the problem that most long-term marriages have of at some point being a little boring.

So, though these couples miss their daily conversations and quiet, relaxing "inactivity," they recognize that the very availability of these routine interactions lowers the probability of stimulating ones. Without everyday contact, limited interactions become more important, focused, and full.

Fewer Trivial Conflicts

Many couples who share a single home argue about small matters or "tremendous trifles" (Blood, 1962). Since commuters interact less frequently, they seem less disturbed by minor infractions. Many made remarks like:

When we're together, we don't fight anymore. We're so glad to have the time together. All the petty stuff seems to fall by the wayside. Like, I just don't care if he pushes the toothpaste without folding the bottom. I know that sounds silly. But when you're together all the time, you fight about trivial things. Now we really enjoy each other more.

In addition, these commuters monitor their behavior because they do not want to waste their limited time on divisive interactions. What they tell us, then, is that some of the shared trivia of living together produces, rather than helps manage, tension. As a result of indulging their relationships, most commuters overlook, or do not even see, these trifling irritants. Thus the anger does not build up, and they are able to focus on more pleasing aspects of their marriages.

Romantic Love

Separation not only helps many of the spouses appreciate each other more, but a few even speak of their changed relationship as "romantic." One husband commented:

I guess the positive side of this whole separation thing is that, in some ways, it is like the new boy–girl relationship. It's an exciting, romantic period.

His wife felt some "stranger effect" in their sexual reunions. Yet, she used almost the same words as her husband when she described the feelings she attached to their reunions:

It's like when you are in college and have a boyfriend in some other school, who you can only see on weekends. There is less routine.

Some commuters even turn their reunions into celebrations, giving each other presents and doing one another special favors. Said one wife:

It's added some romance. There are a lot of comings and goings. We give each other presents. When I come home, there's a huge welcome. And there are tears at parting. I usually arrive looking exhausted. Show up completely collapsed. And my husband has a bottle of wine, no kidding, with a bow around it and flowers or a bottle of Chanel. And he makes a bath for me.

And her husband said:

The only good thing about this arrangement is that when you see each other, it's a big thing. So it becomes kind of romantic. There's a romantic aspect to the marriage that may not have been there before. Except at specific moments. And Amy and I just joke about this. That it's being on a honeymoon every time we see each other.

This contrast between the single-residence marriage and the commuter marriage is similar to the distinction often made between the "companionate love" of marriage and the "romantic love" of courtship. Romantic love gains its intensity from its brevity and anticipation of forthcoming events to be shared. And companionate love comes from the knowledge and experience of daily, routine interactions. Some commuters re-experience, through separation, "romantic love" with its anticipation and courtship. Of course, this is not the same as "tension management" provided by "companionate love." But even if these exciting reunions are themselves tension producing, they clearly yield a type of tension that is experienced positively. The reduction of tension is not always a useful or engaging process — and this is a dilemma of the "normal" American family.

CONCLUSION

The focused, pleasurable interactions these commuter couples speak about contrasts with what many married couples experience. In his work on the dyad, Simmel (1950) long ago described the underlying process to which these intimate unions are prone. The partners in such relationships share what we called "indifferent intimacies" — the details of everyday living which remain hidden from others. The focus of the intimate pair turns inward while the public parts of their identities, what Simmel called "objective, generally interesting features of their personalities" (p. 127), are saved for others. According to his account, these are gradually eliminated from the marriage, ultimately reducing the relationship to a boring routine But, we have seen that commuters experience the loss of daily conversation and companionship — Simmel's "indifferent intimacies" — as a real problem induced by separation. They often speak of their marital partners as the only ones with whom they could share the minutiae of their daily lives, as well as their personal failures and weaknesses. Though Simmel suggested these "intimacies" and "weaknesses" may be the less important part of an individual's personality, they are nonetheless significant parts, causing commuters dissatisfaction when not shared.

At the same time, Simmel's analysis does point to the negative consequences of these needed interactions. By constantly seeing each other, the members of a couple often become too relaxed. They take for granted the presence of their spouses and interact in a way that they would not consider doing with anyone else. The detailed reviews of their days are simply less stimulating than periodic exchanges, with highlights, that are "saved" for others.

This analysis suggests a dilemma. On the one hand, daily companionship, security, and comfort are desired and, in their absence, missed. On the other hand, the daily presence of the partner contributes to less enthusiasm, less appreciation, and, possibly, boredom between spouses. By living apart, couples rediscover each other at the cost of daily intimacies. Here, the costs and rewards of residential separation expose a basic, perhaps irreconcilable dilemma of conventional marriage.

CHAPTER 4

Incapacitation and the Division of Labor

In the previous chapter, we discussed the emotional losses and gains that accompany commuting. This focus on emotional consequences echoes the emphasis of many sociologists who regard emotional support as the family's chief remaining function in modern societies. The losses commuters report, however, suggest that we oversimplify when we discuss the family's function in terms of people's feelings alone. To be sure, the family is no longer routinely a unit of production. But as feminist scholars and family economists now insist, a number of instrumental activities still go on within families. Many of these activities depend on the presence of both spouses within a single home. In this chapter, then, we will look at some of these other activities, the problems faced by the separated commuters due to their truncated resources, and the techniques they develop to deal with these losses.

SITUATIONS OF INCAPACITATION

Sickness is the most obvious circumstance that reveals spouses' dependence on one another. Unlike most others on whom one relies, spouses are available on a daily basis and feel some obligation to provide regular care. In fact, recent studies suggest that the presence of a spouse buffers individuals against physical and mental disabilities (Finlayson, 1976; Paykel, Emms, Fletcher, & Rassaby, 1980).

Many commuters do mention illness as a potential problem. But for a variety of reasons, most of the commuters do not think of it as much of a barrier to setting up separate residences. First, they depend on air and rail transportation that, in times of emergencies, permit rapid reunions. Furthermore, the probability of illness, involving lengthy incapacitation, is highest when individuals become elderly.

As the mean age of commuters was 40 for men and 39 for women, chances were slight that illness would become a pressing problem. (See Appendix, Table A6, for age distribution of commuters.) As one woman in her late 50s commented:

The only thing I foresee as a real problem is that as we get older, you have more health problems. And I would feel very bad if I wasn't there to look after him because he's the most helpless creature in the world when he's sick. He really does need attention when he gets sick.

Moreover, the availability of other primary group members, besides the spouse, helps reduce the problems sickness can present. As we shall see in Chapter 5, although commuters do lose social ties, many feel they could call on others in a real crisis. Thus, because they can arrange emergency reunions, are relatively young, and can rely on other primary group members, commuters are not likely to have serious problems dealing with illness, though they are aware of sickness as a potential difficulty.

Fear of criminal attack is the second major circumstance that highlights the benefits a coresident spouse provides: One person is a more vulnerable target than two. Given their "single" status, commuters, especially in the very beginning, often worry for their personal safety:

I lock my door with all its latches. I draw my curtains every night. I must say as I've gotten used to doing this, I haven't been quite so anxious and have adjusted rather well.

Even if such fears are not related to real threats, perceptions of a threat may themselves cause discomfort. Women, in particular, fear attack and, as a result, are reluctant, at times, to go out alone at night. Typically men voice this fear for their wives, rather than for themselves. Those husbands whose wives live in large urban areas are especially fearful of the possibility of crime. This husband's comment was typical:

I worry a lot about her safety because New York is a dangerous place to live. And a woman alone is a prime target. Not that my worrying does a lot of good. It is one of the main things, though, that I'm worried about.

Like other men away from families in the evenings these commuter men express concern about their inability to protect their wives and children.[1] However, they can and do take precautions and can rely

1. Mott (1965) found in his study of shift workers, where husbands were often required to be away from their families in the evenings, one of the real losses these men

on neighbors and friends for protection. But most commuters need to learn to adjust and apparently do:

In the beginning, I was really afraid at night. I had heard so much about Washington being a dangerous city. I wouldn't even go to the corner store when it was dark by myself. I guess I've just adjusted. I do go out less at night by myself than when I'm with Jack [her husband], but I'm certainly not a complete hermit. If I have a meeting at night, I can't say: "Sorry, I'm scared of the dark." I just go. And I double lock the door when I come home.

Sickness and crime loom as possible threats to commuters' capacities to live alone securely. In American society, the spouse is often called upon for medical assistance and protection. Of course, some adults (most notably singles and widows) regularly do without such help, but few alternative sources of aid are cheaply and readily available to them. They must develop personal systems of aid or remain in a more vulnerable position — exposed to possible serious and difficult problems.

HOUSEHOLD CARE AND MAINTENANCE

While illness and crime illustrate dramatic instances of dependence, domestic chores and household maintenance are the major day-to-day tasks that spouses perform for each other. Such household chores remain primarily the wife's responsibility even if she is employed, as long as the couple shares a single home (Berk & Berk, 1979; Hartmann, 1981; Robinson, 1980; Yogev, 1981). Though wives typically do more household work in the shared home, husbands often do perform particular chores, such as repairs and yard work. Each spouse is believed less capable of performing the tasks of the other. Thus, we asked: What happens to the division of labor, and the sense of capability that accompanies it, when spouses set up two homes?

Before commuting began, a few couples had assigned almost all duties to one partner (usually the wife, but in two cases, the husband), and a few said they had an equal division of labor. But for the majority, both spouses agree that the wife did more than the husband before they began to commute, although husbands in these families probably "helped" more than husbands in traditional single-career

---

felt they faced in their roles as husbands was their ability to provide, or think they were providing, physical safety for their families.

families. Nevertheless, even when the husbands do quite a bit of actual domestic work, the wives typically take the role of household manager:

Although he helped with the inside work, it was sort of understood that I was the household manager, you know. I made decisions about the washing machine being fixed, what groceries we needed, and I usually did the marketing. Sometimes he went with me, but when I was there I sort of planned things even though he may have executed them afterwards.

And this woman's husband said:

Well, I did help around the house. That was only fair. But she was the manager. She made the decisions about what to buy, how to arrange things, plans for when things needed to be done and so on.

So before commuting, wives took the major responsibility for household management, which meant they gave more time, energy, and thought to domestic tasks than their husbands.

Despite variations in the division of household tasks before commuting, while apart most couples develop common responses to cope with the daily maintenance of their homes: They delegate chores to hired help, redistribute responsibilities to each other, and generally lower their standards.

Hired Help

Unlike providing emotional support, maintaining a household does not require a personal relationship between family members. Many dual-career couples, even when they share a single home, hire help (Holmstrom, 1973). For a commuter, the perceived need becomes even greater.

Many of the commuters (but not all) did hire help in the primary home — the home they shared before setting up two residences. However, they generally used hired help only for some of the cleaning and not for the many remaining household tasks. Moreover, almost no one hired help in the second home. This residence was generally small and had few personal possessions. Typically, neither spouse considered it home. And, in fact, less space required less work.

Redistribution of Domestic Labor
and the Learning of New Roles

When commuting began, spouses generally hired help and redistributed household chores. Wives enumerated the tasks that living by themselves eliminated: cooking breakfast, picking up dirty clothes, doing grocery shopping. Many speak of being freed from household administration. Not surprisingly, their reduced work load pleased them:

Before, I did the breakfasts, dinners — often he did the dishes. But I ran the place. I was the person in charge of saying: "This needs to be done." Now, there is just much less with him away in this place, and when I go there, it's just not as clean as I'd keep it, but I do very little housework. So he has to do more.

And her husband, like most others, agreed:

When we're together, she does more cooking and cleaning than I do. Here alone, I'm not as neat, but she isn't around to get things done. I do have to clean up; I do have to eat.

As a result of such redistribution, commuting equalizes the division of domestic labor: Women do less than they had done in the past; men do more than they had previously done.

Because they redistribute tasks, both spouses discover they can learn or relearn domestic skills. Although the women had assumed major domestic responsibility in the shared home, commuting makes them realize that they had relied on their husbands in ways no longer necessary:

With commuting, so much of the role business ended. When he started going away, I found I could do anything: I could pay all the bills, I could keep the bank books, I could do all the gardening, I could do all the mowing, all of the things he used to do and I used to feel somewhat dependent on him for. When we're together, we have things each of us does, though, as I said, my part seems more. But, now when we're not together, I have no trouble doing these things. I used to feel somewhat helpless.

When I'm here alone, I've had to learn to do things. When the faucet starts to leak, I can't wait till Matthew [her husband] comes home to fix it.

As these remarks illustrate, the women both learn new skills and relearn forgotten ones.

The men, though they have lower standards of cleanliness, learn (or relearn from their bachelor days) to keep the house in order and to plan household maintenance. Many begin to cook on their own:

Before we got married, I cooked all the time for myself. Then it was as though I forgot how. She seemed to be better; it made sense for her to do it. Now that she's gone, I'm rediscovering I can cook — slowly. And you wouldn't call the meals gourmet, but I can put food on my plate that's better than the local greasy spoon.

And to iron or to sew:

This may sound infantile, but I never knew how to sew on a button. The other day I was down to my last clean shirt and a button was missing. I fixed it. And what may sound even more silly was that I showed it to Sally [his wife] with some pride when she came home.

So when they shared a home — the "normal" familial situation with its different and unequal expectations for husbands and wives — these spouses had come to rely on one another to perform gender-typed tasks. Like others who share a home, they had come to believe they needed their mates to maintain a household. The shared home, by the very success of its domestic division of labor, retards movement away from segregated roles. The single-residence marriage, by promoting dependence with its specialized division of labor, is the foundation of, or training ground for, incapacities. Precisely because the domestic division of labor breaks down in commuter marriage, this alternative arrangement produces a new sense of effectiveness.

This analysis does not suggest that one individual can get as much done as two or can do it as quickly. It does not mean that people *want* to perform the tasks generally assigned to the other. They may want to remain dependent in certain areas. For example, a woman may not want to learn how to fix a car because then she can be asked to do so; a man may prefer not knowing how to cook because then he may have to. However, as the comments illustrate, by learning to rely on one another, spouses develop an unwarranted sense of dependency, and an overstated sense of helplessness. Living apart for periods of time establishes or re-establishes self-sufficiency.

Lowered Standards

For most couples a reduction in household standards accompanies the equalization of domestic tasks. When alone, the husband's standards are not as high as when the couple shared one residence. The tasks their wives performed remain undone for longer periods of time. Many men claimed:

She's neater than I am, but I do have to clean up eventually.

She has higher standards than I do, but it gets taken care of in time.

So, too, many women, often to their own surprise, find that in addition to having one less person to care for, they also develop lower standards for themselves. Invoking her role as wife, one woman put it:

It's funny, when he's not here my standards go down. If I have to do it just for myself, it doesn't matter so much. It's just when I feel responsible, I start to become compulsive.

Another woman emphasizes a different aspect, disliking herself for imposing what she now sees as unnecessarily high standards in their shared home:

I'm messy when he is not around. My standards just become higher when we live in the same house. And that is something I don't particularly like about myself.

Providing for one person simply requires less time and energy than providing for two. In addition, when another person is present, each mate must consider the other's rights and desires. Alone, the individual can live anyway he or she deems appropriate.

Significantly, however, it is not solely that the other person requires consideration or that there is twice as much work when two people are present. Rather, for women in particular, geographic separation seems to bring a transformation of needs. As the women's comments suggest, much of the domestic burden appears to come from pressure to act like a "good wife." These supposed obligations, although attached to marriage, become fully activated only when both spouses share a single home. Wives feel a sense of responsibility, even a desire, to care for their husbands: to provide a real meal instead of a quick snack and to keep a neat *family* home. As the men's remarks suggest, they do not demand these high household standards. Rather, the wife often feels the responsibility to fulfill her own self-image, regardless of any expressed demands. But while a self-image, it is also a wife's image of herself in relation to her husband. When she is alone, the salience of this image diminishes—her dinner and housecleaning can wait. She thinks of herself outside her role as wife and this, in turn, allows for a reduction in household maintenance.

However, commuters do not regard this reduction in household work as only a benefit. Instead, some of the commuters — both women and men — dislike the lowered standards, especially at mealtimes. Most of the husbands remark that their meals were "primitive" or "just not up to par." Dinner alone is often TV dinners, sandwiches, cottage cheese at home, or a quick dinner at a local restaurant. Both spouses think serious cooking for themselves is not worth the trouble. They miss not only better food, but also the company of their spouses during meals. While they can do less domestic work and enjoy this reduction, they miss its end result as well as the interaction it entails.

PARENTING AS A PRACTICAL TASK

Child care, unlike housework, cannot be set aside. (See Appendix, Table A5, for number of commuters with children.) The parents, who remain in the primary home with the children, often comment that one major problem with commuting is that they have to perform the duties of both parents which amounts to a great deal of work.[2] Here, they are very much like all single parents.

Among the commuters with children, especially young children, almost all believe they need additional adult help. Most hire help who come into their homes daily. A few have relatives or close personal friends help them out and a few use daycare facilities.

However, most of these commuters with children cannot, and do not, desire to abdicate the personal role of parent. In dual-career families, even when they hire help, both parents generally share the work to some extent, though mothers typically do more (Rapoport & Rapoport, 1976; Yogev, 1981). Thus, the commuters find themselves in the position of overburdened single parent. They usually put their children to bed, feed them dinner, and listen to their stories — alone. Since they usually do less, fathers alone with children feel this increase in workload more than do mothers. One commented:

This whole arrangement is difficult. I have to give more to the kids, for the kids, in a way. I have to put them to bed every night when she is away from home. When she's here, she usually does that. For anything, there is just me. It's really exhausting. The housekeeper helps, but she's not here at nights and I can't expect, and don't want her to be, a complete substitute. They need a parent and now it all falls to me.

2. In this chapter we are concerned only with the *work* of child care. See Chapter 6 for discussion of individual parents' psychic responses to parenting alone.

But the wives also often feel like single parents:

I do find it difficult. I have to do all of the shopping. I am the one that has to go to all the school conferences. If a kid gets sick or has to go to the dentist, I have to take them. There are all of these demands on my time.

Providing emotional support for children is part of the "work" of parenting. And whether it involves eating dinner together or talking about their problems, commuter parents do not choose to delegate these tasks to outsiders:

We have a housekeeper who has come to us everyday for most of our lives. Same woman. I, and I think you will find my wife also, give her as much credit as any single person in making this kind of thing initially possible, and ultimately workable, because she takes up a lot of the slack. The emotional side is, of course, much more difficult to assess. I knew I would have to be mother and father to the kids insofar as they needed a parental ear.

In addition, some parents speak of increased difficulties of discipline. As a father who left his wife and children during the week put it:

I'm the disciplinarian in the house. Cindy [his wife] doesn't assert herself. She depends on me to back her up. In my absence, they tend to go wild.

His wife remarked:

The real problem of raising children without a father here all the time is that he is not here to help do some of the disciplining and some of the other things — especially disciplining. They need his firmness. I think when he tells someone to do something, they do it. Now the only way to handle discipline problems is on weekends, but he will only relate to a problem he's personally observed, not one he hasn't seen. That's okay; I understand why he feels that way, but it makes it more difficult.

This overburdening occurs with older children but, predictably, is greater the younger the child. In fact, older children may reduce these very burdens because they help out and because their presence alleviates loneliness. As the father of a 15-year-old daughter said:

It's brought me closer to Amy [his daughter]. She's become a friend. We spend some leisure time together watching TV, going to games. It's good she's around to keep me company. Somebody to have dinner with and talk to. And she helps around the house more than before. Helps cooking, cleaning. The house isn't that clean and meals aren't fit for a king, but we do sort of divide things up.

While both parents value the help children offer, it is fathers who mention that living with their children also makes their relationship closer — an important compensating consequence.

CONCLUSION

This analysis of practical tasks clearly indicates that family functioning involves considerably more than emotional support. Separation makes commuters aware of other aspects of their dependence on one another. In the shared residence, spouses often provide medical care. Spouses, typically husbands, may also be seen as protectors against crime. Because children, especially young children, require emotional care and daily physical care from their parents, an adult living alone — whether unmarried, divorced, widowed, or commuting — faces a difficult burden.

However, such demands are not continuous. Few couples care for young children throughout their married lives and the likelihood of incapacitating illness is periodic, not constant. Even the threat of attack increases as adults grow older, thus, reducing the need for a younger mate's physical presence. Rather, mutual dependence varies as individuals pass through different stages of life. Consequently, commuter marriage, or any state of "singlehood," may be said to "fit" least adequately when children are young or when the adults are quite old.

Additional tasks, such as household chores, increase the desirability of two adults' physical presence in a single home. While two individuals can do these chores more easily than one, household management, unlike the situations of incapacitation, can be handled by phone or can be allocated to outsiders with relative ease. It is obviously cheaper to do one's own housework than to hire help. Spouses may also believe that they are more reliable than hired help. Many of these tasks *can* be performed by one person. As we suggested, the single-residence family invites dependency. When the other is constantly available, husbands and wives come to feel that they cannot provide for all their own daily needs. However, as the commuters' experiences suggest, these skills — cooking, cleaning, sewing, gardening, automobile repair work — can be learned and performed by either husband or wife. Also both husbands and wives can lower their standards. It is *easier* to have two spouses continually available, if both are willing to help, especially if there are high standards. However, it is not *necessary* as alternatives do not cause great hardship.

Recent work on singles (e.g., Stein, 1981), which concentrates on emotional hardships, loneliness, and other problems stemming from the social stigma attached to singlehood, tends to overlook the other functions of the family. One can survive without a spouse and more people every year are choosing to do so (Glick, 1977). Just like commuters, the single enjoys benefits not possible in married life. Yet, as we have seen, today the problems that an adult without a mate faces are not strictly emotional. In modern society, alternative sources of institutionalized aid, from the state social services to private personnel, are often expensive, time consuming and inefficient for simple tasks. Other primary group members often help with such problems, but are not as strongly committed to the regular provision of ongoing practical help. It is this provision of *daily* care that falls to nuclear family members. Commuters—like other adults living alone—face real costs in trying to provide for their own daily needs and those of their young children.

A Caveat: "Doing Marriage" and "Being Married"

In the last two chapters, we have examined the many losses and few gains that commuter couples face when they set up two separate homes. As we saw in Chapter 3, the absence of daily face-to-face interaction reduces the likelihood of needed conversation and limits shared spontaneous leisure, inactivity, and sexual satisfaction. It also threatens the "taken for granted" quality which grounds marital interaction. As we saw in this chapter, commuting limits each spouse's ability to offer protection and medical aid and undermines each one's dependence on the other for help with household and parenting responsibilities. More generally, then, the loss of daily proximity disturbs many facets of "doing" marriage or the performance of marital roles.

However, the experiences of commuters speak to another dimension of marital experience. We can distinguish this "doing marriage"—the actual practice of marriage as couples live it—from what we call "being married"—the idea of marriage that people carry around in their heads. "Being married" refers to spouses' ideas and feelings about being in a relationship: their subjective sense of their union and its meanings (e.g., the relationship is "natural" or "awkward"). This distinction between objective and subjective realities throws the analysis of commuter marriage into relief, allowing us to see what structural underpinnings sustain or threaten the idea of being married, and to what extent this idea functions independently of any particular marital structure.

Commuters' statements about what their marriages mean to them show the resiliency of ideas about marriage. The reality of the marriage and its ability to order the spouses' worlds is independent of their particular living arrangements. That is, the idea of marriage and the feeling of "being married" do not rest exclusively on daily interactions. Rather those who have an ongoing marital relationship may provide one another an interpersonal stability and security without seeing each other every day. In fact, the strength of their sense of the marital unit, as well as that stability and security, may mitigate the debilitating effects of separation. As these couples comment:

It's kind of reassuring to know that no matter where I am there's someone special out there who cares for me.

I have never been lonely with her gone in the sense I might if she didn't exist. I think there is some security just in that.

I think I am the type of person who likes everything to look very unstable and have a very stable little core. That's what getting married meant to me. You know, I know he's there and I know he'll continue to be there. I mean we've said we like each other forever. I'm embarrassed to tell anyone that, but it's true.

I guess I am pretty dependent, you know, just the knowledge that she is going to be there is some kind of comfort to me. Even when we aren't in the same place. She's there and she cares. It gives me psychic comfort.

For these separated spouses, it is reassuring to "know" that there is one special person "out there" who thinks of them as their life partner. Some might make the same remarks about friends who live in separate locations, but the permanency, salience, and rights and obligations of friendships are more diffuse, less assured. The marital tie is unique and its uniqueness does not rest solely on daily face-to-face interactions. One of the primary characteristics that distinguishes it from other relationships is the conception that marriage is a long-term or permanent bond which, unlike blood kin, is based on individual choice rather than ascription. One husband said of his wife:

Dianna has been and is the only kind of big constant in my life. Other than that, things, places, relationships change. But being apart doesn't make Dianna and me less permanently linked. Our decision to be each other's central relationship isn't destroyed by distance.

As such, marriage structures daily life:

We have a permanent commitment. I have that with close friends too, but there's more of a sense in which we'll plan to do things together whereas with my friends, you know, we see each other, talk to each other, but we don't plan trips together or what we are going to do with a sabbatical or even how we are going to structure a week.

There is the sense that regardless of physical separation one's life is permanently intertwined with one's spouse. This is comforting and promotes a sense of order on a higher level, in the long run rather than in the short-term or daily basis. The spouse, thought of as someone who cares, who shares in the planning of one's life, fuels this "idea of marriage." As we have seen, this idea of marriage is not unassailable; it does respond to threats to its structural underpinnings, although it is also somewhat independent of them.

CHAPTER 5

The Commuter as Social Isolate: Friends, Kin, and Lovers

Up to this point, the discussion of commuting has focused on its consequences within the nuclear family. But despite claims to the contrary, the nuclear family is not isolated; it is embedded in a network of other personal relationships. These other relationships — with friends, kin, and even lovers — are significant sources of support, aid, and, occasionally tension (Bell, 1981; Fischer, 1982; Lee, 1980). Since commuters cannot rely on spouses to the same extent as those who share a home, we might imagine that they would turn frequently to these other relationships.

In this chapter, we examine several different types of relationships. First, we ask if commuters turn to friends for both psychological and material support that they would normally get from their husbands or wives. Second, we discuss their ties to kin, in particular to their parents. Third, we look at sexual relationships outside of marriage, whether or not they become more frequent, and what they mean for those who do (and do not) have them.

THE LOSS OF FRIENDSHIPS WHEN APART

By altering the structure of their marriages, commuter couples also alter their relationships with friends. They discover, often to their own surprise, that one of the great costs of their separation is the restrictions it places on meeting and socializing with others. There is a change, but the change does not involve finding substitutes for the spouse, so much as a general weakening of friendship ties. Why?

Relationships with Couples

Perhaps the most difficult relationships for commuters to maintain are those with other couples. Many couples assume a commuter marriage is a marriage in trouble or about to dissolve. Others express disapproval, and occasionally such responses result in the disintegration of friendships. However, the breaking-up of friendships does not come simply from skepticism or disapproval. Rather, previous research on individuals living apart from their spouse — military wives away from their husbands (Price-Bonham, 1972), divorced men and women (Hetherington, Cox, & Cox, 1976; Weiss, 1979), widows (Lopata, 1979) and widowers (Gerber, 1977) — suggests that there is a general pattern of exclusion: A spouse living without a mate faces difficulties in maintaining or developing relationships with couples. The commuters' experiences further confirm this pattern.

Most commuters make comments about the "coupledness" of the social world and their resultant exclusion from other couples' leisure activities. Those who remain in the primary home have difficulty maintaining couple friendships that had developed before their spouse began to commute:

You would be amazed at how little I've been asked out this year. I think people have not asked me because I am single. The same people that asked us together last year won't ask me because Janet [his wife] is away.

For those who moved to new locations, the problem more often involved an inability to develop new friendships with couples:

Being single makes it more difficult to get to know people. So, I think I do find it more lonely. People tend to think about inviting me only when I'm with my husband.

Note that both of these commuters, like most others, referred to themselves as "singles" when discussing their social worlds. They remain a couple in both a legal sense and an emotional sense. But they are not couples in a social sense. In the absence of a husband or a wife, the marriage — for the purposes of making and keeping friends — does not exist. Other couples will not initiate friendships with them nor will they maintain previously established friendship ties.

In part, this social exclusion may be explained by a perception of the single individual as a sexual menace. Duberman (1974) found that couples, believing that unattached individuals may be sexual threats to their own relationships, do not include them in social gatherings. Some of the commuters' comments suggest that they themselves could see this happening:

Everybody seems to be just a little bit on guard with me because a single guy around, or a guy without a wife, is always a dangerous quantity in any crowd of people.

However, the perception of sexual threat is only one element contributing to the coupling of the social world. Another element involves the need or, at least desire, to maintain the gender balance that many people seem to see as essential to the smooth flow of leisure activities. As one woman said:

To be a single woman who has a husband somewhere else makes you an absolute social outcast. You simply don't fit into the very rigid kind of military social system, you know, with wives talking to wives and husbands talking to husbands.

Singles "don't fit in"; they destroy the symmetry of groups composed of pairs. Or as a man put it:

They don't invite me because I am single. And I can understand it. You try to balance social events. I make it uneven.

He understands the desire for symmetry. But that shared social code precludes his own participation in social gatherings.

"Proper social etiquette" requires equal numbers of each sex. These norms in themselves discourage couples from becoming friends with unattached individuals. For the "single" individual, the consequence is loneliness.

Relationships with Singles

As we have suggested, married couples socialize with other married couples. Moreover, Stein (1976), in a study based on intensive interviews, documents that singles socialize primarily with other singles. Because they describe themselves as "singles," we might expect that the commuters could at least form friendships with others who are unattached. But though apart, commuters have an ambiguous status: they are, for social purposes, neither single nor married. The lack of clarity in their position is illustrated in this man's remark:

They don't know what to do with you. You're an oddball when it comes to social activities. Because they have to pair you off with someone, a woman, and here you are married but not, if you get what I mean. So, how can they pair you?

As "married singles," then, they are usually unable to form independent ties.

Again, sanctions against sexual relationships may explain this isolation. Singles can legitimately ask one another out and even couples can invite the unattached to social gatherings in equal numbers with other singles. But such cross-gender relationships are not available for the "married single" commuters. They cannot legitimately enter into such relationships or at least feel they should not. As one man remarked:

Um, I am married, so I am not in a position to go out with a woman just for a drink and spend the evening talking. I feel the inhibitions and the community is small enough so any time I go anyplace, I see somebody I know.

But not only small communities prevent such interactions. A woman, living in New York, expected she would become friends with two of her single male colleagues. But she was disappointed:

Here are these two single divorced men who I would like to say to: "Come over to supper," and they would not have to think about it because I am married. But there is something in the situation that doesn't allow that. They are really confused about how to relate to me. I'm not single, but my husband is not here.

This limitation on cross-gender relationships may be especially problematic for women professionals who are likely to find themselves in a job situation where men outnumber them.

But many commuters not only have trouble developing friendships with those of the opposite sex, they also have difficulty developing friendships with single people of the same sex. As Merton (1957) has argued, participants experience social interaction as rewarding when they share similar statuses and, therefore, similar values or assumptions. Of particular importance here is that marital status seems to contribute to the establishment of a particular set of values and concerns. Often commuters do not share interests with unmarried persons or feel that their personal concerns and needs are different. A woman remarked:

There's a woman here, a single woman, who I guess I would like to get friendly with. But I get the feeling she cares about different things because she's single. Like she wants to meet men. And she wants to talk about meeting men or not having met them. We just haven't seemed to get that close.

And a man said:

Well, there's this one single guy in the office whom I like. But when we're outside the office, we just don't see each other. We just don't seem to be able to really get it together. I guess our life situations are just too different. Funny, you wouldn't think marriage would make that kind of difference.

There were, however, a few exceptions to this pattern. Some commuter wives seemed able to form supportive relationships with other women, who tended to be single. When they were able to meet such women, the freedom implied by separation from the spouse promoted the development of the new relationship:

Relationships when you're apart develop faster. They're easier. Just because of the fact that you spend more time with them. I mean for instance there's this one woman, in particular, we have coffee together in the morning and often dinner. And we sit and talk late. Much more concentrated seeing of each other. If Tony [her husband] had been here, she and I wouldn't spend that much time together.

Such relationships can become more intense in the absence of the spouse:

When we were together all the time, I didn't have the time or energy and the freedom to just pick myself up and go out with a friend like I do now. Ellen and I get together every Tuesday night and go out to a really nice restaurant. Afterwards, we might go to a movie. Blow a wad of money. Or just sit and have a real good talk. We have a ball. A blast!

But these are exceptions. Such friendships seem to develop only under a number of highly restrictive conditions. First, commuters need the opportunity to meet single individuals, which not all commuters have. Second, they must have a common ground—like the same occupation—that provides similar interests and values sufficient to overcome differences in marital status. Third, they must have a desire to spend a large part of leisure developing such friendships. Not all do. As a result of these restrictive conditions, very few commuters form friendships even with single individuals of the same sex.

Commuters Perpetuate Their Own Isolation

When couples share a single residence, they typically socialize only with those whom both spouses like (Hess, 1976), even though husbands and wives often disagree about who their friends are or should be (Adams & Butler, 1968; Babchuk, 1965). But, when they are apart, commuters seem to be in a position to develop friendships without considering their spouses' likes or dislikes. However, very few take advantage of this special situation.

Some commuters attribute their unwillingness to pursue friendships to their lack of material resources. Their second homes are generally small and lack facilities to entertain in. As a result, they suggest that the spouse who travels is not in a position to have people into his or her home. The lack of resources is not, however, limited to the inadequate space and comfort of the second home: Even the commuters who remain behind, or who have a good living arrangement in the second home, do not entertain. Not material resources, but what might be called social resources, prevent them from doing so.

The most important of these social resources is a spouse whose presence permits a division of labor in entertaining. Some described a conventional division of labor that required the presence of both:

If I am planning to have a dinner party or something like that, it's easier when he's here. It's hard to do alone. When he's here, well, then he can be the host, shake hands, make drinks and so on while I cook.

But for others, while labor was not divided along conventional gender lines, it was nonetheless divided:

When we have people over, when we're both here, we each do different things. While one is cooking, the other can talk. I think it would be awfully hectic to do it alone.

Though there may or may not be a gender-typed division of labor, there is usually a sharing of tasks to which the commuters have become accustomed and continue to assume is necessary. In the absence of a spouse, socializing becomes burdensome.

Even if they have adequate facilities for entertainment and are not worried about the added labor, they still seem to feel uneasy about asking people over. One man, commenting on his unwillingness to entertain alone, said:

It just wouldn't feel right without Rebecca [his wife].

Another remarked:

Because Barbara isn't here, I don't really pursue things. Because I can't, don't want to pursue things alone. I need her for that. It's sort of like waiting. So I've developed acquaintances, not friends. Not people I really see, who I initiate contact with.

These commuter husbands conceive of their marriages as vehicles for socializing. Here, they seem to be speaking not so much of a practical division of labor, but of an emotional division of labor. Perhaps each spouse takes a distinctive role in conversation, in the creation of smooth interactions. When the wife is away, the husband feels unable to replicate the style of interaction he has become accustomed to and now depends on.

Some women, too, said that they do not feel "quite right" inviting people over when their husbands are away. But women add something more:

I must say I don't entertain at all when Ben is not here. I mean, in terms of social obligations, I don't feel I am obliged to because he is not here.

For her, invitations mean additional work—unnecessary in the absence of her husband. While it is more difficult to socialize, the social obligations of a person living alone are diminished. Part of marriage, at least for a middle-class wife, is the development of a household where entertainment is not only appropriate but expected. These expectations are dropped when the husband is away. One consequence of these decreased expectations, however, is fewer friendships.

The problem is the same though heightened for single members of the opposite sex. In those cases where a married person does have a friendship with a single, that relationship is generally fused with the marriage (Hess, 1976). For commuters, this is impossible. Their comments suggest that they do not initiate such friendships because they feel external pressures and internal pressures against doing so:

Helen and I developed some close friendships with single women when she was here. I just don't see them much anymore. If I invite them, there is a certain artificiality of the relationship that even the greatest honesty in the world can't erase. Sexual faithfulness is not a big thing on my scale of priorities, but that doesn't remove the problem at all with regard to friendships.

A woman expressed the same inhibitions:

I don't feel like I can go out with a man here, invite him over to dinner or something like that. Well, to be honest, I'm afraid of their intentions and sometimes I'm afraid of my intentions. Sex is always there between a woman and a man. And why place yourself in a situation where it is more likely to be.

For the commuters, too, friendships are arranged to reinforce the solidarity of the couple. Cross-sex friendships in the absence of the spouse reduce that solidarity.

Thus, commuters extend few invitations to both singles and married couples, and as a result, further decrease the likelihood that they will receive invitations. In this sense, then, commuters perpetuate their own isolation.

THE LOSS OF FRIENDSHIPS WHEN TOGETHER: PRIORITY OF THE MARITAL RELATIONSHIP

Up to this point, we have only discussed the reduced ability to socialize when spouses are apart. But what happens when they are reunited? Apart much of the time, commuters choose to be together as much and as intensely as possible when they are together. When others are included, the intensity of their own interaction diminishes. As Simmel (1950) points out in his analysis of the dyad and triad: "No matter how close a triad may be, there is always the occasion on which two of the three members regard the third as an intruder . . . the sensitive mood of two is always irritated by the spectator" (pp. 135–136). Commuters focus intensely on one another when they reunite, forming just such a "sensitive" union. Third parties are likely to be excluded.

Some commuters' comments illustrate this process of exclusion. One couple, both in their early 30s, spent much time with friends before they began to commute. They enjoy and value such activity but find it appealing only when they also have a great deal of time to share alone with one another. While commuting, they believe that their leisure time should be predominantly for the two of them. Though the wife developed a close friendship with another woman in her husband's absence, she feels that friendships should be curtailed when he returns home:

We used to be very groupie people and spend a lot of time with our friends. Now we only have weekends together. We get kind of selfish with our time and spend at most one evening with other people. That's kind of hard on us.

Her husband agreed:

When we're together, there is a desire to spend time by ourselves, take advantage of these marvelous mountains, catch up on all the things that have happened during the week. We really can't be doing these things when other people are around.

Another older couple, both in their 50s, had often entertained before commuting. The wife was a gourmet cook who prepared elaborate meals when entertaining. However, with the onset of commuting, she and her husband became increasingly family-oriented during their short time together. They no longer invite or accept most invitations. As she commented:

It's fun to have other people in sometimes and to go out or something but now we spend 75%, maybe more, of the weekends by ourselves. Because we have to.

And her husband remarked:

We really don't have time to socialize. There's already so little time together. That bothers me; it bothers me a lot.

When commuters are together, they generally feel that the intensity of their own interactions will be reduced if others are included. They jealously guard the privacy of their already limited reunions. Most of the commuters in this study put a priority on their marital relationship; they reveal their high commitment to their marriages in their willingness to give up other relationships to be together. However, this decision has its costs. Though the choice to eliminate others is made voluntarily, the loss is still felt as very real indeed.

As these findings suggest, either being single or married in a shared residence provide the basis for integration into friendship networks. However, for those who are married but do not share a residence, the situation is very different. For, at the same time that marriage encourages certain types of relationships, it excludes others. Commuters, who are temporarily single, find themselves excluded from the usual friendships of both the married and the single. For them, marriage plays a role that cannot be played by alternative relationships. Without a shared home, they find it difficult to substitute other people for the spouse and to maintain old friendships. For them marriage is not simply one among many alternative relationships equally available for the distribution of emotions. Rather, there are structural constraints that preclude attachments to others, even when an individual has the desire, available time, and energy to form them. The "coupledness" of the social world, the segregation of singles and marrieds, the requirement of the full marital unit for entertainment, and the priority of the marital relationship are limits that undermine the full use of individual's "affective energy."

Social theorists, analyzing the functions fulfilled by the family in contemporary society, focus on the tasks that involve only the marital dyad and their children. For example, Parsons (1965) argues that: "The home, its furnishings, equipment and the rest contribute the logistic base for the performance of family functions" (p. 37). However, Parsons (1955) also suggests that the family's functions are limited to the microsociological level, stating:

> The family is not a major agency of integration into the larger society. Its individual members participate . . . but they do so as *individuals not in their roles as family members.* (p. 16, emphasis added)

As the analysis of commuters' friendships suggests, this perspective is limited and omits a major area of family functioning. For married adults, integration into social networks is not "as individuals" but as partners in a marriage. Consequently, the physical separation of spouses has a limiting effect on the breadth and depth of their personal relationships with others.

RELATIONSHIPS WITH KIN

If friends do not provide company and aid to commuters' spouses, we might expect relatives to. Research on those without a spouse, including both the divorced (McLanahan, Wedemyer, & Adelberg, 1981; Weiss, 1979) and widows and widowers (Arling, 1976) suggests that while they cannot rely on coupled friends, they can and do rely on kin. However, our research suggests that commuters are much less likely to do so. For some, even these relationships become strained. Some of their kin, like some of their friends, take the conventional marriage as a standard and, in doing so, see the commuters as negligent.

But such strained relationships are not typical. Instead, with regard to kin, most commuters resemble the "typical" American middle-class family. Most middle-class couples live at some distance from their relatives. Still, despite their geographic separation, relatives continue to visit with one another and to talk regularly on the phone (Adams, 1966; Lee, 1980; Litwak, 1960). So, too, commuters tend to live at some distance from their relatives, but they continue to visit with kin (an average of about four times a year) and, more often, talk on the phone (an average of once every two weeks). In short, these relationships were similar to those they had with relatives before they began to commute. As a result, for most commuters, kin certainly could not act as substitutes for the spouse, either in providing daily emotional sustenance or practical help.

A significant minority (about 25%) did, however, come to rely on their kin, especially their parents, in extensive ways as a result of commuting. They were able to do so because their relatives lived nearby—either because they lived close before commuting began or because the traveling spouse commuted to a location near kin. In fact, in a few cases, one of the spouses actually moved back in with parents, establishing a home there again. For these commuters, this arrangement includes financial aid and helps alleviate loneliness. As one man, who moved in with his parents while commuting, said:

I don't have to worry about anything except my work. I let my mother take care of everything else. She feeds me, you know, everything a mother does. Obviously, it could not be permanent. It wouldn't be good for me or for them. But we have a good relationship. I don't have to come home to an empty house. It doesn't cost me anything. It's the optimal arrangement for me right now.

For him, commuting had fewer negative consequences than it did for most: his mother replaced his wife in helping with domestic duties and providing company. However, most others living with their parents do not see this arrangement quite so positively. There were advantages, but also disagreements and conflicts:

I have a friendly relationship with my parents. But we're very different. They don't understand how I lead my life, like smoking dope or living away from Tina [his wife]. When they're around, I pretty much avoid them. But they're trying to be nice. And it does give me a place to stay. And food in my mouth when I want it.

These relationships had, in the past, been established on the basis of inequality, with the parents having authority over the child. Just as the divorced have difficulty readjusting to sharing a home with parents (Brown, 1979), so, too, do commuters. Because returning to a parental home is sometimes convenient, a few commuters do take advantage of its availability. But when they do, tensions seem inevitable: It is difficult to keep an adequate distance between the two adult generations who now have lives of their own with different values and routines.

Those situations most easy to adjust to involve cases where relatives live nearby and only provide occasional help. Most importantly, they provide emotional support:

My brother lives nearby and when I am lonesome or want some conversation, I call him or go to see him. It's a pleasure to get reacquainted and to find we really like each other and, I must say, it's nice to know they are here.

I go see my parents every weekend. It makes the commuting thing easier for me. I know they are here and we are a really close-knit family.

In several cases, when the commuters have young children, their nearby parents provide much needed child care:

My mother-in-law lives near here and if I need help with the kids, I can just call her up. And Arnold's [her husband] father helps Joey with math. He gives him some kind of constant father figure. It would be much harder to do this whole thing if they weren't available.

As we discussed in Chapter 4, the spouse left with the children often experiences burdensome difficulties in trying to provide for them. If relatives live nearby, generally, they are trusted surrogates.

Most of the commuters remain in contact with their families across distances. Unlike friendships, these relationships do not require the presence of both spouses. However, as their relatives are usually living at some distance, the commuters cannot turn to them as substitutes for the daily contact typically provided by a spouse. And, in most cases, when the kin live nearby, commuters tend not to want, or to have, daily contact. Just as Shorter (1975) has remarked: "Kinfolk today extend and complement the conjugal family's egotistical emotional structure. They don't rival it or threaten to break it down" (p. 244). So, too, these kin relationships cannot replace the bonds of spouses.

EXTRAMARITAL RELATIONSHIPS

Marriage, we have said, provides access to nonsexual relationships. At the same time, it discourages outside sexual relationships.[1] Individuals are restricted by norms prescribing sexual fidelity and, some would suggest, by constant visibility to their spouses (Bell, Turner, & Rosen, 1975; Maykovich, 1976).

But what of those couples who live apart at least some of the time? Commuters say they are constantly confronted by others who expect that they will discard monogamy and take advantage of their new found possibilities for sexual freedom. So, too, our popular conceptions would have sailors meeting lovers in every port and traveling businessmen seducing their colleagues. These clichés assume that marriage erects a barrier to extramarital affairs only when the behavior of a husband or wife is under the scrutiny of the other.

For commuters, the spatial and temporal boundaries typically provided by marriage are reduced, resulting in less scrutiny and wider opportunities for extramarital relationships. Furthermore, because the couple is separated, they cannot engage in sex together as often. Do their marriages, with their changed structures, cease to operate as a mechanism of social control over sexual activity? More specifically, do commuters find new sexual partners in the absence of the spouse? And if so, do these relationships replace the marriage as their central emotional relationship?

Does Freedom Cause Affairs?

Nearly one third of commuters had affairs while commuting. Those who did but had not before living apart, believe that their increased freedom made these other relationships possible. For example, one man was married 10 years before he and his wife set up two separate residences. During that time, he had had no other sexual relationships. But he felt commuting changed all that:

1. Though sexual affairs are more legitimate today than they were in earlier decades, most people still hold the ideal of fidelity. In a recent Roper poll, adults ranked sexual fidelity as a component of a good marriage, below only being in love and being able to talk about one's feelings. And Singh, Walton, and Williams (1976), in a study using a national sample, found that the overwhelming majority of Americans (approximately 75%) disapprove of extramarital affairs.

*I'm having one [an affair] now. I wouldn't be doing it if we weren't commuting.
It's simple. My behavior is just less constrained, sexually and otherwise. It's lots
of fun. It's like being a kid and going out to play baseball when you feel like
playing baseball.*

A woman, married for six years, clearly saw the separation as an occasion to have sex with another man. Soon after two homes were established:

*I was really feeling my oats. Felt really single for the first time. I probably wouldn't
have done it if Thad [her husband] and I had been together. I was sexually turned
on to Jack [the "other" man] and I was not about to pass up the opportunity.*

Indeed, all but one of the spouses who had affairs while commuting,
but not before, believe that commuting made these other relationships
possible. They accept the common sense — and sociological — explanation that reduced spatial and temporal boundaries led them to reject
sexual boundaries.

However, an analysis of the behavior of the other commuters suggests that interpretation is incorrect, or at least inapplicable, to the
majority. The analysis shows that commuters were not more likely
to have affairs after they set up two homes than they were while living together. More than half (about 60%) of the commuters never,
either before or while commuting, engaged in extramarital sex. This
figure is very similar to the range found in the general population —
50% to 70% (Athanasious, Shaver, & Tavris, 1976; Hunt, 1974;
Ramey, 1977). These figures suggest that commuting does not lead
to affairs. But more interestingly, for the purposes of this analysis,
we can make a distinction between a "stable" and an "unstable" group
of commuters. The stable group is composed of those individuals who
exhibited no change in their extramarital behavior, including those
who had no affairs before or while commuting (60%) and those who
had affairs before commuting and continued to do so (21%). The unstable group is composed of those who exhibit change after commuting
began. This group includes both cases quoted previously — who did
not have affairs before but did while commuting (8%) as well as
those who had affairs before commuting and did not do so afterwards
(11%). The combined total of the two stable groups (81%) is approximately four times greater than the total of the two unstable groups
(19%). As the majority exhibit stable behavior, this analysis suggests
that physical proximity is not the characteristic of marriage that enables

it to serve as a mechanism of social control. In other words, commuting does not cause extramarital affairs.

Finally, there is even more striking evidence that separation does not cause affairs when we see that the majority of those in the unstable group changed in the direction of monogamy. That is, more commuters had affairs while they shared a single residence than did so after they set up separate homes. The rationales they gave for this unexpected behavior change vary greatly. For example, one woman said she had an affair before commuting because she felt hostile toward her husband since she had no job and, simultaneously, he was very involved in his work:

When we were living together all the time, I got involved with this other guy. Ted [her husband] works very hard and when he works, he doesn't talk. He gets up, leaves the house in the morning, comes home, eats supper and works 'til 3 or 4 in the morning. I was very dissatisfied with that; I was lonesome. I didn't have my own work and so I got involved with this other guy. As soon as I got the job, and knew my life wasn't washed up, it disappeared. It was very dumb. I won't do it again.

Others said that with their present jobs, they are too busy to have affairs. And still others could come up with no explanation for the unexpected change:

We decided before marriage that marriage wouldn't interfere with that kind of thing. He had some and I had some. And I figure I am getting terribly old because I haven't met anybody in the last few years that I find interesting.

I've had extramarital affairs. But it hasn't happened since we've been apart. It's crazy, isn't it? I have all the opportunity in the world now and the appetite doesn't seem to be that great.

Many commuters who did not have affairs, however, found that their sexual fantasies increased. Women said:

I find myself noticing men's bodies a lot more. Thinking about possibilities in bed. But it stops there.

I daydream more of sexual encounters. Less sex, more fantasy. That makes sense. But no more sex.

Men said:

Now, while we're apart, my fantasy quotient is probably up. Separation has made me think about it more probably because of my repressed libido. Made me think more in sexual terms about people I'm interested in. But our marriage couldn't take it.

Sure, when you're apart, you want it more. I notice other women as sexual beings more.

However, for these people — as for most — these fantasies are not translated into activity.

It is clear that other elements — besides time and space apart from their spouse — lead some commuters to extramarital activities. But it is unclear why those who had affairs only after commuting began did so. There are many differences among them. Half are male; half are female. They range in age from 27 to 55. Some see their spouses every weekend; others less frequently. The only thing they clearly have in common is the explanation that increased freedom accounted for their affairs. But because they are such a small minority, the belief that freedom causes affairs remains an inadequate explanation.

These findings suggest that the small minority who believe decreased visibility and increased freedom lead them to affairs are simply using a rationale that helps them understand, and perhaps excuse, their behavior. In most cases, attitudes (that exist prior to separation), rather than the opportunity brought about by separation, seem to be the primary determinant of extramarital liaisons.

Norms against Sexual Permissiveness

An examination of the rationales of those who remained monogamous throughout their marital lives will help explain why the increased opportunity for an affair does not, in fact, typically explain its occurrence. Commuters in this stable group use two types of explanations for their abstinence. Some commuters express an overall commitment to an ideology of monogamy. One man said:

Naturally, I've felt desires. Normal I would say in wanting to, but I haven't primarily because I just don't believe in it.

His wife commented:

Neither one of us, as far as I know, has ever had a sexual relationship outside of marriage. I guess cause we just don't believe in them. When you're married, you're married.

For the individuals in this group, sexual faithfulness is an essential component of their definitions of marriage.

These commuters are aware of changing sexual mores in contemporary America. Defining themselves in opposition to such changes, they frequently made remarks like: "I'm old fashioned"; "I guess I'm just a traditionalist"; "I'm puritanical." They are not "traditionalist" in that they choose to establish two separate residences. But one type of "deviance" does not mean that they tamper with all traditional marital norms. Restrictions on sexual activities prevail whether their spouses can see them or not.

Not all of the commuters who did not have affairs believe monogamy is the only way to run a marriage. A second group of sexually loyal individuals expressed the fear that they would feel jealous and they would be imposing pain on their spouse if they had affairs. Intellectually, this group thinks sexual liaisons outside of marriage are acceptable. Yet, emotionally they feel that they *themselves*, as individuals, are incapable of such activity and could not deal with it if their mates had affairs. Women were much more likely than men to offer this rationale — to say that they had not engaged in extramarital relationships because of the pain and deception it would involve. As one woman put it:

On a really intellectual level, I think I can say it is perfectly acceptable for people to be involved with other people. I don't think it would work very well for me. The main problem is deception. And I guess the problem is jealousy of the other person and having to avoid that, having to deceive and to lie about it. It would hurt him very badly.

In contrast, her husband spoke of the more general meaning of marriage and simply said:

I don't believe in sexual freedom, at least for married people.

Another women expressed the personal orientation, rather than the ideological, in the following way:

I'm not for it or against it. But we love each other too much to impose that kind of pain. I know being away gives some people a release, makes them turn on.

I have just the opposite reaction. It's like losing your appetite. When you're not hungry, you don't eat. I guess we're just not hungry.

In this case, contrary to what she suggested, her husband was "hungry," but not willing to have an affair:

I think it has probably crossed my mind more frequently when we are away from each other. There is a need there. But I can't, at least not with another person. It would hurt me if she did it and I think it would hurt her if I did it.

Of course, these are individual attitudes. Spouses differ not only in their rationale for abstention, but, in some cases, their actions: One is opposed to and does not have affairs, while the other does. For example, one woman had an affair when they shared a single home and did not tell her husband. It had been short-lived and she did not feel it "was necessary to dwell on it with him." Her husband, however, did not have affairs because:

I haven't and I wouldn't because it would hurt Judy [his wife]. I don't like the idea of doing something and not telling her. It's not something I could personally do. I mean I love Judy and that's the reason for not having an affair.

He, like others in this second group, is afraid of the pain an extra-marital liaison would cause his wife.

Though this second group may be more likely to change, the end result, for the present, is the same for both groups: none of them engage in extramarital relationships. Marriage is a unique relationship and their commitment to it is unchanged. A changed marital structure — with less proximity and responsibility toward the spouse — does not change the normative attitudes about sexual exclusivity. Rather, these expectations continue to serve as boundaries for sexual activity.

Who Does Have Affairs?

Let us turn to the second stable group: those who had affairs before commuting began and continued to do so while living apart. Given their willingness to have affairs, commuting made it somewhat easier:

If I'm not home by 6:00, she doesn't know and doesn't worry. It obviously makes it easier. I can't tell her. Once, before I started coming up here, I tried and she

*got incredibly upset. Started screaming at me and crying. And there is no way
she is likely to suspect it now.*

He was wrong: his wife did suspect it. Her response was to follow suit
and have her own flings. But it was her husband's activities, not the
residential separation, that led her to do so. Again the increased opportunity brought by separation did not determine such behavior.

      Attitudes and rationales for extramarital affairs vary widely. Some
commuters suggest they have affairs because of dissatisfaction with
their marriages:

*We're very different sexually. She is really not interested in sex. Liz [his wife]
is sexually excited about a half-dozen times a year. I'm sexually excited about
a half-dozen times a week. I'm not trying to boast. I sometimes seek other people
because I miss sex. I would prefer not to. But sometimes I have to.*

In this case, dissatisfaction with the marriage provides the legitimate
condition to search for alternative sexual relationships. For others,
those conditions are provided by the discovery that their spouses are
having affairs. They, then, feel they will as well.

*I became aware that Richard [her husband] was considerably more active than
I had thought. In order for me to put that in perspective, I have my own relationships. I can understand the significance or lack of significance of them. I
don't feel done in or trapped.*

Here, a sense of fairness, or even a desire for revenge, overrides the
particular attitude toward affairs. Finally, still others simply reject the
norms against extramarital sex. They have, instead, a counter ideology:

*I knew from the beginning of our marriage what I wanted for the future. I guess
the main reason is I like variation. Why not? You need to develop sexual relationships to have intimate relationships. Now we both agree about this. I don't
see why such a big metaphysical fuss is made over this.*

His wife did agree:

*Affairs are not correlated with our being apart. We agreed long ago that we were
going to have the kind of marriage that included the right for both of us to have
sex with other people.*

      Importantly, these couples who do have affairs, both before and
after commuting, maintain a set of normative guidelines for their be-

havior; they maintain a primary commitment to their marriage. They speak of affairs as "additions" that could not replace their more important marital ties. Therefore, attempts are made to confine such activities to those whom they believe posed no real threat to the more permanent and valued relationship with their spouses:

It's better to have an affair with a happily married man who is not looking for a life's partner or anything like that. The single man is always falling in love. That's difficult. I choose people who don't threaten my relationship with Jerry [her husband].

I like having physical relationships with other women. They are nice while they last. But I know there is no future. I wouldn't break up my marriage for them. When they get too serious, that means trouble. I don't allow that to happen. I pull out.

These couples have decided that their relationship with their spouse is special and the distinction made between it and other relationships is not solely sexual. Such other relationships do not affect their desire to maintain a permanent marital commitment. Among this group, marriage still remains subject to a set of normative guidelines, those that Bernard (1973) argues are the only ones viable in contemporary society: "permanence and nonexclusivity." Thus, while those who have affairs speak to the pluralistic character of the normative system, they in no way suggest that norms are unimportant.

Responses of outsiders to commuter marriage involve conceptions of sexual freedom as well as sexual activity. The commuters themselves say people periodically make comments to them about their new found liberties. This popular view, reiterated in the sociological literature on extramarital sex, suggests that marriage acts as a constraint not because of the norms attached to it but because of the daily face-to-face character of its structure. But, as the commuters' experiences suggest, this view is a simplistic one.

Of course, there must be some opportunity. If there were not, there could be no affairs. But, it could be argued that the opportunity for affairs is always available. Few spouses are together 24 hours a day. Most can, and in fact do, interact with members of the opposite sex on a regular basis. Affairs do not have to take place at night in some secret hideaway in order for spouses not "to know." But obviously, even with the relatively high rates of affairs, not all individuals with such opportunities take advantage of their supposed freedom. Instead, they abide by a strongly held set of beliefs. Just because the structure of marriage changes, the rules or guidelines for behavior need not.

Yet we must view these findings with some caution. Perhaps there is the sense among some of these commuters — especially those who had affairs before commuting but not afterwards — that they must compensate for their separation with greater sexual fidelity. Alternative relationships might be more threatening since there is a greater chance for them to become real substitutes. Commuters have already tampered with the marital bond by living in separate residences. To tamper with these bonds even further by starting or even continuing affairs might strain them beyond what the spouses consider acceptable. Yet, the patterns that appear — some continuing to have affairs and others continuing not to do so — are at least suggestive, if not definitive. These patterns suggest that physical proximity is not the determining factor controlling or causing extramarital encounters. Rather, the attitudes of the individual spouses, whether together or apart, are the primary cause. What determines these attitudes cannot be explained by this study. What these data do indicate is that the typical marriage provides access to friendship while it prohibits access to sexual relationships that could replace it.

CONCLUSION: THE COMMUTER AS SOCIAL ISOLATE

We expected that commuter couples might come to rely on other personal relationships, and even substitute these for their relationships with their spouses. However, in most cases they are unwilling and/or unable to do so. Though the spouses suffer losses in their relationships by being apart, their marriage remains the primary source of aid and support.

Though they may desire to increase the amount of interaction with others, separated spouses typically cannot do so. As far as friends are concerned, social structures and conventions preclude their providing alternative aid and support. Because most live at some distance, kin cannot serve as substitutes for the absent spouse. As for extramarital affairs, normative prohibitions prevent access to sexual partners other than the spouse. As Litwak and Szelenyi (1969) argue:

> Under the impact of modern industrial societies, primary group structures tend to assume a variety of structural forms. Furthermore, these different structures can handle different tasks most effectively. (p. 465)

The "normal" nuclear family, because of its daily face-to-face interaction, is a unique institution that other groups cannot replace. As a result, the physical separation of spouses results in a drastic overall reduction in the amount of interpersonal interaction for each spouse.

The loss of old friends and the inability to make new ones, the failure to substitute kin or lovers may have consequences for the commuters' marriages. In the absence of friends, lovers, and kin, the commuters turn in on one another. These heightened expectations further diminish their ability to get what they want. Ironically, because they are apart, they depend on each other more. The result, perhaps the most difficult part of commuting, is a frequent and pervasive loneliness.

CHAPTER 6

"His" and "Hers": Separation and Individuation

Recently, social scientists have begun to focus on the ways in which the intact nuclear family reduces the satisfaction of its individual members. Earlier formulations, depicting the nuclear family as an emotional haven, now seem little more than idealizations, not only misleading but also the source of impossible, even harmful expectations. Some feminist critics, in particular, identify the family as a key institution responsible for the subordination of women. As now structured, feminists argue, the family requires a full commitment to the needs of husband and children at the expense of women's own power, autonomy, and independence (Easton, 1979; Epstein, 1982; Hartmann, 1981). More recently, "male liberationists" have argued that men also suffer emotionally because of the asymetrical responsibilities imposed on them as husbands (David & Brannon, 1976; Lewis, 1981; Pleck, 1982). Many other social scientists and therapists, without focusing on gender-linked difficulties, have argued that at the moment values promoting "personal growth" and "self-actualization" have surfaced, marriage, at least in its conventional form, "spells the end of self-development" (e.g., see Kammeyer, 1977).

A central theme runs through the discussions of all these writers— marriage is a mechanism of social control. But often it remains hidden *how* marriage becomes such a mechanism. What the comparison of commuter and conventional marriage reveals is how traditional marriage becomes such a mechanism. The analysis of commuter marriage suggests that it is shared physical space, coordinated schedules and a division of labor that leads to social control. Commuter marriage—by reducing shared time and space—is a form of individuation and may be, at least, partially liberating. As a result, it may yield benefits for each spouse individually that are not realizable in most homes where family members are together every day. In this chapter, we look at how the "normal" American family — with its characteristic single residence and gender-typed division of labor — obstructs individual functioning. But we will do so by looking at what commuter spouses, who leave the conventional home situation, reap for themselves as *individuals*. Finally, we consider how and why these gains vary by gender.

SIMPLIFICATION OF DAILY LIVES AND THE INTENSIFICATION OF PROFESSIONAL WORK

Most dual-career couples organize and routinize their lives in well-planned, tight schedules. With the demands of job and family pressing constantly, the spouses expend a great deal of energy compartmentalizing and coordinating both sets of responsibilities (Rapoport & Rapoport, 1976). But when they are alone — away from the immediate responsibilities of family — both husbands and wives experience new freedom in arranging their daily lives.

Commuters enjoy the simplification of their days apart. Away from their families, they avoid much of the detailed daily planning that characterized their lives together. As a result, they have much more time and energy to pursue individual desires. Many spoke of the pleasure in less structured lives:

There is a great luxury in coming home whenever you want and then doing just what you want to do.

One woman spoke of the change in highly charged emotional terms:

I was really unprepared for the fierce joy I have felt at being my own woman, being able to concentrate on my own activities, my own thoughts and my own desires. It's a completely selfish, self-centered existence. It's almost a religious experience when you're fifty years old and have never felt that before.

Simplification means selfishness, and selfishness means "fierce joy" for these individuals who had previously led coordinated, routinized, lives. Both men and women talk about the pleasures of eating when they want, of working late without worrying about the time, of reading or watching television late at night. Typical remarks were:

I like to read and I can do that anytime. I don't need to be responsible to anyone but myself.

If you want to listen to the radio late at night, you can, I can. If I want to sleep late, or go to bed late, I can. Just those little things, I'm free to do what I want when I want to do it.

Any time an individual is alone, there are fewer demands and fewer constraints. Certainly, as suggested in Chapter 3, not all demands are experienced as problems: a "demand" to talk or to relax with one's spouse may be quite welcome. But as the commuters' comments suggest, periodic release from such temptations (and obligations) is a type of freedom.

Interestingly, men and women do not value this simplification equally. Though a few men make such comments, almost all the women do, and it is women who celebrate the attendant joys. That women are more likely to express this sentiment should come as no surprise. In a shared residence, women are more likely to be responsible for a greater number of daily family demands. As a result, they are also more likely to experience separation as freedom because separation removes them from those demands.

That the simplification of daily life, and the concomitant release from family responsibilities, is far greater for women than men becomes particularly clear when we examine changes in their daily professional lives. Both men and women were asked if commuting led to an increase, decrease, or no change in the amount of work they did. Women were almost twice as likely as men to increase professional work involvement (76% vs. 43%). In contrast, men were almost twice as likely to say they experienced no change (34% vs. 20%). Moreover, about one quarter (23%) of the men decreased their professional work involvement as compared to only 4% of the women.

As these figures indicate, not even half of the men actually increase the amount of time they work. Most who do so are those who "help" around the family home or share equally in domestic chores while sharing a single residence. When alone, men, too, often let housework and cooking standards decline. They also do not have anyone with whom they can spend (or "waste") time.

Yet, for most men, the time saved and obligations avoided are not great enough to free significant time for work. In fact, many stated quite simply:

It's had no effect on the amount of work that I do.

I thought that I would spend more time working living apart, but I don't think that I do.

Some of their comments suggest that they had been working to capacity while sharing a single residence. As one man put it:

I work hard together or apart. I can't work all the time.

Indeed, a surprising number of husbands claim that while alone they actually decrease the amount of time they work. Some of these men provide a simple explanation: without a wife to provide domestic services, household work impinges on professional work. In general, the husbands' professional roles set the parameters of their daily existences even when they shared a single home with their wives. For them, family life did not intrude, but instead supported their professional lives.

Others explicitly state that because living in a family unit relieves strain, it simultaneously promotes intense work involvement:

I probably work less now. I think I spend more time moping around. Maybe a bit more drinking. Not excessive, but a bit more escapist.

I might work less because, of course, when you are living with your family, you can, say do some work for the next day for an hour, then put the children to bed, get involved with the family and then go back and be re-energized to do some more work.

As we discussed in Chapter 3, marriage provides — especially for men — the sense of order that makes productive work possible. Without sharing time and space, some of these men are clearly disoriented for some of the time and, as a result, become less productive in their hours alone.

This inability to concentrate, to work productively in the absence of a spouse, is far less characteristic of commuter wives. As seen, the large majority of these women increase the amount of time spent on work when they live alone. They do so because the time they previously reserved for leisure companionship they can now direct to professional activities. These women also work more because, as we suggested in Chapter 4, they invest less time in household chores in a separate home. Almost all women said things like:

Every night I bring work home. If he was here, I'd have to let it go. I would have prepared real meals. Made sure the house was neat. Had much more laundry to do. Oh, you know, the whole list. But being alone, it's just easy to work. I'm kind of lured into it.

Finally, wives also work more because their own schedules are no longer determined by their families' schedules or needs:

I love my work and here apart I can really enjoy the freedom to put as much into it as I want to. If I were with him and wanted to put in extra time, I would run into real conflicts.

I guess I have done more professionally. In some ways, I have more free time. I have one less person to contend with during the week. I am more of a night person and he is more of a day person.

As their comments suggest, these women are not only able to increase the amount of time they spend on work, but they can focus better, with fewer interruptions, when alone. For many of these women, then, living alone does not introduce the sense of disorder or strain that characterizes so many of their commuter husbands. Quite the reverse — without interruptions and conflicting obligations, commuter wives enjoy greater involvement in professional lives.

Women who leave children with their husbands note the reduction of responsibility and intensified professional involvement most emphatically. In all of these cases, the amount of time spent on work and the ability to concentrate increases dramatically. One woman, who left her young daughter with her husband, said:

I can treat myself with all the luxury that a student can. Now I work when I would be with my little girl.

Another remarked, as did so many, on her sense of guilt and sense of release:

I do feel guilty leaving my children behind. But I can concentrate on my work here with no interruptions. I can work 14, 16 hours a day. And I'm not torn between, say, going to a breakfast meeting because I have to make sure the children are off to school.

In contrast, the group least likely to increase their work output were these women's husbands: Those men left with the children. Here the benefits to the spouses are the most clearly asymmetrical. Women left with the children generally recognize some added domestic obligations, but typically were already used to heavier child-care responsibilities. The time they had previsouly spent with, and doing for, their husbands could now be used for their jobs. Thus, most women left with children are still able to get at least the same amount accomplished. But as we saw in Chapter 4, the men left with the children generally find themselves spending much more time helping, talking to, and playing with them than in the past. And, the effect on their work was negative:

It necessarily reduces the amount of time available for work. I have to take both mine and my wife's responsibility for the children. Somebody has to have dinner with them, talk to them, and help them with their homework every night. You can reduce sleeping from 8 to 7 to 6 hours, but at some point, you can't handle that anymore.

For commuter husbands, housecleaning standards can be lowered and chores can be delegated to outsiders. But when the children are left with the husband, they require immediate and regular attention. When the wife, typically the major provider of child care, is absent, the husband has no choice but to fill the gap. Thus, in terms of professional involvement, the wife is the prime beneficiary.

AUTONOMY, INDEPENDENCE, AND SELF-ESTEEM

Not only does living apart reduce familial responsibilities and simplify the commuters' lives, it also provides these husbands and wives with a new and positive sense of themselves. Spouses are quick to discover the benefit of increased independence and autonomy when they enter a commuter marriage. This new-found self-esteem is especially apparent in activities traditionally done by either husband or wife. As discussed previously wives learn they are able to fix dripping faucets, change tires, or mow lawns. The men learn to vacuum or sew on buttons. Before commuting, many felt as though they had to ask for help in what was defined as the spouse's area of expertise. With separation, they learn to cope alone, thereby gaining a new sense of self-effectiveness.

Their increased sense of autonomy not only comes from the discovery of an ability to perform tasks generally done by their spouses, but also from the very fact of being able to live alone. Many of the commuters had never lived by themselves or had not done so for many years. Before commuting, they had been afraid to do so. Now, they discover, often to their own surprise and elation, that it is possible. As one woman commented:

I've learned to live with myself, by myself, which I couldn't do before or at least was afraid I couldn't do. So many people can't be alone without feeling lonely. I've learned to enjoy that.

A man remarked:

We've both discovered that we have some resources that we may not have used for a while. One of the things that worried me to begin with was that I was going to get uptight at the idea of being alone. I have proved to myself that I can be alone.

Sharing a residence assures spouses of the constant availability of one another and a sense of need grows from this habit. Before commuting, spouses were frightened at the prospect of "being all alone." After commuting for awhile, they reassess their own needs and discover that they can be "alone but not lonely." While a husband's or a wife's presence may have been pleasant and comforting, it is not essential. They may miss one another, but they also find compensation in a new sense of self-sufficiency.

Some even translate this compensation into a desire they had never known or recognized: a desire for private space. Their discussion of "private space" is not metaphorical, as in popular usage, but instead quite literal. They discover, as Virginia Woolf did before them, a need for "a room of one's own." As one woman remarked:

I never had a place of my own or a real space of my own. I didn't know it was what I wanted. That was a real discovery for me.

When asked about loneliness, another woman said:

No, in fact, I would say that one of the problems with being married is that you don't have enough chance to be on your own. You don't have the same kind of privacy. And commuting has certainly changed that. You call it loneliness and I call it privacy. And I see it positively rather than negatively.

Perhaps most importantly, learning to live alone and discovering an ability to cope with varied tasks leads to a sense of independence. Certainly the fact that they were willing to set up a commuter marriage in the first place suggests that these couples are not overly dependent. But the discovery that they are able to provide so well for themselves often increases their self-confidence. That is, commuting not only affects how participants structure their daily lives but how they fashion their identities as well. Conventional marriage, with its elaborate, and often fixed, division of labor, shared space and co-ordinated schedules, brings a sense of dependence; commuting, in breaking down these connections, increases independence and competence.

However, this benefit is not experienced equally by women and men. Women, in particular, express the new sense of self in a variety of ways. Women learn to hammer nails or change tires, and they take some satisfaction, however slight, in these new-found abilities. Even more important, though, is that, for women, commuting allows full participation in the professional world. Because achievement in a career is so highly valued in our society, success in that realm provides a heightened sense of worth. A typical comment about the full professional involvement that commuting permits was:

Last year, I was thinking to myself that I am all washed up and had nothing to offer. He was the one person who made our world. Now, I am much more secure. I regard myself up here having a job as a neater person.

Finally, in part from this fuller participation in their professions, and in part from living alone, women renew their sense of individual identity. Reflecting on their lives before commuting, some wives said they had felt invisible. This sense of dependence expressed itself in their relationship to others outside of marriage: These women felt that others perceived them solely as extensions of their husbands. They did not experience this as a benefit, as a "status rub-off," or as a vicarious achievement, but as a denial of identity.

In contrast, commuting provides a sense of visibility. As one woman, contrasting her commuting experience with her experience in the shared home, said:

I guess the best way to explain it is that I am an individual in my own right. And partly because I am not playing the role of wife, I like the idea that other people will like me, or they don't like me, but for my own characteristics, not because I am my husband's wife.

Another woman said:

I got something back that I lost when I was part of a team all the time. People know me as me and not as part of the team of which Harry [her husband] is the captain. And just being me, and reacted to as just me, for at least part of the time, that feels good.

Commuting has far fewer consequences for husbands' identities. A few do learn to do some household chores they had been unable to do before. And, to be sure, they do take some pride in these accomplishments. But none of the men talk about changes as fundamental to their sense of self as those cited by the wives. Because they had always participated in a professional world, none talk about a new sense of confidence deriving from participation in that world. Also, not a single husband mentioned that before commuting others had responded to him as an extension of his wife.

However, if the husbands do not benefit directly from a new sense of identity, many do benefit indirectly from their wives' higher self-esteem:

I like having a professional wife. Someone I feel proud of and who feels proud of herself. Commuting made that possible.

Having this job has restored her self-confidence. Sharpens her. It makes her better company. That's a bad expression. It makes her more interesting.

In this sense, the men benefit as individuals because their wives do.

At the same time, such individual benefits do have potential costs for the unity of the couple. Of these, commuters are keenly aware. In particular, they believe that a sense of independence could, ultimately, undermine the marriage itself. Some commuters speak of a delicate balance between independence and dependence. As one man remarked:

You are freer for certain lengths of time and there is certainly some satisfaction in that. But I wouldn't push it too far. There is a certain point at which it could turn the other way. You become too free. I don't think it has happened yet, and I hope it won't, but I think it would be silly to think it would be impossible.

A woman spoke in very similar terms:

I've learned I can function on my own, can face life on my own, even enjoy my independence. And obviously that has a potentially debilitating effect if you see it as something that would lead you not to be able to function in a close relationship. That hasn't happened. But I see that it could be a logical progression.

Periodically, then, the commuters worry that the very advantages they find as individuals could in the long run weaken their marriages. They enjoy their autonomy and freedom, but also value being married. Wanting both, they are afraid their desires are contradictory and that eventually growing independence may undermine their need, or their spouse's need, to remain married.

IDEOLOGY OF INDEPENDENCE

Up to this point, we have discussed the experience of increased autonomy and independence as benefits that emerge almost automatically when couples live apart. But, married couples have not always sought independence. Just 20 years ago (and re-emerging in some quarters today), the predominant ideology of a good marriage was "togetherness." This ideology celebrated the fusion of partners, the subordination of individual needs and desires (see Friedan, 1963, and from a different point of view, see Schlafly, 1977). Today, we see a plethora of books, speeches, and articles advocating a different ideal: the independent pair. Today, those who have taken it upon themselves to offer advice, suggest that spouses take separate vacations to develop their own identities, maintain their own separate interests, and follow their separate goals. Beginning in the early 1970s, psychoanalysts promoted independence as an avenue to psychic health. Thus Otto (1970) writes: "The criterion of a successful solution to marital and family relationship problems is not the experience of the relationship but rather the experience of freedom, confirmation, and growth on the part of each participant." He went so far as to advocate that "'seeking spouses' . . . try such things as living apart from time to time" (p. 49).

In this context, it became possible for commuters to see independence as a virtue. Many of the commuters endorsed the ideology of independence, at least in part, before they set up two separate homes. But once they began to live apart, most of them elaborated it, making independence a personal ideal. To quell their fears about the potential dangers of too much independence, these couples seize the modern model of marriage as justification for their own lives.

Many of the commuters' comments indicate that they developed such a view over time, that it was not an immediate achievement. For example, one woman said of the first few months of commuting:

I think in the beginning there was much more of a frantic quality to it, at times. And I would think to myself, I don't know whether I can live this way.

But gradually she, like many others, began to elaborate an ideology to support her style of life:

Then I would think: You damn well better learn to live this way because it's terrible to be that dependent on another human being. The relationship shouldn't be that kind of dependency. That's better. A marriage shouldn't be based on attachment that develops because you can't function on your own. It's awfully easy for a marriage to deteriorate that way.

She reminds herself how she "should" run a marriage. That reminder alleviates some of her doubts. Others even suggest that the marital model of "togetherness" was itself the cause of discord, and by implication, the absence of "togetherness" the cause of marital satisfaction:

Independence is very important to me. Being self-sufficient and in control of my life. I wouldn't now give that up. I mean personally I believe that a lot of marital trouble stems from forced dependence when really if each person were just treated as an individual, a lot of disagreement could be avoided.

As noted in previous chapters, these couples have an image of what marriage should be. They first endorse, and then come to believe quite firmly, in both equality and independence. In this context, separation becomes admirable and morally validating. Indeed, for many, this ideology proves extremely helpful. Women, in particular, use it to assuage guilt they might otherwise feel for stepping outside of the boundaries of appropriate "feminine behavior." Most spoke of some guilt and the way they conquered it:

For a while I was working on this thing about responsibility to my marriage and family. So if I got to pursue things intellectually and to work, that was luxury, extras, icing on the cake. I was going through a lot of guilt about wanting to do it. What I have come to, I guess just in the last year, is working through feeling guilty about it. Accepting it, liking it, seeing myself in a process of individuation which is important and beneficial to my family.

Thus, individual benefits become family benefits. Many women recall efforts to contend with competing ideologies and how the "modern" one took hold:

Sometimes I feel guilty about doing this. I think I should be at home being the good wife. But then I quickly realize that this is wrong. He is my husband but he is also a human being. I am his wife, but I am also a human being. I think we've both come out with the idea that the world is just filled with individuals. And the family is a group of individuals that are related, that are concerned with one another, but that should never have to deny their own individuality to be a member of a family.

Not all of the commuters advocate this ideology of independence so fully. For example, one commuter wife feels enormously guilty for pursuing her own career at some distance from her husband. As she remarked, in stark contrast to most others:

As a result of this being free and independent and really liking it, it makes me feel extremely selfish. I just don't feel like I am thinking in terms of us anymore as much as I am thinking in terms of myself. It disturbs me a great deal, you know, because I don't believe a couple ought to be two individuals. I don't think it's healthy. That frightens me.

Though she "really likes" her independence, she simultaneously senses that her pleasures are somehow wrong, "not healthy," even "frightening." She has not accepted the new ideology of marriage, at least for herself, and cannot find compelling justification for what she perceives as her "selfish" behavior — pursuing a career in a location far from her husband. As a result, she constantly questions herself, feeling great anxiety and self-reproach. Her idea of a good marriage influences the way she feels she is "doing marriage." Given her more traditional ideas, what were benefits for other commuters became costs for this woman.

The problems of guilt and anxiety — a reticence in fully supporting an ideology of independence — surfaced much more often for those couples with children. Many of these commuters believe that they are not acting as responsible parents. To be sure, many parents today have fears, worrying that their actions will cause permanent psychological damage to their children. But commuters' concerns extend beyond the typical concerns. They are afraid that they have stepped outside even the broad range of norms now acceptable for "good parenting." They are also subject to beliefs concerning their total influence as parents over every aspect of their children's development.

Feelings of guilt are strongest for the parent away from home, especially so for mothers, and they increase the younger the child. The only couple with an infant daughter voiced particularly strong fears about the potentially damaging consequences of separation. Away from his wife and daughter, the father said that this was the greatest problem of commuting:

There are times when our daughter's behavior will cause me to have some questions about whether we are doing the right thing. I'm perhaps more conscious of what I consider atypical behavior that doesn't seem to be quite the way I wanted it and you know that shakes me up. I think: I should be there, not here.

Parents fear that their young children will have trouble with "rejection," with "anxiety," with "insecurity." These words appear repeatedly
in their discussions. They even search for indicators of such problems.
One woman described her own past, so different from her present life:

*I was brought up that a mommy stays home with her kids. My mom was a full-
time mommy from morning 'til night. And way into the night. And one way I
didn't go under was that I always knew that I was first with someone.*

Because of her ideals for good parenting—based on her mother's behavior—she worried:

My daughter isn't sure she is first.

As a consequence, she was especially attentive to any sign of difficulty in her 7-year-old child:

*She has her insecurities. They are not worse as far as I can tell—and I take a
lively interest—than the insecurities of other kids whose moms are here. But I
always think that they might be. I am always worried that they will be. There
are just tremendous guilts living this way.*

So, too, another man poignantly described his search for indicators
of breakdown in his children (aged 7 and 8). He discussed the same
fears:

*My son keeps saying every time I call "Come home." He keeps saying "Daddy,
live here. Daddy, when are you coming home?" I do look for changes and I don't
find any. But I'm sure my children will have trouble with rejection. I can just
see my daughter with a husband. He is going to have something to deal with.
Oh, I don't know, it's hard.*

Not only did these parents of young children have to deal with
their own sense of guilt, but some face pressures from others. A few
recount how their children come home from school, telling how they
are teased or questioned by other children about the absence of one
of their parents:

*One problem has been dealing with other children's remarks. Junie the little one
[9 years old] has had kids say to her: "Oh, you don't have a father."*

Some of the women commented that other women expressed disapproval:

To my husband, they say: "How can you stand taking care of Trudy alone?"
People are always asking about it. And women often wonder how I can leave
our children alone.

Other women show their disapproval that I am leaving the kids with Frank. They
won't come right out and say it, but they'll ask supposedly subtle questions about
the effects on the children.

Just as the commuters look for indicators of problems in their children,
they easily interpret the questions of others as disapproval. These questions and comments compound the anxieties the commuters already
feel about their adequacy as parents. As their comments make clear,
an ideology of an independent marriage is far more difficult to endorse when young children are at home.

However, commuters are able to develop, to some extent, their
own rationales to cope with their sense of guilt. Some comment that
the quality of childrearing is more important than quantity:

As a justification, I must say I spend a great deal more time with them on week-
ends. A professional man comes home late at night and rushes off to his office
on weekends. I spend more time with them than those men. But, more impor-
tantly, it's concentrated time.

Others suggest that they are providing their children with a positive
alternative role model:

I realized that my daughter could look at it in terms of anticipating her own future
role. And she feels very strongly that she would like to have the options I have.
I heard her say, when she grew up, she wouldn't want to feel that she had to
stay home. She hadn't decided yet, but she would like to feel that she had the free-
dom.

Many commuters speak of the benefits to the children's own development. Van Mering (1971) found that professional women tend to emphasize the importance of independence in their children, while housewives tend to emphasize protection. Commuters specifically argue that
commuting helped children develop a sense of self-sufficiency:

In a way, it makes her stand up for herself more. I think it makes her feel more
of an individual.

Let me tell you one of the plusses I see out of this is the children are extraordinar-
ily resourceful and independent. I really can count on them to be able to cope with

any situation. They have almost adult responses. When confronted with something, they know how to manage.

The commuters carry even further the conception of reduced child care that is already held by many women professionals. Such an ideology helps the commuter parent, like other professional spouses, cope with an atypical life situation. But, it does not do away with their guilt entirely. Those without children are much more committed to the ideal of independence because independence for adults is a more accepted standard than independence for children.

"HIS" AND "HER" MARRIAGE

We have discussed certain advantages for the individual that commuter marriage allows, as well as the development of an ideology that enhances and sustains these advantages. We have seen that women are able to benefit in ways their husbands cannot. But we still might ask: overall, do women evaluate commuting differently from men? Indeed, they do.

In overall evaluations of the commuter arrangement, husbands' judgments are typically more negative than those of their wives. In 62% of the couples, the husband dislikes commuter marriage more than his wife. In 22% of the couples, both spouses share the same evaluation. In only 16% of the couples does the wife dislike the situation more than her husband.

Remarkably, this pattern—where the husbands are less favorably disposed to the commuter arrangement—holds up regardless of the specific conditions of commuting. For example, we might expect that the partner who travels between the two homes would make the more negative evaluation of commuting. But as Table 6-1 shows, this is not the case. The figures in Table 6-1 are, of course, at best suggestive. But they do indicate that whoever travels—the wife, the husband, or even if both spouses alternate—the husbands tend to dislike separation more than their wives.

Although we have noted the guilts of the parent who lives away from his or her children, we might also anticipate that the parent who remains with them has more difficulty because of increased child-care burdens. But as Table 6-2 shows, in the cases where couples had children, the pattern persists. Regardless of which spouse stays with the children, husbands are more likely to have a lower evaluation of the commuter arrangement than wives.

TABLE 6-1. Evaluation of Commuter Marriage by Who Travels

EVALUATION OF COMMUTING	WIFE TRAVELS	HUSBAND TRAVELS	BOTH TRAVEL[a]	TOTAL
Husband disliked more	12	14	5	31
Spouses evaluated equally	2	6	3	11
Wife disliked more	2	4	2	8
Total	16	24	10	50

[a]"Both travel" refers to those couples in which neither the husband nor the wife traveled more frequently between the homes, but rather, they alternated that travel.

In most cases, the commuters themselves are aware of the differences between their own evaluations and those of their spouses. Yet their comments also show that they fail to see these differences as a function of gender but instead see them as a function of their particular situations. For example, in one case, a husband was the one to travel 300 miles between the couple's two residences. He said:

I've been sad commuting. Sometimes traveling back and forth, I feel alienated from myself. I think about the other men at my age and feel sorry for myself. I describe myself sometimes as the Willy Loman of academia.

His wife acknowledged that her husband was more dissatisfied with commuting:

For me, this is just not such a big deal. It's had very much less of an effect on me than on Peter. I don't have all the exhaustion of traveling.

In a contrasting example, the wife was the one who did the traveling between the couple's two residences. But she said:

TABLE 6-2. Evaluation of Commuter Marriage by Whom Children Stay With

EVALUATION OF COMMUTING	CHILDREN WITH WIFE	CHILDREN WITH HUSBAND	TOTAL
Husband disliked more	13	9	22
Spouses evaluated equally	1	2	3
Wife disliked more	2	1	3
Total	16	12	28

The situation has been much harder for Stu. You know, it's always harder for the person left behind.

Her husband said:

This lifestyle just doesn't appeal to me. Just aren't any benefits. A husband and wife should live together. Unfortunately, we can't right now.

Here, in each case, both members of the couple differently assess the impact of travel arrangements. In one case, the happier spouse was the one who traveled and in the other, the happier spouse was the one who stayed behind. In both situations, it was the husband who liked the arrangement less.

Other couples explain their different evaluations in terms of which spouse keeps the children. For example, one husband traveled between the couple's two residences while his wife stayed in their primary residence with their two children. As he saw it:

Commuting is just not a tenable way of life for me. I think she is a bit more in favor of it. But I feel lonely all the time.

He had evaluated his wife's attitude correctly. As she said:

It's more detrimental to Hal than to me. I don't get lonely because I have lots of things to do. The children are here with me. And he's all alone down there.

Many of the commuters suggest that when the husband leaves the family behind, it is his consequent loneliness that accounts for his lower evaluation of the commuter arrangement. Yet, typically those husbands left with the children also find commuting more difficult than their wives. For example, in one family, the two children stayed with the husband. He said:

It's just a difficult situation. I assume it is even more so for me than for Sara. I've got all the responsibility as a parent during the week.

His wife, living alone during the week, explained:

People say: "How can you do it?" And I say: "I feel great about it." There are heavy costs familywise. But that's only half the picture. I have a far easier time of it than Richard. It's much harder to be at home with all the family responsibilities.

Again, the husband is more dissatisfied, but now the explanation is reversed. Here, it is not the loneliness of the spouse who travels that causes the problem, but the husband's greater responsibility for child care. However, as we have seen, in families in which the women are left with the children, the men still experience the situation as more stressful.

In sum, no matter what the situation, wives typically evaluate the commuter arrangement more positively than their husbands. The commuters base their evaluations in their particular, at times idiosyncratic, circumstances — which spouse travels, which spouse keeps the children, the particular personalities involved. Yet our analysis suggests a broader explanation: Women garner more benefits from commuting, while men benefit more from "traditional" marriage in a shared home.

CONCLUSION

In this chapter we have discussed the consequences for individuals in commuter arrangments. In past decades, few sociologists thought to include both husbands and wives in their studies of marriage. Implicit in their research was a conception that each marriage was a single entity and that, consequently, either the wife or the husband could act as an informant for the experiences of both. Moreover, there was an idea of transcendence embedded in this methodolgy, an assumption that marriage has a life of its own which exists apart from the lives of its individual members. Because of this assumption, sociologists of marriage and the family were unable to ask the question that is routinely asked of other social institutions: Who benefits?

Relying on a range of literature, Jessie Bernard addressed this question in *The Future of Marriage* (1972). In this influential book, she argued that every marriage contains not one marriage, but two: "his" and "hers." In contrast to both sociological and popular images — marriage as a whole is either good or bad — Bernard claimed that a husband and wife not only experience their marriages differently but also derive unequal benefits from it. Albeit with an occasional exception (e.g., see Glenn, 1975), evidence has accumulated to suggest that men are the prime beneficiaries of the single-residence marriage: Women are more likely than men to have regrets about marriage, to experience marital problems, to feel they lack understanding, and to be irritated with spouse's behavior (Locksley, 1980; Rollins & Cannon, 1974; Rubin, 1976; Schafer & Keith, 1981).

Our findings on commuters add further support to this framework. Though commuter marriages clearly involve losses for both spouses, many of them, especially the women, see benefits for themselves as individuals that were not possible when they shared a single home. Since these changes occurred within a supportive ideological climate, wives can perceive and articulate them in a fashion that helps alleviate guilts and anxieties often associated with deviant behavior.

With the evidence from this and other studies, we can make a stronger case for the hypothesis that the typical nuclear family, with its shared residence, restricts women more and rewards them less than it does men. By separating, or approximating singlehood for part of the time, women commuters are able to overcome some of the specifically "feminine" burdens of marriage. Yet, these women are still married and may receive some of its rewards, such as stability and security. They know others will label them "married," which is obviously still *the* legitimate status for adult women in our society. That is, they can maintain the status of "being married" while having some of the practical advantages of "doing" singlehood.

The commuters' experiences seem to suggest that there are several components to the role of wife, in her "doing marriage," that make it less satisfying than the role of husband in the intact nuclear family. Demands stemming from the husband's career, such as geographic mobility, receive priority in the family unit. Consequently, the wife is required to be the more dependent family member. It is she who suffers professional setbacks, losses of self-esteem, and consignment to relative invisibility even when she attempts to pursue a career. When a woman is employed (as some of these commuters were before they lived apart), she typically continues to perform more than half of the domestic tasks at home. When apart, the domestic tasks necessarily are redistributed and equalized. Consequently, a woman's professional work output increases when she is living in a separate home, while her husband's is less likely to do so. In addition, it is typically the woman who makes greater marital adjustments, acting as the flexible and supportive family member. When away from her husband, she may simplify her daily life, paying more attention to her own needs and priorities. Because women are more likely to be engulfed by familial tasks detrimental to their own needs, they benefit more from separation than do their husbands, who in a shared home could pursue their own needs as individuals and as members of a couple.

Our analysis does not suggest that commuter wives view their distinctive gains as adequate compensation for the considerable strains commuting produces. Most would prefer a world in which it was possible to have these benefits while sharing a home with their husbands. Most experience some guilt because they pursue their own individual desires. But this analysis does suggest that "allowing" women to work is inadequate as a means to equalize the costs and benefits of marriage when spouses share a single home. If such costs and benefits are to be equalized, the marital relationship itself must be more thoroughly equalized in its internal division of domestic labor, in the psychic adjustment and support offered by each member, and the independence and autonomy possible for each member. Living apart for periods of time, husbands and wives alike are, by force of circumstance, more likely to make equal contributions. In this situation, if not in the conventional family, wives, along with their husbands, discover the virtues of independence.

CHAPTER 7

Commuting:
What Makes It
Easier or Harder

For commuters, the decision to live apart solves the problem of work demands that send them in different directions. Yet, as a solution, living apart creates its own problems. As we have seen, most commuters view the advantages of geographic separation as an island of benefits in a sea of costs. However, certain factors lessen the effort it takes to live apart and make commuting more tolerable. In this chapter, we review conditions which affect the viability of commuter marriage. We ask: What characteristics and conditions make it easier or harder to set up two homes?

First and foremost among those factors are the conditions of separation itself—how far apart the spouses live, how frequently and regularly they reunite. Second, we shall see that characteristics of their marriage and work are important limiting conditions as well. The length of time the couple has been married and whether or not they have children (as well as the ages of those children) affect their responses to living apart. Work-related factors that figure into the cost–benefit calculus of these spouses include what career stage they have reached, their employers' attitudes—how supportive they are—and the flexibility of their work materials and relationships. Beyond these structural factors are the couples' own coping devices, which seem to operate independently of their particular demographic profiles or their commuting patterns. Here we see that the extent to which spouses are able to separate work and family demands influences how successfully they cope with the strains of living apart. So too does their perception about how long they will "need" to live this way, that is, how temporary or permanent they think the separation will be. Each of these factors will be addressed in the discussion that follows. But first let us consider generally what viability might mean in the context of commuter marriages.

COMMUTING AND MARITAL VIABILITY

At its most basic level, viability means the absence of divorce. Ideally, to assess the likelihood of divorce, we would want not only a randomized study design but longitudinal data as well. While we have neither, we do have some data that address this issue: our study did include interviews with seven individuals who divorced while in the process of commuting.[1] Although our ability to generalize from these data is obviously limited, the statements of these seven respondents do suggest that commuting alone is not sufficient cause for divorce.

All of these spouses said that although the establishment of two separate homes may have led them to seek divorce more quickly than if they had remained in a single home, geographic separation was not itself a key factor in the actual decision. One husband put this quite succinctly:

The commuting just clinched it. I was divorced in my mind already. It in no way caused it.

This idea that the marriage was already in jeopardy before commuting began and that commuting enabled the break-up of what Waller and Hill (1965) call the "habit system" of marriage was a common refrain among this group:

Commuting made me see I could live alone. But you can see we weren't happy with each other for a long time before that. There was just much more pain than pleasure.

This woman's ex-husband seemed to be, essentially, in agreement:

I think we both knew a long time ago that the marriage was bound for an end. But we just kept living in the same house — side by side — but not really together. I guess we convinced ourselves that a bad marriage was better than no marriage. I know I just thought it would be a pain in the ass to start all over again, to

---

1. These seven ex-spouses were interviewed because they had divorced while commuting. That is, these ex-spouses were not a part of our main commuter sample, but are, instead, an entirely different "subsample"; see Appendix for discussion of this group.

date and all that garbage. When we started living apart, it just became clearer to me and Becky, too, that it was time to go to see lawyers. Not that that was an easy thing. It wasn't. But, anyway, if we'd really had a good marriage before commuting, I don't think living apart would have killed it. Of course, I don't really know. That's just my feeling.

Though not itself causal, then, the distance allowed spouses time and space to re-evaluate their relationships. Living apart exacerbated the marriage's problems, but did not create them.

We must remember that these spouses' statements are postfactum explanations. Possibly, these dissatisfied couples would not have been forced to face and act on their feelings and might have remained in "empty-shell" marriages; perhaps their relationships would have improved eventually if they had continued to share one home. But the growing divorce rate suggests this is unlikely. Instead, though it may not initiate the problem, the divorced commuters' comments suggest that geographic separation may facilitate the actual decision to begin divorce proceedings.

Clearly though, divorce is only one measure of the viability of a particular marriage structure. Short of dissolution, the question of whether commuter marriage is viable cannot be answered with a simple yes or no. Rather there are limiting conditions under which it can be said to work well or not so well.

CONDITIONS OF THE COMMUTE

Several features of the commuting arrangement affect how the couple responds to the rigors of traveling between two homes. Obviously how far the distance is between them limits how often they can get together and, as we saw earlier, the longer the time apart, the greater the awareness that "it is time" to reunite. Moreover, not only the pattern of separations, but also the pattern of reunions — their regularity, timing, and duration — seem to affect the experience of a commuter marriage.

Greater distance increases the strain of living apart in three ways. First, when the distance between them is longer, spouses must necessarily spend more money on travel and phone calls. Second, actual traveling calls for increased and sometimes trying energy outlays.

I mean sitting on a plane for five or six hours or door-to-door, six to seven hours — that really shoots the weekend. You've got less time together and you've got to recuperate on both sides.

Third, and most importantly, the increased cost and energy required for greater distances lengthens the time most couples spend apart. Most of those who saw each other infrequently traveled the farthest, although a few of those far apart could have afforded to reunite more often. (See Appendix, Tables A8 and A10, for distance separating spouses, and Table A10 for frequency of reunions by distance apart.) Those couples who were apart for longer periods of time experienced the greatest stress. For example, a wife who saw her husband every weekend, minimized the inconvenience:

Commuting isn't that big a deal. When we live together, we spend an awful lot of time apart anyway because we both do so much work. Now we see each other on weekends and feel really good about each other.

Though, as we have seen, men are less likely to see advantages in commuting, the following husband, who lived apart from his wife only four days a week, said:

Now, it's not so bad. Four days apart is a short time to be separated. We like some degree of solitude and we find that when we return, like Friday evening, it's kind of exciting, news, things to report, just seeing each other.

Sharply contrasted with such statements are those of people who are apart for more extended periods of time. A husband whose separation from his wife usually lasted for an entire month told how he had reached the point where he was willing to give up his job and move to where his wife works. An academic, he thought he could read and write at home until something closer to her became available. He insisted:

Commuting is just not tenable at all. I don't see how two people who love each other very much and want to see each other all the time, want to live together, and want to discuss their lives as they unfold, can live apart. It would be much more viable as a stop-gap if we could see each other on weekends. We've just suffered a great deal this way.

In this case, his wife agreed:

We miss each other awfully much. I can, of course, only speak for myself. But I have every reason to believe we both miss each other. But I know my own life first. I miss my husband awfully much as a companion, as a lover, as a friend. In every respect. It's a terrible handicap to me. There's something terribly wrong with this business of being apart. I'm an emotional person and I need my husband. I miss him very much. But do you know how long a time a month is to go without seeing your husband? I know couples who are apart three or four days a week. Now that looks like nothing.

Another couple dramatically illuminates the impact of different distances on a couple's relationship, for they had experienced two different types of commuting arrangements. First, they had lived over 2000 miles apart, at which time they only saw each other at most once a month. At the time of the interview, they were separated by only 100 miles and were apart only four days a week. As the husband compared the two situations:

The problems with it depends on how much time you are apart. Now we are apart only four nights a week. It's not as serious a headache. We can talk on the phone without spending too much money. We can still keep up with each other's days. When we were apart four or six weeks at a shot, it was just much, much harder. If you'd interviewed me then, I would have given you a long list of why commuting is impossible for a couple that wants to have a marriage.

His wife agreed:

Now, it's like a luxury compared to what we had before. And it's really not a disastrous situation. There are even some very nice things about it.

As these examples illustrate, when the time apart increases, so too does dissatisfaction with the commuter arrangement: Losses to the couple — in their conversation, shared leisure and inactivity, as well as physical contact — are high while rewards are low. The balance produces increased stress.

In addition to the length of separation, the timing, relative duration, and regularity of reunions affects the quality of the commuting experience. Couples who see each other every weekend not only have the obvious advantage of being separated for shorter time periods compared to couples who cannot get together every weekend, they also have a pattern of separating and regrouping that roughly parallels the work–leisure pattern for most of society. They are away from each other when others are working and together for weekends which they, like others, devote to shared activities. The "weekends together" pattern, then, is least discrepant from the work–leisure rhythm of their coresident dual-career counterparts (Rapoport & Rapoport, 1976). It is the pattern of separation relative to other patterns that is least likely to threaten their sense of what marriage "is." For it is weekends that most middle-class Americans learn to define as time that not only is, but should be, shared. As a result of these assumptions, individuals perceive a Saturday night alone as lonelier than a week night alone. Consequently, commuters who do not reunite on weekends experience the pains of separation most intensely:

You know, I feel most alone on Friday and Saturday nights. I'm not invited out when my wife isn't here. And I find myself turning on the TV or radio just for company. That isn't the case during the week. Then I'm alone but not lonely, at least not nearly so much.

Moreover, the duration of reunions — especially relative to the duration of separations — seems to color the experience of living apart. The same amount of time together, for example, a weekend, is experienced differently if it comes after a long or short separation. A weekend visit after a long separation may be too compressed a period to accomplish what spouses expect, especially since expectations seem to grow as time apart increases. Several spouses complain that the time together was not what they had hoped for. They seem perplexed by this fact, as if they could not quite understand how something they so looked forward to could disappoint them. A wife who saw her husband less than once a month for only a couple of days at a time said:

When you have only a couple of days, you never get it to be comfortable so there's a strangeness, that letdown, like: "Why aren't I enjoying this more?"

Short reunions, especially after lengthy separations, then, provoke a sense of spoiled time:

Our expectation level was so high because it was so important that every minute count and everything be perfect and it just wasn't. The pressure was always on and it was a real strain and we both felt it.

Finally, irregular reunions, that is, getting together when either one's schedule permits, challenges the relationship's taken-for-granted quality in ways that regular regrouping patterns (e.g., every weekend) do not. Couples who are together each weekend seem to accommodate themselves to the routine of this pattern and take comfort in its regularity. They tell of taking a specific train, arriving at a certain time, and of a schedule of events throughout the weekend, all of which seem to fortify their relationship.

While the pattern (and not simply duration) of reunions affects the viability of a commuter relationship and while, as we would expect, personality traits affect the amount of time couples believe they can live apart, there does seem to be a real limit to the amount of time they can live separately. Most who were apart only a week or even two at a time found the situation tolerable (and even in some ways beneficial) for their relationship; those who lived separately for a month were much more likely to find the situation extraordinarily stressful. In fact, a month, as the limit on separation, kept coming up again and again in the interviews:

Seeing each other once a month is just ludicrous. It would be much more liveable if we saw each other every weekend or even every other weekend. But a month at a time, I mean, this is the other end of the world. It's not really a commute. I mean it is really living apart. Our worlds are so separate.

We have some friends who commute between Illinois and Virginia. They're lucky if they see each other once a month. We couldn't do that. It all becomes sort of surreal.

There was an awful long period when we didn't see each other for a month. That's too long. By the end of the month, your patterns of not seeing each other are too well-established.

Apparently, if couples are apart for a month or more at a time, this way of "doing marriage" begins to affect their idea of marriage — their sense of "being married." Their marriage begins to resemble a non-marriage. The relationship becomes less of a structure around which they can order their lives; it lacks time and place constancies that allow daily connection and the sharing of "trivia" which undergirds the foundation of marriage.

The way we do it, seeing each other, at most, once a month, just can't work. If you're apart a week or two, you've got a chance. But the longer you're separated, the more mechanical it becomes. We're married, we speak to each other. But, I don't see any of what I was raised to consider a marriage to be: The mutual understanding, the discussion of everything that goes on, the companionship, just knowing about each other's lives.

Yet, important as these conditions are, so, too, are specific characteristics of a couple's marriage, which may either aggravate or mitigate the strains produced by commuting.

CONDITIONS OF MARRIAGE

One of our major conclusions is that characteristics of the familial and economic systems must be considered in tandem to reveal their mutual effect. The interaction between family and work outside the home is immediately apparent because the family characteristics that matter most — length of marriage and presence of children — not only covary but also tend to covary with career stages. Young couples married fewer years, are likely to be childless or, less typically, have very young children, and are in the early stages of their careers. For older couples, just the reverse composite is typical: married longer, they either have older children or children away from home, and at least one spouse is likely to be advanced in his or her career. These family–career composites reveal three types of commuter couples: "adjusting," "balancing," and "established."

While all of these couples share some common concerns, there are important variations in their experiences. The youngest wives and husbands grapple more with conflict about whose career needs should predominate; what we call career politics or career ascendancy conflict. Compared to the older couples they expend a good deal of effort "adjusting" to the lifestyle. Older couples, who have children at home, contend more with conflict over increased child care and domestic responsibilities for the spouse who stays with the family. They must strike a balance between the demands of their jobs and their families. Finally, the "established" couples — those whose children are no longer at home — have cemented their marital relationship and face neither the guilt nor anxiety associated with parenting in separate homes. At the same time, they face fewer conflicts over the priority of careers. Though not without difficulty, these couples' commuting lives are the least stressed because they are the most "established" in both their work and family lives.

Adjusting Couples: Youth and Career Politics

For the young wife, to have her professional identity attended to at all, for it to be a factor causing the difficulty separation entails, means that she is getting a "benefit" denied the traditional wife. She is thus "special," and she knows it. Yet, this is not an unalloyed advantage, for there is some guilt attached to the recognition that her "specialness" causes her husband disadvantages if compared to other husbands. Her sense of advantage is mitigated and undermined by an attendant guilt, leaving her with a burdensome, perplexing sense of somehow having wronged him.

A wife in medical school expressed these conflicting emotions— satisfaction because she could devote herself to her work, unfettered by the usual wifely commitments, and guilt because she felt responsible for hindering her husband's potential:

I am extremely tired but really enjoying myself and I come home at night and fall into bed. I am very aware of the fact that if he were here, you know— relationships take time. There's a good side and a bad side to that—if you don't have time and energy. So I think, "Well, while I'm doing surgery, maybe it's better that Dave's not here."

Later she added:

I know he has lots of dreams for what he wants to accomplish in his lifetime. I really have sensed in him this fall a sudden realization that he was getting older—that there's certain things he wants to get done with his life and somehow the way we're living, the separation, is demanding too much. It's too much of a sacrifice.

For the young husband, on the other hand, what contributes to his wife's sense of "having something special" at the same time creates his sense of loss. Although they both take pride in his "liberation," such pride does not compensate adequately for the deprivation he feels relative to the traditional husband role. After all, he is "giving up" the subordination to his needs usually enjoyed by the male, the breadwinner, the "necessarily" career-oriented member of the couple. For all his efforts to suppress the resentment, he still feels somewhat deprived. It is not the ministrations of a doting wife he misses—neither one of them ever expected to be "picked up after" or physically catered to. Their belief in equal partnership precludes such a response, or at least, reduces its salience. Rather, what the husband misses is a wife willing to acknowledge his "inherent" right to first place, to initial consideration. Of course, her career "counts" and is seen as important. It's just not *as* important as his. He both yearns for subordination and castigates himself for wanting it—because he realizes such subordination flies in the face of his other standards for their marriage. Still, at least in this sense, he feels more denied, more "taken from," than a woman who knows she is being given an option not typical of a wife's claims on her husband. As one young husband put it:

I thought her getting the degree was going to finish it all and that would be it. She went up there to be a potter, she got the MA and got seduced into high art and wanted to be a sculptor. Intellectually I was very supportive of that; emotionally it was something I couldn't handle easily. I don't like being alone.

Furthermore, he cannot acknowledge such feelings openly because, on the face of it, he "wants" full development of her potential. This is his reasoned, intellectual objective. Emotionally, however, he feels bereft, the loser of a benefit he had learned to anticipate from his concept of a "wife." As another young husband explained his irritation:

I think it had to do a lot with who was put out, who was making sacrifices. I just decided that from my stance it had nothing in it for me. It took me a while to become aware of it.

Another young husband explained the effort it would have taken to pass up the opportunity his present position affords. Thinly veiled resentment and irritation for having to wrestle with the decision in the first place permeate his account. He did not want to sound resentful or irritated and seemed upset by the way the words were coming out. Yet, it was clear, even to him, that these were his emotions. His struggle also conveyed a sense of diminished, or at least tarnished, self-esteem for the ambition and egotism his decision implied. Even more important, he was uncomfortable with this threat to his picture of himself as someone "concerned with his wife's needs":

We know this professional couple who have made a decision to alternate, giving each one's career a turn in deciding where to go. But that would be very hard for me. I wanted Barb's location to fit in with my plans, but we couldn't work it out. I felt that it worked out that I had to be away from her. I needed for her to see that it had to be this way. I just couldn't have let this go by.

Here the issue is not whether the wife should have a career. As we have seen, most husbands in these families did not discourage, and a significant group encouraged, their wives' ambitions — a stance consistent with the high educational level and professional orientation of both spouses which anticipates and even presumes her professional interests. Yet, each recognizes, at least covertly, that living apart is a response to her need to be somewhere he cannot. This realization is expressed especially well by a phrase used independently by both members of a couple. They each said that they frequently mused privately, as well as confronted each other directly (sometimes playfully, sometimes accusingly), with the question, "Who left whom?"

Though the wife actually had moved out of their apartment in Arizona to attend law school in the Midwest, she had done so on the assumption that he was to follow as soon as their affairs were settled. They had agreed to this arrangement. At the last moment, he decided he could not give up some powerful incentives his company offered him to stay. Now she sometimes feels he left her because he did not follow as planned. He, in turn, nurtures the view that since he stayed where *they* were, the issue is not clear. This dialogue, to which they both alluded, framed the tensions created by their mutual awareness of the antagonistic pulls of their respective careers.

The career ascendancy struggle, viewed by young couples from the perspective of traditional husbandly prerogatives and wifely responsibilities, is exacerbated by two additional factors: Their marriages have not endured long enough to exist as a solid reality, and the rewards of firmly established professional identities are not yet theirs. They are, thus, more vulnerable on two counts. First, as marital partners, they are still conscious of themselves in the process of creating a sense of "we-ness" and cannot yet count on a set of shared experiences to act as an emotional reservoir from which to draw. Second, as struggling, newly-minted professionals, they do not have the confirmed sense of competence that buttresses the egos of their older counterparts. The concern they share with other dual-career couples — "Is my marriage as important as my career?" — is not yet counteracted by a sense of the marriage as one which can, in fact, endure the tensions they see beleaguering it. Because they have not yet successfully created a marital unit involving two professional careers, they are not at all convinced they can. Hence, the inner nagging: "What kind of an emotional freak am I? Why is my career as important to me as my marriage is?"

I think that's how we both see it. We know that neither of us is willing to give up the course we are going on so we can't ask the other to. Yet implicit in that is the realization that somehow you are making the statement that at least some aspect of your career is more important than being together. I think that's a real issue for today. I get really angry and feel like why do I even have to make these choices, one against the other. It doesn't seem right. There's obviously still a lot of pain.

Such searching is intensified among those adjusting couples who have children. Most of the couples do not yet have any children; those few who do tend to have very young children and, for them, the questioning is all the more painful. They not only ask "Why is my career as important to me as my marriage?" but also ask "Why is my career as important to me as my children?" As we suggested in earlier chapters, the presence of young children adds problems for all commuters, but these are especially great for those couples who face the squeeze of a relatively new marriage, young children, and a not yet stable career.

The strains from the power struggle over whose career commitments should prevail weigh as heavily on these adjusting couples as does the fact of living apart. For these sophisticated, highly educated young people, varying from the norm of sharing a home, though troublesome, pales in significance to varying from the norm that the husband is the primary breadwinner whose career needs should come first. Because they can neutralize pressures for living apart by disengaging from questioning relatives and friends, couples find these pressures are not a source of profound discomfort. Much more basic to the tone of their relationship, and to the marital bond they are still fashioning, is the struggle between them. True enough, their own career struggles reflect societal views about the role of husband and wife, but they experience this as an issue of power between them. The power issue is all the more unsettling because these liberated young people consciously eschew notions of dominant husbands and submissive wives and because their education instills the idea that alternative arrangements can be more appealing than conventional ones.

Balancing Couples

Clashes resulting from the antagonistic claims of marriage and career are less disturbing to older couples married for a longer time. Older spouses very much realize the importance of a backlog of experience for coping with separation:

We had enough of a base beforehand. I think if we had done this when we were married two or three years, we never would have made it. We have a lot invested emotionally in one another and I think we had a strong enough reserve and had enough smooth times before to make it. I think our bond was strong enough that it overcame all the problems and trauma.

In contrast, a commuter who had been married and living with her husband for only one year remarked:

I'm afraid it's dangerous for us to be living apart. After all, we've only spent one year in the same house.

Other studies of separated spouses corroborate the importance of a long marital history. Looking at families separated during wars, McCubbin, Dahl, and Ross (1974) found that the longer a couple was married before separation, the greater the likelihood of a successful reintegration. Apparently, families evolve into stable units over time. Young couples must establish a basis of trust and a shared history before setting up two separate homes. Becker (1960) points out, in another context, that the time devoted to an activity creates commitment to the continuation of that activity.

Still another factor related to length of marriage mutes any career ascendancy conflict. Older couples often sense that the wives are correcting an imbalance in the marital relationship. Since they have been married longer, the past usually includes more time when the husband's career did "come first," while the wife stayed home to raise the children and/or worked a "job" to enable him to succeed. Now that the wife finally has decided to pursue her own career, they both look forward to the results. In fact, in these instances, the husbands explicitly say, "It's her turn now!"—a sentiment the wives clearly echo. Each feels a sense of accomplishment because the decision to live apart gives the wife "her turn." The husbands in these marriages are most likely to say that the "best thing" about living apart is the opportunity it affords the wife to measure up to her potential, "to fulfill herself," "to be the person she's capable of being." These older husbands are able to respond to the difficulties of commuting as returning the advantages they previously enjoyed. While we saw in an earlier chapter that most husbands like commuting less than most wives, the older husbands' sense of burden is tempered somewhat by the real satisfaction they get from seeing their wives develop.

Yet despite their common reservoir of experience and sense that they are correcting a previous imbalance, these older couples are still not free of painful resentment. Parental responsibilities trouble these older mates. We have already seen how parents left with the major responsibility for their children's practical and emotional needs feel overburdened, much like other single parents—especially if the caretaking parent is the father. So, even couples with the advantage of a longer marriage, if children are still at home, experience resentment, overload, and guilt. Husbands proud of their wives' accomplishments still resent the increased child care and household maintenance burdens. A quite typical remark from an older husband with children was:

There are chores and running of errands and I felt the anger of the frustration of the needs and demands placed on me by the three kids. More than anything else, the need to be at a piano lesson, to go to the doctor. I'm not sure I was angry at her as much as I was just angry that the need was there, that I couldn't share that.

Wives, in their turn, miss their children and worry about their lessened input into their lives. Given the tenacity of the equation between parenting and mothering in our culture, these mothers find it especially painful to leave the family home and to relinquish day-to-day responsibilities:

I don't know how you balance it. I don't know how to balance two or three years of wanting to stay and watch my kids against 20 years of my life.

These greater domestic and child-care costs are, for "balancing" couples, the counterpart to the career ascendancy conflict which troubles younger couples. However, the trade-offs each type makes are not equally discomforting because older couples do acknowledge more sources of satisfaction: the solidity of their relationship, the faith that they can endure the demands of living apart, and the recognition that they are compensating for the wife's past efforts on her husband's behalf.

Established Couples

It is the third group of couples — those established in their marital, parenting, and work lives — who experience the fewest strains while commuting. They already have a long marital history which sustains them during their separations. As one commuter, who had lived with his wife for 20 years and whose only daughter was now in college, put it:

Time means a lot to me. It's partly a clue to my attitude to my wife. I don't understand how someone at age 50 can pick up and go off and make another relationship. I mean you know them so well; the relationship has been cemented by the time we've already lived together.

More importantly, the children of these "established" couples are grown and out of the home which leaves their commuter parents with a sense of accomplishment and freedom. As they see it, these spouses can now optimize their career involvement. As one woman whose youngest child had just begun college put it:

If we had children at home, it would be very difficult. This is really, from my standpoint, the first year it could have worked. I don't know how we could have done it before. Now I finally think we have the right and time to live this way. It would have been so much harder with our children still at home.

However, even these "established" couples — precisely because they have shared so much — experience some sense of regret because they live apart. The very fact that their lives are more connected, that they have built up a sense of common identity, makes the separation that much more of a trial:

I don't relate intimately to a lot of people, but by now I do to her, so I've lost a great deal when she's gone.

I really don't handle aloneness well because I'm so used to having someone to come home to.

Overall, then, it is this group of older couples, without any children at home, who see the greatest advantage to commuting. Yet, despite compensations, even the accounts of most of these couples suggest that they cope with the lifestyle more than enjoy it. For each type (and for each spouse) a compromise has been fashioned, but it is "no bargain" either.

CONDITIONS OF WORK

Another set of work-related conditions figures into the bargain these couples fashion. First, low income precludes even the possiblity of commuting. As we have seen, traveling and long-distance phone calls entail considerable expense as do the requirements of a second residence and of hired help. Many families simply would not have an adequate income. But even with an adequate income, those in the lower ranges have more difficulty with the commuting arrangement, as this husband's ($25,000 family income) comments reveal:

We're not poor. Obviously our joint salaries are good. Compared to being students, we thought we'd feel rich. But that was before we started living apart. I mean if we were more advanced it wouldn't be nearly so much hassle. We have to drive — it takes six hours each way. And even then we have to worry about gas and tolls. We have to really think twice about calling each other, and when we do it has to be after 11:00 when the rates are cheaper. I don't exactly live in a palace. And Marsha had to chose between a hovel or sharing with someone else. And even with that, there's very little money left for anything.

A second job condition, which increases the strain of commuting, is the inflexibility of some working schedules. A job involving primarily individual, rather than cooperative effort, is more appropriate for commuting. For example, an academic faculty job is more compatible with commuting than a managerial position in a business corporation. Many academics can take part of their work home, away from colleagues. They have greater say about when and where to work as well as more and longer vacations than many other occupations. Though vacation time may be spent on work, academics often do not need to be near their college or university. This holds true even if only one of the spouses is an academic and he or she can do all the traveling. An administrator in a large organization expressed this common view:

I would say ours, among the variety of commuting marriages, is about the easiest one in that Fred [her husband] is on a very flexible schedule, namely an academic schedule. His primary interest is his research and that he can work on here. The academic year is quite short and he doesn't have to be in his place of work five days a week.

If both are academics, this further eases the arrangement.

The academic calendar is especially good for commuting, especially since our schedules don't coincide. Like my spring vacation isn't when his is. So next week, I can go down there for a week. Then he'll come here for his. Then in the summer, we'll be together for the whole time. Although it doesn't always seem like it, we don't spend that much time apart.

Contrast these comments with those of a couple where the work conditions and schedules of both — she is an editor in a publishing house; he, a manager in a large chemical plant — are more constraining. He stated:

I'm a product manager, have responsibilities for a product. I have to be in the office five days a week, at least nine to five because those are the hours everyone else is working. My job isn't so flexible that I can very often decide to just pick up on Thursday instead of Friday night. Neither can Mary. It'd be much easier if one of us could.

Finally, the immobility of work-related materials limits the ease of commuting. For example, a laboratory researcher must stay much closer to a specific location than someone doing library research with materials that are widely available, where the required sources may be carried with him or her, or may be partially stored in two locations. However, though not even library work can be done any place, any time, an ongoing lab experiment demands more constant attention in one specific locale.

COMPARTMENTALIZATION

Up to this point, we have discussed the viability of commuting in terms of the pattern of separation and reunions and the structure of family and work, identifying life conditions that lighten or increase the burdens of commuting. The mechanisms that operate regardless of the couple's particular demographic profile or pattern of separation and re-union are also important. Here we see that the way couples intentionally alternate the priority of work and family life shapes their commuting experience.

Because they work in locations completely separate from their spouses, commuters have greater opportunity to compartmentalize their work and family roles. When apart, they can focus on their jobs; when together, they can focus on one another. And, as discussed earlier, such compartmentalization has its rewards for the couple — heightened communication, lowered conflict, and possibly more romantic exchanges — while it simultaneously allows the pursuit of individual career goals.

Most commuters' discussions of their weekly routines clearly suggest such alternating emphases. Both spouses typically share this pattern. For example, a wife with a heavy research and teaching load believed in setting aside most of her weekends to be with her husband:

I structure my time in a different way on the weekends than I do during the week. During the week, I'm usually pretty well lined up and don't have time to sit and chat. I couldn't relax enough to do that. But during the weekend, it is mostly leisure time, shared time. It's a very conscious thing.

Her husband, also an academic, said:

During the week, I work very hard. Work is what I do. But weekends are the times to be together, to share with Joanne, to focus on one another. Sometimes we both do some work then, but much less at home than when we lived together.

Most couples not only set aside work when they reunite, but, as we discussed previously, they also curtail other personal relationships. As most commuters perceive it, time in the shared home is for the marital relationship — not for work or socializing with friends.

Those couples with children have more difficulty compartmentalizing their time so that when away from work, they could focus solely on one another. The parent remaining with the children has family responsibilities even in the other spouse's presence. The parent who traveled to a separate residence comes home to both children and spouse. Time and energy have to be shared with all family members. But even with children, some compartmentalization could occur, bringing emotional benefits — "quality" time — to the family. For example, a wife with a husband and two children, who commuted to her administrative job, said:

When I'm at home, I really want to be totally with the children and family. But I like the change of pace. The ability to concentrate when I come to work. I may work 14 or 16 hours a day and I'm not pulled between my family obligations and my work obligations. I ought to be thinking I'm responsible for my children regardless of my location, but there is an intensity of both sets of activities. I work very hard here but not at home. So I can also focus on the children and be super mother. Up in the morning, making lunches, doing all the things we need to do together. And we do these things as a whole family now. I seem to function very well keeping all these activities very intense and very separate.

For many of these dual-career couples, balancing family and work demands began even before commuting. Then, guilt occurred when either activity was the central one, especially for women. In these cases, the clear separation of work and family obligations which commuting promotes makes it easier to manage competing obligations. As one wife, an academic, with three children put it:

I burn the midnight oil more when we're apart and I'm more involved with the family when we're together. I went to a few things at the kids' school during the day which is something I didn't do when I lived there all the time. I was so tied in with the administration. So there the problem was; it was much harder to reduce competing obligations between job and home. It wasn't just a question of meeting classes, but all of a sudden an emergency meeting would be called at 8:00 at night, and I'd been away the two previous evenings. I felt very ambivalent. And it's very nice once you make the decision to commute. It makes things simpler. Because of the concerns over things like: should you be at home or should you be at work? The priorities are now clearly established.

But not all couples are prepared to compartmentalize their lives. For the minority who do not, commuting brings no intensification to their marriages. Several husbands and wives told how they were irritated by their spouses' lack of attention when they did reunite. Voicing such a complaint, a husband said his wife did not change her routine when he came home for the weekend, that is, did not turn her attention to their relationship. He responded first with anger and then with resignation:

When we started commuting, I got into a tantrum that must have lasted a couple of months. I felt quite sorry for myself. I felt misused. I just thought somehow things should be arranged differently. And when I come home on weekends, at least we should be able to spend time doing things, and she'd be busy doing her work. So I'd come back all full of anticipation about seeing her and she was always very glad to see me and we'd have a good dinner and all this and then she'd say, "Well, I've got to go back to work." I began to feel, "Oh, this is awful. Nobody cares for me down there and nobody cares for me here. I'm just a poor, little abandoned fellow." I guess I'd just finally come to terms with it. I don't have much choice. But it is frustrating.

In another case, the husband wanted to continue socializing with other people just as they had before the separation. His wife was upset, because she felt the need for more involvement with just him during their short reunions:

He still wants to have people over, go places with other couples and stuff like that. Of course, I do, too. It'd be nice. But, I don't think we should 'cause we don't have much time just for the two of us. It makes me feel he doesn't care enough. I need him when I come home. I must say this is a point of contention. I'm feeling particularly angry this week because this past weekend we were with other people the entire time I was home. This is something we are going to have to work out.

For a very small number of couples, neither spouse felt any desire to change their routines when they met in a single home. These couples placed little value on their relationships before commuting and did not particularly enjoy even their limited, shared time. For them, marriage had been, and continued to be, a convenience:

When we're apart, I don't really think either one of us cares. And when we're together, it is certainly nothing spectacular. Just humdrum routine kinds of things.

Her husband felt the same way:

It started going downhill a long time ago and being apart certainly hasn't made it go back uphill. There simply isn't any warmth left, much less real love. So why should we be different when we see each other?

These couples did not divorce only because it was easier to remain married. For them, commuting brought neither losses nor gains to their relationship. When they reunited, the dissatisfactions remained; too much disinterest, even hostility, had accumulated. In such cases, a geographic separation could not revitalize the relationship and compartmentalization was neither desired nor used.

To conclude, residential separation leads most commuters to change their expectations about the allocation of time; both spouses try to set aside other activities during their reunions. Doing so, they find they can cope with the commuting arrangement, indeed, it brings many rewards. But such compartmentalization is not automatic. A few couples lived "as usual," experiencing neither increased satisfaction nor dissatisfaction. However, when the spouse's expectations for the reunions are discordant, the result is disturbance: the needs of the couple as a unit are not met.

Finally, to end discussion of the benefits of compartmentalization, we should note an apparent inconsistency between the emphasis here on the gains derived from the separation of work and family spheres and our earlier assertion that the initial decision to commute depended on an ability to connect work and family satisfactions. Both points are valid. An essential ingredient of the decision to commute, the strong association couples make between their work and family identities, is a link that makes them want to satisfy the demands of both spheres simultaneously. At the same time, what expedites living in a commuter arrangement is just that ability to disconnect the two spheres so that the demands of one do not encroach on the other — to the detriment of adaptation to both.

TEMPORARY DEVIANCE

The relative comfort or discomfort of commuting is also affected by the extent to which living this way fits into the larger picture these couples have of what marriage "is." Overwhelmingly, commuters define the situation as temporary, no matter how unsure they are about when it will end. To these spouses "being married" means living together. Consequently, to maintain a sense of their marriages as whole, even real, they view their separation as a temporary aberration, which they intend to correct. Some believe that they knew from the beginning exactly when it would end: completion of a law clerkship, a graduate program, internship or some such time-limited activity. However, some of these couples understand that the completion of this stage in their career might simply usher in another situation — when both or either of the spouses would be looking for another job — once again requiring separate residences:

Who knows — I wouldn't like it — but if she graduates and doesn't find a job near here, we may have to do this all over again.

Moreover, many could not even try to specify when they would live together again. By continuing to look for other positions and by establishing themselves in their individual careers, they hope their situations would change and they would be able to share a single residence again. This is dramatically illustrated in a case where it is highly unlikely that both spouses can ever work and live in a single community — she is a TV anchorperson on a local station and he, a city manager. Potential conflict of interest (they both agreed) precluded living together. Nevertheless, each spoke of the arrangement as "temporary" and looked forward to the time it would end.

As we have seen, most of these spouses were strongly attached to each other and did not want to become commuters. They would have preferred to pursue their careers while living together. As many commented:

We did, after all, get married to live together.

They said:

There is something schizo about this whole thing. But as I look at it as something temporary, it doesn't bother me as much.

I think the only way I can handle this is that I know it is temporary, that we won't be doing it for the rest of our lives.

It doesn't bother me so much because I know, come hell or high water, it is going to be over in the not-too-distant future. You can do amazing things with your psyche as long as you know there is an end.

Their commitment to one another, remaining high during separation, leads them to perceive their situation as a transitory stage; the very anticipation of change alleviates the stress.

Defining themselves as "temporary deviants" not only relieves their own anxieties about "how long they could stand this," but also helps them fend off negative imputations about their marriages. Especially mothers who left children with their fathers, but many others as well, knew that living apart set them off from other families and invited speculations about inadequacy as a parent or impending divorce. Assuring parents, friends, and colleagues that they would not be living this way "for long" helped avoid censure. The ability to justify the arrangement as necessary, but temporary, makes it easier for commuters to accommodate the ways they are "doing marriage" to their implicit idea of what a marriage "should be."

CONCLUSION

Over the years spanning our involvement in this research, each of us has been asked by scores of anxious spouses contemplating a commuter marriage, "Does it work?" As this chapter makes clear, there is no simple answer. It is not lack of will or methodological caution keeping observers of marital separation from spouting simple judgments about its effects. Rather, knowledge of its complexities clearly reveals commuting to be a difficult arrangement. However, it is manageable, and under certain circumstances, even rewarding. Further, most who try to live this way view the costs and benefits as "worth it," even though the costs can be considerable and although it usually is more "effort" than "pleasure."

In this chapter we suggested that the basic limiting condition of a commuter arrangement is the amount of time spouses must spend apart and can spend together. Most couples who see each other every weekend, or even every other weekend, do not perceive the situation in totally negative terms or see it as overwhelmingly painful. In fact, in some ways, the brief time away enhances the value of the time together, making their weekend reunion a time "to look forward to." But for most of the couples who reunite only once a month or less (because of the long distances between them or work schedules), the separation is extraordinarily stressful. In these cases, living apart seems to corrode the relationship, while the strains of separation limit the satisfactions couples can draw from their time together. The marriage approximates a nonmarriage.

Certain conditions of the job, in conjunction with conditions of the commute, may also prevent couples from functioning as a close emotional unit. When either characteristics of the job or of the commuting arrangement force couples to expend a great deal of money and energy on reuniting, or, more importantly, require that they be apart for more than a month at a stretch, the costs of separation clearly come to outweigh the rewards. Though spouses may benefit from *some* break in their face-to-face interactions, that separation cannot go on too long.

Almost as important a determinant of the costliness of the arrangement is the couple's particular family constellation: the stage of the family and their respective career stages. Here the number of years they previously shared a residence and the presence of children are key factors. Those couples who have been married 10 or more years are most clearly in a position to enjoy the benefits of separation. More generally, the longer the marital history is, the easier the commuting. Though they, too, typically miss the daily interactions, "established" and even "balancing" couples have developed a strong, stable bond of trust, or they have come to take one another so much for granted that they are well served by loosening, for short periods, the dyadic tie. Then, too, the fact that they are older means at least one is likely to be advanced in his or her career, and not as anxious about "achieving" as a younger person might be. This difficulty is greater for couples married only a short time, when both may be just beginning to achieve professional recognition. Those married only a few years must develop a "habit system" and focus on their marital relationship. So, too, the presence of children acts as a limit on a couple's ability to provide each other with the necessary emotional support during their short periods together. When children must be included, the marital relationship, itself, cannot be the central focus. Parents, especially of young children, often feel overloaded and face losses in their spousal relationship, while at the same time experiencing greater guilts over pursuing their own individual career goals.

The balance struck then by juxtaposing a given commuting schedule, set of work-related conditions, and family constellation, determines whether a particular couple perceives the arrangement as basically "liveable" or not. But additional mechanisms, which could be though are not necessarily used by all commuting couples, can help ease the strains of living apart. Couples may compartmentalize their time, focusing on their work (or individual) needs when apart and on the relationship when together. Taking pride in being able to manage a difficult situation, because it shows how much each one spouse respects the other's right to a serious career, is reward in itself. Also, the couples may define their situation as temporary, so that they, as well as onlookers, can minimize the arrangement's "deviance."

This analysis provides the configuration of characteristics which yield a fairly sanguine prognosis: The couple is older; have no young children left at home; get to see each other every weekend or so; work in flexible settings at good-paying jobs; are able to set aside work and devote themselves to each other when they reunite; assure themselves that they will not always be living this way; take pride in being able to commute to advance each other's careers; reaffirm the importance of "being married" in spite of the way they find themselves "doing marriage." If these characteristics are incorporated into the commuter arrangement, the couples will endure it with less discomfort and some satisfaction. They will probably feel that it is "worth it" to separate residences to serve both family and career goals simultaneously.

CHAPTER 8

Living Apart:
A Comparison of
Merchant Marine and
Commuter Couples

Married couples live apart in a variety of circumstances: Business and military personnel, immigrants, and Merchant Marines — as well as the types of commuters we have concentrated on — all spend substantial periods of time away from their family homes. (See Chapter 1 for discussion of the variety of circumstances that require couples to live apart.) Many discussions of commuter marriage (e.g., Kirschner & Walum, 1978; Orthner, Sullivan, & Crossman, 1980) have noted these examples. But, in doing so, these researchers assume that the very existence of precedents, testifies to the viability of such a way of life. Therefore, commuter marriage must be viable too. However, these writers did not ask, but presumed to know, just how viable other types of separation actually are.

In alluding to other examples of married couples living apart, these writers make another suspect assumption: Geographic separation affects all marriages in the same ways. Yet, commuter couples — by definition dual-career couples — might well respond differently to living apart than do couples who separate because of the husband's career alone. These differences could obscure the effects of separation per se. Both how much separation itself *and* how much other factors determine responses to living apart need to be studied.

To this end, we interviewed Merchant Marines and their wives. These families live apart because of the husband's career alone. In these families, who refer to themselves as "sailing families," the husbands sail as licensed personnel on commercial fleets on the Great Lakes.

(See Appendix for a fuller description of the Merchant Marine sample.) Until recently, these sailing families regularly separated for months at a time during the nine-month sailing season, reuniting only for sporadic, brief vacations — as little as six to eight hours at a time when the ships were in port near their family homes. Today, a union-negotiated family leave policy allows for regular reunions during the nine-month season with set periods of work (e.g., 60 days) followed by vacation periods (e.g., 20 or 30 days). However, though it is now possible to return to the home for several weeks at a time during the sailing season, many men do not take their scheduled vacation. (See Appendix for further discussion of schedules.) In any case, these sailing families reside continuously in one home only for the three months when seas are not navigable (from January to the end of March). As a group, then, the separations these families endure are longer and they have lived this way for longer periods than most commuters.

Most Merchant Marine couples have lived apart since they first married, an average of 15 years. Moreover, the social backgrounds of Merchant Marine husbands and wives are quite different from those of the professional commuters. Both the sailing husbands and their wives come from working-class families, and the large majority have only a high school degree or less. However, while the wives do not tend to be employed, a major attraction of sailing for both spouses is the high income the husbands earn. Over half of them make at least $50,000 a year — more than the combined family income for most of the professionals who commute.

But perhaps the most important difference between Merchant Marine and commuter couples is their different models of marriage. Recall that for most commuting husbands and wives, having an egalitarian marriage was one of the major factors they believe responsible for their decision to live apart. A belief in equality justifies the decision to set up two homes and bolsters the arrangement once it begins. In contrast, sailing spouses expect the husband's needs to take priority in their marriages. Both sailing husbands and wives tell how the husband had tried other jobs, but had come back to sailing because of its satisfactions. Often the wives said, "he just loves his work" or the husbands said, "I really love sailing" to explain why they live this way. This consideration, in addition to the recognition that the family's support directly depended upon the husband's job, assured it priority. Because the husband's job is primary, the wives are expected, and indeed expect themselves, to adjust to the husband's prerogatives. As we shall see, these different models of marriage — the traditional and

egalitarian — as well as the different patterns of separation have consequences for the experience of living apart.[1]

By comparing these Merchant Marine families with commuter
families, we can judge the independent effects of geographic separation and the effects of the interaction of separation and other characteristics (like career status and models of marriage) on married life.
This chapter discusses the results of that comparison. While in previous
chapters we examined the general consequences of commuting on dual-
career couples, here we examine the particular effects of geographic
separation on different types of couples. We look first at consequences
attributable to living apart per se — those common to both commuters
and Merchant Marine families. Second, we discuss consequences
found only among Merchant Marines and analyze what factors produce these dissimilar outcomes.

COMMON CONSEQUENCES OF LIVING APART: SHARED EXPERIENCES OF COMMUTERS AND MERCHANT MARINES

A Common Cost of Separation: Emotional Distance

As we have shown in previous chapters, living apart jeopardizes psychological intimacy. Commuter couples are aware of the psychological
distance in their relationship and explain that they sometimes feel
"weird," "strange," or "awkward" when they reunite. Our analysis suggests that such feelings indicate a threat to the order-constructing
quality of marriage. Marital interaction, the day-to-day sharing of the
minutiae of life, we argue, validates and nurtures the roles and selves
of spouses. This function of marriage results, in part, from the fact
that living together allows couples to share space and organize their
daily time commitments around each other's schedules. Shared time
and space help produce the order-sustaining quality of marriage, the

---

1. We use the terms "traditional" and "egalitarian" to reflect the same distinction
Harding (1981) makes when she uses the term "hierarchical" and "egalitarian." (Merchant Marines are "hierarchical" or "traditional"; commuters are more "egalitarian.")
Her discussion provides a useful explication of the different values and stategies these
two types of family structures imply. As she suggests and we shall see, these two world
views imply differences in dividing labor and distributing power between husbands
and wives inside of the home, as well as for assigning priority to spouses' commitments
outside the home.

subjective expression of which is the feeling that the relationship is "normal," "comfortable," and "unself-conscious."

Sailing husbands and wives recognize the same emotional nuances in their reactions as do commuters—a recognition that signals jeopardy to the order-constructing quality of marriage. They, too, used words like "strange" to describe the distance they feel from their mates when they first reunite:

I can't put my finger on what the feeling is, but it's kind of strange. You know, like you kind of hold back. You know him so well, but yet you don't think that's maybe the same person. I just can't explain all that. It's a strange feeling.

Her spouse is a stranger—a social and psychological anomaly—and so she says, "you know him but you don't." As a stranger, someone new and different, the spouse cannot provide a sense of ongoing order in their lives:

It feels like he's a stranger, like I don't know him, as if something might have changed him a bit and I just don't know what happened or anything.

A husband put the same feeling quite simply:

It's like meeting a new woman each time.

This awareness of psychological distance between spouses is caught graphically by the wife who said:

It's like yelling across a cavern at first. You say: "Hi, sweetie, should we go to the movies tonight?" "Oh sure," he yells back.

She goes on to suggest that the psychological distance is not un-bridgeable, but takes time to overcome:

You feel just like you get back together one step at a time. It's like you're walking down the street and you're on one side and he's on the other and you kind'a come together at the corner.

Or as another put this process of reorientation:

When you're not used to having another person around, it's sort of a strange feel-ing for the first couple of days. It goes away.

It is marriage that they expect, even want, to take for granted. In-stead, they find that they feel strange and unnatural. Consequently, these separated spouses feel disoriented: For a time, they see their spouses as strangers and find that feeling itself strange. Though temporary, this response is nonetheless unnerving.

Reunions require shared time and shared schedules that bring a new and different order to daily lives. In explaining why it is difficult to adjust, one wife commented on the newly shared schedules:

Well, like he has a different schedule that I do at home. I don't eat three meals a day when he's gone and it's very different . . . it's like you have to start all over again. I have to keep reminding myself that we are a couple and it's not just me.

Reunions bring shared space that is now noticed, not presumed. In talking about the necessary adjustments she feels she has to make, a wife recalled a conversation with her husband:

I said: "I feel like when the phone rings, you're there listening to me." And he has a perfect right to. It's his house, too.

Many spouses spoke of sleep disturbances, resulting from the need to readjust to a shared bed, the most intimate of areas symbolizing space which is theirs together and only theirs: "I'm not used to sleeping with someone" was a common response of both husbands and wives.

Like the commuters, then, the separation of Merchant Marine families means that husbands and wives do not arrange their daily regimens (like morning departures, meals, and evening activities) around each other's schedules while they are apart nor do they occupy a common space where each comes to experience the others' presence as "natural." These sailing couples, just like commuters, register reactions signaling a felt threat to the naturalness of their relationship. In this way, living apart jeopardizes the psychological intimacy expected of marriage.

A Common Benefit of Separation: Heightened Communication

For a distinct subset of sailing spouses (about a third of the wives and a little less than a quarter of husbands) there is another side to the emotional distance introduced into the marital relationship. Like some commuters, these sailing spouses believe that living apart prevents the boredom or dullness that they see as characteristic of coresident marriages. Like commuters, they speak of a sense of freshness and spontaneity, of heightened communication, rediscovery and interest in each other when they reunite. One of these men remarked:

I think that you probably appreciate each other more than others. It's not like the same face day after day.

Many use the term "honeymoon" to characterize this aspect of their relationship. The frequent use of this term during the interviews (as well as in informal conversations with groups of sailing couples) suggests that it has become a conventional response. When they want to tell each other, or an interested party, about a benefit their marriages have that others lack, it is this honeymoon quality they mention. As one husband put it:

It's always like a honeymoon. It's always new — your relationship with each other.

And as a wife said:

Every time they come home, it's like a honeymoon — really. I mean it's a grand time. If anybody is having trouble with their husbands, send them away. When they come back, they're so glad to see her. I always say its just like a honeymoon when they come back.

Indeed, just like some commuters, some sailing spouses even seem to suggest that separation was the cause of marital satisfaction and by implication, its absence, the cause of marital dissatisfaction:

I think it helps marriages, because a lot of them whose husbands were home, aren't married, they're divorced. This way, when they come home, it's a honeymoon and I think it's better for marriages.

As was true of commuters, living apart provides another side to lost naturalness — the ability to ward off routinization:

Really, it's kind of neat, this deal of come in the door and, "Oh, gee, honey, I'm so glad to see you." He doesn't come in and sit down and pick up a paper and put his feet up and ignore me.

For all these couples who live apart, a cost perceived from one perspective becomes a benefit perceived from another. Or, to state it differently, we see in both commuter couples and Merchant Marine couples a dilemma of marriage: Living together produces intimacy but also a taken-for-granted, sometime dull, routine. But living apart renews stimulation and lessens routinization at the cost of daily, desired intimacy.

Autonomy and Independence

The complex of advantages and disadvantages Merchant Marine wives balance becomes especially clear in their frequent references to loneliness, on the one hand, and independence on the other. While living apart causes considerable loneliness, it also increases competence, especially in those gender-typed activities which would be assumed by the husband in a shared home:

I'm pretty handy. You learn to be. You know if you're by yourself, you learn to try. You just try it. I can use lots of tools now. I had to become more independent.

Sailing husbands, however, were not as likely as commuting husbands to mention increased competency in these types of activities, probably because aboard ship domestic functions are still largely performed for them. At sea, they are not required to make their own meals, clean their living quarters, or be responsible for much more than their own laundry and mending, which all of them do. Opportunities then, for cross-typed activities were not as great for sailing husbands as for their wives or commuter spouses.

For wives, recognition of increased self-reliance is not limited to performing particular chores. Both sailing and commuter wives also recognize a more generalized sense of independence—sometimes even suggesting that they had become "too" independent. The negative side of independence—the sense that it has gone too far—is stated much more strongly by the sailing wives than by the commuter wives. In articulating the negative side of independence, sailing wives either mean that they resent how much responsibility they have to bear alone or that their independence creates problems when their husbands return. Perhaps sailing wives feel this more strongly than commuters because they are required to assume primary responsibility for household management and child care for a longer period of time than commuter wives. Perhaps, too, sailing wives—with less education and coming from working-class backgrounds—anticipated more traditional marriages and, therefore, may have expected to be dependent wives. With some regret, many recall earlier times when they were not independent, claiming that their new found independence is a result of necessity rather than desire:

I think it's probably made me far more independent than I wanted to be. I would've loved to be a clinging vine and be taken care of. But, it's forced me into being a stronger person I suppose.

Thus, while both commuter wives and sailing wives become more independent they evaluate this common outcome differently.

Another outcome shared by wives who live apart from their husbands is also not experienced in the same way. Living apart not only brings transformations in their marital relationships, but also changes their place in the community; commuter wives and sailing wives respond to this in somewhat different ways.

Social Isolation and "Being Different"

In both groups, wives report feeling like a "fifth wheel" at social gatherings.[2] The sailing wives (and husbands talking about their wives) feel others do not include them in events as often as they might if husbands were home. Or wives admit that they exclude themselves, expecting that they will feel uncomfortable at gatherings consisting of couples.

Ambiguity characterizes the social status not only of commuters but also sailing wives:

You're a single and you aren't a single. You belong and you don't belong.

The people we know accept the fact that Joe is gone. And occasionally we will make plans as a group to do something and they'll say, "Come on anyway, Rose." Well, I hesitate because I usually feel like a "fifth wheel." But they don't make me feel that way. I'm uncomfortable, but, what I mean is, I don't do it. In fact, I think I'm more apt to exclude myself in a big hurry, saying: "No, I'd rather not do it because Joe isn't here."

As these comments suggest, living away from one's spouse produces loneliness at the same time as it increases competency and autonomy — advantages prized to some extent by both sets of women. But the cost

2. See McCubbin *et al.* (1976) for similar findings about military wives.

of personal autonomy is social isolation that results from fewer opportunities to attend events and celebrate occasions in a "couples"
world.

Moreover, it is not only the coupledness of social events that
threatens these spouses' integration into the community. In addition,
both commuters and sailing families realize that others think of them
as "different," and both must defend themselves against the label of deviance. However, this problem is more serious for sailing families than
commuters, despite the fact that commuter marriages, with career-
oriented wives, appear to depart more from norms about conventional
marriage.

Commuter couples are not misunderstood when they account for
their living apart. Their explanations sometimes occasion a response
that the listener would not "put up with" or "get away with" such an
arrangement. But, for the most part, commuters deflect such negative
responses without much effort, because, in general, they are not particularly concerned with others' reactions to their lifestyle.

In contrast, sailing spouses frequently mention a lack of com-
prehension when they try to explain their way of life. For sailing
families, the reason for separation — the husband's work — is not what
raises eyebrows. Rather it is the *length* of separation that elicits skepticism. Not spending as much time together as conventional ideas
about "being married" imply makes others see them as, and sailing
couples themselves feel, different:

*You try to explain the time they spend on the boat and the time they spend off
and they just kind of stare at you, like, "Oh, really?"*

What they have to contend with in this respect vividly comes through
in the following account given by a wife who tells of the problems she
had when appearing as a witness in a friend's divorce proceedings.
The friend had also been married to a seaman and she described how
difficult it was to describe their husbands' schedules to the court.

*Well, that was a trick and a half to try and explain to them what this Marine
business is actually like. It was just unbelievable. You had to start from the very
beginning and tell 'em how these boats run seven days a week. There is no time
off, there's no night, no day; their time just rolls all together. There's no time
off for a holiday because somebody is getting married. It goes on and on and on.
It was unreal trying to explain this lifestyle. They could not comprehend the fact
that these men are gone, period. If Christmas comes and goes and you're out on
the lake, that's just too bad. It was terribly hard trying to explain that to them.
It's almost like you can't believe it unless you do it.*

The fact that more than half of the commuters live apart during the week, but reunite on weekends, is pertinent here. At least for many of these commuters, the rhythm of their lives — at work during the week, at home on weekends — is not completely different from the typical pattern of most couples, especially those that are also dual-career (Rapoport & Rapoport, 1976). Even for those commuters apart longer, very few stay apart for more than a month; if they do they reunite for at least a weekend and sometimes longer. Also, as we saw, commuters have something else to mitigate the effect of imputations of deviance. They could comfort and protect themselves from the inquiries of others by knowing that their "deviance" was temporary. Because they believe they would eventually return to living together, commuters can define themselves as "temporary deviants" in a way sailing couples who realize that separations are an enduring fact of life cannot.

Many sailing spouses said they had "given up" trying to explain their pattern of separation and reunion, because the topic caused so much incredulity. They prefer not to have to contend with the deviance implied by their way of life and try to avoid defending the logistics of their time together — which many agree makes them "strange":

It is a strange, strange life.

We are different, you know.

A small group of sailing spouses handled "being different" by denying the legitimacy of the charge and recasting their time with each other in a more favorable light. Like commuters in this respect, they speak of "quality time," meaning that the time they have together is better used and more appreciated. Since husbands are home "all day" during reunions, they argue that "on balance" they have "as much time" or even "more time" with their families. Here they note the many vacations they could take as a family; the father's ability to spend "all his time" on winter sports activities with the children. So, too, they specify not only how they are exceptional, but what they share with other marriages; they often refer to other occupations, like doctors and truck drivers, that keep men away from their families even "more."

So while commuters have to contend with reactions to their lifestyle because their separation is a nontraditional one — deference to the wife's career — sailing families have to account for a very unusual pattern of separation and reunion. Sailing families deflect these responses less successfully, because most sailing spouses measure their own marriages with their detractors' yardstick — agreeing they are indeed "different" from the traditional families they, themselves, value.

In addition, sailing families have more trouble defending themselves against imputations of deviance because other elements of social disapproval are tied up with the public image of sailors. Most husbands and wives acknowledge that the general image of sailing still retains elements of a way of life long since supplanted by better working conditions and a different population (at least among commercial ships on the Great Lakes). They lament that the general population knows so little about commercial sailing as an occupation and, therefore, tends to have outmoded notions about sailors. The old-fashioned stereotype of the sailor as rowdy, unstable, and generally unsavory no longer applies, they say. Here they note with pride the long hours of study undertaken for examinations sailors must pass to advance in their job, and the modern, clean, automated, and complex machinery with which they work. They note their stable family lives and relatively high incomes as evidence that the stereotype is inappropriate to their circumstances as licensed personnel and officers in the Merchant Marines.

In part, this additional negative stereotype, the longer separations they endure, and their own acknowledgment that indeed their family life is "different" makes sailing families speak of the issue of deviance with more emotion than commuters. Although all recognize the advantages of their generally high incomes, sailing families are clearly more defensive than commuters about their way of life.

SAILING FAMILIES: CONSEQUENCES OF LIVING APART NOT FOUND AMONG COMMUTERS

We have seen that living apart brings a series of consequences common to both commuters and Merchant Marines — changes in the marital relationship, changes in the sense of self, changes in their relationships with others. But we have also seen that some of these common consequences are experienced differently: Sailing wives are more likely to be troubled by their independence and more likely to feel, and to defend themselves against, a sense of deviance than commuters. Moreover, these Merchant Marine families face other consequences not at all characteristic of commuters. Here, we find that geographic separation does not affect all families in the same way.

The one phrase, more than any other, distinguishing the accounts of sailing husbands and wives from commuters is the formers' emphasis on "necessary adjustments." The Merchant Marines' greater discussion of necessary adjustments can be, in part, accounted for by the differences in their patterns of separation (which as we saw above also affected the responses of outsiders). The periods of time sailing spouses live apart — as well as their reunions — typically are far longer and far less predictable than those of commuters. Equally important, differences in their models of marriage — what they think a marriage "should be" — help explain why these two types of families do not experience their separation in the same way. These different ideologies for marriage, in concert with different patterns of separation and reunion, color the experience of living apart, producing more "necessary adjustments" for the sailing couples than for the commuter couples.

Patterns of Separation and Reunion

A whole set of problems unique to sailing spouses results from the unpredictable schedules they contend with during the sailing season and the predictable, long winter reunions they face when it ends. During the sailing season, the boats these men sail on may return to port in the home areas as frequently as every six or seven days. Particularly husbands, but most wives as well, expect that the women will either meet their husbands at the dock or be home if their husbands can get there. Their time together may be just a few hours (rarely as long as twelve, typically five or six) and the husband may arrive in the middle of the night or midafternoon. As a consequence, both spouses believe that wives cannot have commitments that might reduce their availability to their husbands.

Largely because of this demand to stay available at unspecifiable intervals, husbands and wives agree that the women cannot hold jobs, at least not demanding jobs that would prevent them from being with their husbands. Understandably then, the few (one-fifth) who do hold jobs, work part time. (Only two out of twelve employed wives work full time.) The jobs they hold typically require low skill and offer low pay. Their positions are governed by "arrangements" and "understandings" with their employers that allow them to be with their husbands when they do come in. The majority, however, are not employed and several recount giving up a job because "it didn't work out."

More generally, the indeterminacy of the husbands' schedules during the year means that wives make plans and arrangements with the understanding that the ship's arrival may cancel them. A few wives said they went on with their plans, but most suggest it is "only right" that they be available for the few hours their husbands are home. Their development of dependent lives in a context that simultaneously requires independence is part of a process with which they must struggle. Yet, most sailing wives do finally adjust:

I guess maybe you'd call it habit, being alone and never knowing when he's coming home, cause you don't know and we just have to cope with it. You'd be straight up a wall if you didn't. I'm sure that if you let it bother you, well, the first years that we were married, I'd think, My God, this is a crazy schedule. Then all of a sudden, I realized there wasn't any schedule.

Most accept the loneliness and limitations; they accept that the rhythms of their lives are predicated on their husband's work. But they do so recognizing that such acceptance developed gradually and not without discomfort. The terms they use — "coping," "adjusting," "getting used to" — all suggest a process, a gradual understanding which developed over time.

Thus, unlike the commuters, the sailing couples must adjust to haphazard patterns of reunion and separation. The very regularity of most of the commuters' separations and reunions helps diminish the stress. But still another aspect of the pattern of separation — perhaps a more serious problem — distinguishes the sailing couples from commuters.

When the husbands come home on a full-time basis at the end of the sailing season, prolonged absences become prolonged reunions. Though a few families use this time to travel and a few husbands take other jobs, for most the winter brings an extended period during which family members must readjust to each other at home. The readjustment is complicated by the fact that the couple is now together 24 hours a day. The very presence of the husband, especially since he now has no structured activities while his wife's activities continue (and even increase), creates tension:

He's either gone completely, never here, or he's here constantly. Well, you know, in the beginning he'd say, "Well, I'm coming home. I'll be home for the winter. I'm going to relax, that's it." Well, after a week we were driving each other crazy.

You can't go from working constantly, day in and day out without a work day off and then come home and sit down and do absolutely nothing. It's just not a good thing, just like retiring and doing absolutely nothing. Because too much time together is just as bad as not enough.

This "feast or famine" is the crux of the matter. Many used exactly this phrase or others such as "all or nothing" or "all of a sudden." As one wife described why the winter's reunion is not unconditionally pleasant:

He's on vacation and I'm not.

But wives' feelings about the husbands' presence are complicated: While they have a sense of frustration upon his re-entry into their lives, they also know how much they want him to come home. Thus, they experience contradictory, only partially understood, impulses. Wives seem perplexed and embarassed by the admission that, in some ways, it is easier when he is away, that they sometimes look forward to his return to duty. The following account of a conversation a wife recalls having had with her husband illustrates these complex ambivalent feelings:

"Your vacation in the last couple of years has been literally a hell," I said. "I almost wanted to laugh on the way back from the airport. And I feel so guilty the minute you're on the plane. I feel so bad. It's like I'm afraid I'm going to say the wrong thing, do the wrong thing." It's like being on ice all the time.

As her comment implies, the ambivalence also restricts criticism of their marriage.

"Too Much" and "Too Little" to Do

While commuter wives have professional careers, the sailing women are principally wives and mothers. They fill their days doing tasks related to these two roles. For commuter wives, demanding job-related obligations set and fill their daily schedules. In contrast to sailing wives who tell of a need "to *keep* busy," commuter wives "*are* busy" — a revealing difference in the way they talk about their lives. Over and over again, sailing wives report strategies to combat boredom they developed over the years. Either they explain the mechanisms they use to avoid boredom or they complain about its effects. "I've learned to keep busy," echoes persistently throughout these interviews:

Keeping busy that's the name of the game. I think I spend most of my time working to use up time.

In the same breath, sailing wives speak of being overburdened, "over busy" with the responsibilities and obligations of running a household and raising children, for all practical purposes, singlehand-edly. Given their situations, these are not inconsistent responses. They are, in fact, both "under" and "over" involved:

I think the hardest thing is to be totally responsible for everything and making sure things get taken care of, you know, all the things.

Especially when the children are young, but even when they are older, these women's lives focus on their activities. In part, the children's com-ings and goings are a welcome filler to what would otherwise be a void. However, managing the children's schedules is also a tiring respon-sibility, producing "too much" and "too little" to do at the same time.

Commuter parents who live with their children (recall that only 50% had children living at home, whereas 86% of sailing families had children) also acknowledge feeling like single parents. (See Appendix, Table A5, for numbers of commuters and Merchant Marine spouses with children.) But again, because of the longer period of separation, nearly all sailing wives said they had, at times, felt like "single parents." While much has to do with increased child-care responsibilities in the absence of husbands, sailing wives also have the psychological burden of making decisions alone:

Just somebody to say you've made the right decision even if he says: "Sure honey." It's just so nice to know. Or if the kids are out in the car, there's somebody besides you who's sharing your concern.

Their isolation from coupled activities compounds the uneven, "too much/too little" activity levels of sailing wives. Not feeling free to involve themselves fully in the activities of friends and neighbors, and since they do not have work colleagues, their loneliness accentu-ates their boredom and vice versa. Many of these women work hard at "keeping busy" and appear reasonably successful in doing so, but their necessity to *keep* busy distinguishes them from commuter wives who *are* busy.

Renegotiating Spousal and Parental Control

We saw that, like commuter wives, sailing wives feel more independ-ent as a result of living apart from their husbands. But for sailing wives, much more so than for commuter wives, this increased independence is the trait that often makes "adjustments" necessary when their hus-bands return. The very quality which both recognize as the sine qua non for a wife's successful adaptation to living without her husband can make it more difficult for her to live with him:

I'm very independent. And, of course, he is, too. So there's conflict over who is going to be the boss — that type of thing.

A few of the sailing husbands recognize the difficulty caused by their sudden entry into the home:

I come home and try to function like I always have. I would imagine it was harder for my wife to adjust to me being there. She's used to running things her way, while I'm gone for eight months of the year. Then, all of a sudden, I'm there again, you know. She has to make an adjustment to me. Just to have a man around the house again — all of a sudden.

While some husbands do recognize the problem of sudden, yet prolonged, presences and absences, most husbands suggest the major problem for them revolves around their attempts to resume control in the household. Though the husband quoted understands his wife's difficulty in contending with another person, he also implies the problem is not just his being there. He focuses on the difficulties resulting from his attempts to control the routines of the household:

Oh, yeah, there'd be difficult times. I'd tell her to do something and she'd say: "Well, who made the decisions while you were away?" She'd come out and tell me it was an adjustment for her to make and I realize it.

The adjustments — her accommodation to his desire to resume a controlling role in family affairs and his inability to accept easily her desire to retain partial control — call for considerable marital negotiation, which both husbands and wives acknowledge. The husbands usually focus on their resumption of control vis-à-vis the children:

It's a hard life for my wife and I know for other boat people, I am, I'm God on the boat. All I have to do is mention something and it's done and that's the way it's supposed to be on the boat. That's the way it has to be. I come home and I'm only a deckhand. I see my kids doing something and I tell them to do something else. Do it my way or a different way; or whatever, and it's a big problem because the wife has been home with them all the time. She knows what they're doing and it doesn't please me. So I tell them something else. My way to do it. And I expect them to do it. And they're used to being a little bit loose with their mother. And if she tells them to do it, well, they might do it when they get around to it. Well, that's not the way they operate on the boat. If I say do it, you do it and right now.

Wives believe that the problems revolve around the father's functions away from home, too, but also recognize their own problems in having to consider another adult's wishes in decisions they previously made alone:

I was handling it and then all of a sudden he comes in with his opinions and you kind of resent that a little bit.

The group of wives who voiced the greatest concern about this problem were wives of captains. Apparently, the fact that captains have so much authority and status on the ship and exercise so much control there, spills over into their domestic lives. The effect of captain status shows up in our analysis of overall satisfaction levels. When we sorted wives into groups that are ranked as high (21%), moderate (62%), and low (17%) in satisfaction with the lifestyle, we found that all of the captains' wives were in the lowest group. These women, as a group, give the most poignant accounts of the lifestyle's restrictions; these wives use the most vivid imagery to describe their situations. They say they feel as if they are "in a prison with bars," "a cage," "a coffin," or as below, "in a jar with the lid screwed on":

I think they want you to change and let them do all the thinking and taking care of everything. But, it's like I said one time: "You can't be smart nine months and stupid three." I said, "You can't become a robot at the end of nine months and let somebody put you in a jar and screw the lid down and then emerge when they leave and start taking over everything again."

Yet, we cannot conclude even for these captains' wives that their marriages suffer irreparably from the continous need to realign the spousal power structure in the home. As a group, these women do not describe lives of desperation, but rather voice strains to which they must adjust. The realities of their lives fit with their conceptions of what marriage and family life requires, providing a consistency which blunts the criticism they might otherwise register.

MODELS OF MARRIAGE

Consistency between ideas of what "being married" should mean and the ways couples actually arrange their lives affects the responses to separation of both commuters and sailing couples. That is, a couple's model of marriage — their ideas of what marriage "should be" — influences how they come to terms with what their marriage actually "is." As we have seen, commuter couples ascribe to an egalitarian model though they nonetheless find themselves heir to traditional models. In contrast, sailing spouses — both husbands and wives — ascribe to a traditional model of marriage though they find themselves living in untraditional ways. Let us first examine the influence of traditional views of marriage on sailing couples.

Though sailing wives may chafe at their husbands authority, in principle they accept the idea of the husband's right to control. More generally, these sailing couples accept a view of marriage which frowns on wives' complaining about the "breadwinner's" efforts. Just as Rubin (1976) found in her study of working-class couples, these Merchant Marine wives value the roles prescribed in traditional marriage, accept the husband's claims to authority as legitimate, and consequently devalue whatever ambivalence they may feel. In their view, a husband's work obligations "ought to" take precedence, especially since they are acutely aware of the financial benefits. ("Money" was the most frequent response given to a question about the "best aspect" of this lifestyle, and many told of relatives and neighbors who earned considerably less.) While a few do complain about the effects of the husband's work, most cannot call too much attention to its negative aspects without compensatory statements about its benefits:

It's his work you know. He's not out there fooling around.

A keen sense of the monetary advantages they enjoy, in concert with their traditional views about marriage, mute the expression of doubt.

Their traditional models of marriage, then, different from those of commuters, detract from and bolster the sailing wives' adjustment to living apart. The sailing wife's life is very circumscribed by her husband's work: Her schedule revolves around his short visits or intermittent and unspecified exits during part of the year; for the rest of the year, she must accommodate his constant presence. Yet precisely because the husband/breadwinner is expected to shape and dominate family life, these sailing wives are reticent to express too much dissatisfaction. Instead, they adjust:

This whole life is a bunch of adjustments. Adjustments to his being gone. Adjustments to his being home.

In contrast to such traditional views, we saw earlier that commuter spouses' egalitarian views about each one's right to pursue professional careers are part of what enables them to decide to live apart in the first place. Further, we saw that the vast majority of these dual-career couples believe the adjustments they must make are worth the effort because living apart allows them to behave in ways consistent with their developing ideas of what marriage should be. These views imply a marriage in which both partners' rights and needs determine the choices both make. This perspective comes through clearly from a husband who describes how "tough" it was to have his wife live away from him and his two young children. He wanted the interviewer to understand, though, that the alternative — not supporting his wife's commitment — would be unacceptable:

I think the best thing is that Sarah is in a better place and as my partner, it makes for a better relationship. There is just a lot of coming into her own and experiencing success — and that is good for both of us — what we both want.

Such a stance not only would be highly unlikely for Merchant Marine husbands but also for most of their wives, the majority of whom believed that wives should not work. Their model of marriage requires that the wife be home and available to her husband when he gets there. (That the mothers were like single parents was also used to justify why the wife should be at home, but even those without children accept that the wife be home-centered.) Because the sailing wives felt that their primary responsibilities were to their husbands and children, they more easily resigned themselves to some of the difficult consequences resulting from living apart. Whether spouses view marriage as basically "traditional" or "egalitarian" affects how they come to terms with their lot.

Yet, important qualifications must be made about this sorting of families into traditional and egalitarian categories. For both types of families, certain aspects of the other world-view enter into their response to living apart. In some ways, traditional views affect commuters' responses, while some of the Merchant Marine wives clearly struggle with views of their own needs at odds with what they feel a wife or a family "should be."

We saw in the case of commuters that, though these partners endorse views that imply quite liberal ideologies, such views did not free them from troublesome resentments and guilts. These spouses, though more egalitarian than Merchant Marine families, retain vestiges of traditional structures in their idea of what marriage "should be."

Though both spouses appear to reject traditional marital roles, with the wife's role subordinated to the needs and demands of the husband's, the commuters do use traditional role relationships as a point of reference against which they judge themselves. Although both spouses recognize positive and negative features of living apart, each understands that some of the advantages specific to one are disadvantages to the other (e.g., she "gets" to pursue her career while he "has to" make do without the support he expected from a "wife"). This dilemma manifests itself in resentment over the felt disadvantage, but also in guilt for the resentment, clouding the enjoyment of the advantages. This complex mixture of feelings stems, in part, from the way in which husbands and wives each view their own roles. They do so by taking traditional marriages as the vantage point from which to assess their own nontraditional marriage.

For all their conscious rejection of them, traditional roles still provide the primary model of a marital relationship for commuters. They think of traditional relationships as a standard, and they battle with their variation from this standard; this is what they "know about marriage," even if they want to reject it. Knowing he used traditional marriage as a reference point came through forcefully in one husband's response to the question asking what advice he would give to a couple embarking on such a relationship. He said:

The first part would be, make sure you have the husband–wife relationship straight. Know what's going on, why you're separating. Secondly, also get clear why one is staying and the other needs to go, wants to go. I think beyond that there's an underlying assumption about marriage or interpersonal relations that the degree of freedom that one demands must also be freely given to the other. The traditional variety is where the husband has much more freedom than the wife has. I think that is becoming less and less tenable.

But the ongoing relevance of the traditional marriage has another, contrasting, consequence. The fact that traditional marriage is a backdrop for their innermost feelings makes these couples feel a sense of accomplishment at "pulling off" a nontraditional lifestyle — a positive aspect of commuting that they talk about enthusiastically:

We are patting ourselves on the back for being able to do this and pull it off successfully.

Thus, they feel the coincidental impact of different emotions: pride and guilt. But the very fact that they take pride in being the kind of people who "care about each other's careers" and who can cope successfully with the inconveniences and hurdles of this arrangement again means they use traditional marriages as a reference point. Without any other model with which to make sense of their own experience, commuters use traditional marriage. They recognize the lack of fit, but have little recourse because they do not have one better, in the sense of "more real." Simply, because this traditional relationship impedes and sustains their world-view, commuters simultaneously feel proud and guilty.

Parallel to traditional reference points in commuter marriages is the sailing wives', if not their husbands', awareness that living apart threatens the traditional model. Their ambivalent reactions to how separation affects their own needs for independence represent the basis of this threat. The awareness of a disjunction between their own needs and those of their family may stem from feminist arguments in the last decade. But, their own reality is just as important for these wives: Living alone requires that they become independent and autonomous to a noticeable degree. Here, we see how structure influences ideas. The structural transformation that occurs, once they live independently, undermines their traditional views, and produces emotional static. They "know" they cannot be as "dependent" as their values and their husbands require them to be.

However, we must not make too much of this discord. For the most part, sailing wives use their "idea of marriage" to rationalize and support their situation, and most are successful. Most adjust to the demands of living apart—including subordinating their own needs. Here values overwhelm structure, if not always completely.

In general, then, both these examples—commuter couples and Merchant Marines—attest to the independent importance of *ideas* about marriage which influence reactions to living apart. How partners view that separation, the "meaning" it has for them shapes the viability of separation. Spouses' views reflect the internalized sex-role prescriptions. Among commuters, lingering sex-role traditions color their expectations and tarnish the benefits of a more liberated partnership. Conversely, among Merchant Marine wives, the consciousness that they are "people too" undermines their complete acceptance of the legitimacy of wifely subordination. Yet they adjust because they think they should.

CONCLUSION

We introduced this chapter by suggesting that journalists and academics have, in their zeal to defend commuter marriage, located precedents among others who live apart. These writers assumed that the existence of these other cases, like Merchant Marines, testifies to the viability of a commuter arrangement. But, they presumed when they should have investigated if separation has the same meaning and the same consequences in each situation.

This chapter compared Merchant Marine families with commuters in order to specify the effects of living apart. This comparison suggests that these couples do share much. For both groups, living apart transforms the couple's emotional relationship, hinders their involvement in a couple-centered social life, enhances for individual spouses, especially wives, a sense of autonomy and independence. However, there are other changes that Merchant Marines and commuters do not have in common. These differences depend, largely, on the basic, definitional distinction between the two groups. Merchant Marines live apart because of *the husband's* work. Commuters live apart because *both spouses* have professional careers. The different career involvements of these couples imply very different ideas about marriage (egalitarian vs. traditional) as well as different resources (education, income, and interests). Moreover, differences in the duration and pattern of separation limit the possibility of analyzing the consequences of separation per se. Thus, we found that a full understanding of living apart requires, first, a refinement of what separation consists of and, second, a consideration of other salient factors, like career commitment and models of marriage.

More generally, our analysis suggests that "historical precedents," in which spouses spent time in two separate locales, should not be used as testimony to the viability of commuter marriage. Instead, these precedents entail, at best, a series of hardships and strains to which spouses must make "necessary adjustments." Indeed these precedents may be even more difficult, especially for women, than the modern form of geographic separation commuters undertake.

More specifically, we uncovered some common responses — changes in the couples' emotional relationship — characteristic of both commuters and Merchant Marines that clarify what coresident marriage provides and denies. Living together brings intimacies and with them the routinization of the relationship. This "taken-for-granted" quality of marriage derives in part from the sharing of time, schedules, and space. But in concert with this routinization comes a certain measure of boredom and dullness. In contrast, living apart threatens the "naturalness" of the relationship, and as a consequence, spouses are disconcerted. But, at the same time, by living apart spouses rediscover each other though at the cost of daily intimacies. Thus, both types of marital separation reveal an irreconcilable dilemma of marriage.

Beyond common changes, interpretation of the common consequences shared by both commuters and Merchant Marines must consider how their models of marriage color the consequences of separation. Thus, while wives in both groups become more independent as a result of living apart, this independence has a different meaning for each group of women and for their husbands. When sailing wives say they value their independence, they are really speaking more about personal autonomy — the freedom to arrange their daily schedules while apart — than the freedom to do whatever they want. Moreover, they are more circumspect about the benefits of such freedom. Many Merchant Marine wives, but very few commuters, use the phrase "too independent" to qualify how they felt about the changes in their lives. Because they accept and expect control over their lives to come from outside sources, the sailing wives are as wary of extending the habit of autonomy as they are pleased by it. They know their husbands will come home and expect to resume the responsibilities they assumed in their absence. Thus, sailing wives express a tentativeness about their independence that commuter wives rarely communicate. Because Merchant Marine husbands and wives accept a view of family life which at least prescriptively allows husband's dominance, departures from wifely subordination are troublesome.

In contrast, commuter wives are more able to enjoy their relative independence because they expect women and wives to be more independent, and they know their husbands share this expectation. Since commuter husbands and wives accept the legitimacy of more egalitarian norms about roles and relationships, these wives are more able to enjoy changes that represent departures from traditional expectations about marriage. To be sure, they too wrestle with the discrepancy between their egalitarian expectations and more traditional norms, because traditional marriage is a compelling standard from which they gauge their own marriages. But though both groups use traditional marriage as a reference point, they do so differently, insomuch as one group (Merchant Marine) accepts the legitimacy of this complex of norms, while the other (commuter) cannot yet entirely reject it.

So, too, with the remaining consequences — relative isolation and imputations of deviance — differences in the wives' positions (more subordinate among Merchant Marines, more egalitarian among commuters) result in different responses. Subordination for Merchant Marine wives, as we have seen, means that their husbands' work requirements circumscribe their lives, most importantly, in that they are unable to pursue interests of their own which would keep them from being available whenever their husbands can meet them. Most do not have jobs, let alone careers, which make work a "central life interest." So while most are resourceful and energetic in their efforts to "keep busy," their accounts lack the zest commuter wives convey about their work, how it absorbs and protects them against a loneliness and isolation that might otherwise overwhelm them. Whether or not Merchant Marine wives would want careers is beside the point (although most do not). It seems clear that for commuters, employment mitigates loneliness and isolation while sailing wives have no such interests to absorb them. In these families, children and domestic routines become full-time responsibilities mainly because these wives are alone so much. But as children grow these responsibilities wane, leaving sailing wives with neither career nor equally satisfying interests to which they can turn.

In fending off imputations of deviance, Merchant Marine wives also fare less well than commuter wives. Because sailing wives accept traditional marriage as a standard, and because their pattern of separation is more extreme, they are more defensive about imputations that they are not "normal" families. Ironically, they live apart *because* they abide by a traditional model of marriage which implies support of a husband's career. But, in supporting their husband's career, their own lives become different from the model of a normal family they believe in. The challenge to their "idea of family" is greater than it is for commuters, for whom traditional norms are nonbinding. Commuters know their family life embodies a rejection of traditional norms, but their "idea of family" not only allows for separate living, but requires it.

Moreover, as we have seen, commuters tend to neutralize imputations against themselves with greater dispatch. They shield themselves from censoring views and define their deviance as temporary. It is ironic that the group of couples who are better able to protect themselves from the ravages of living apart are those less likely to have to do so for long periods.

Finally, we see that despite the difficulties associated with their pattern of separation and reunion, these Merchant Marine couples manage to maintain commitment to their marriages. Expecting their husbands' jobs and children's demands to restrict their lives, the wives mute their complaints and celebrate their adjustments. To do otherwise, given the structure of their relationships, would invite emotional disaster. They need the family they create as badly as it needs them.

So do commuters. In this sense, both groups' efforts to create "family" in the face of conditions which threaten its operation, testify to the importance of the "idea of family." Both groups, wanting a family, devote considerable energy to its realization. Both groups, wanting to be family members, underplay the strains of living apart. Thus, we can see that the idea of family is as fundamental to their sense of self and sense of place as are the structures in which they live.

CHAPTER 9

The Articulation of Family and Career

The conventional nuclear family permits and promotes daily face-to-face interaction. But, in so doing, it may discourage its members from full commitment to their careers. In contrast, commuter marriage allows both husbands and wives to meet career demands. And for this reason, the few social scientists (e.g., Douvan & Pleck, 1978; Kirschner & Walum, 1978; Orthner *et al.*, 1980) and many of the journalists (see Chapter 1, Footnote 1) who have previously examined commuter marriage are enthusiastic about it. Like commentators on the burgeoning of other "alternative lifestyles," they celebrate the increasing diversity of American life. Unlike earlier sociologists of the family who argue for the functional necessity of a conventional residentially intact nuclear family, many recent observers welcome the rise of commuter marriage as an expansion of available choices for marriage and personal freedom within marriage. They see it as a healthy adaptation to the tensions of conventional marriage with few costs for the individuals involved.

While we have hardly argued for an uncritical acceptance of conventional marriage, we find such an interpretation of commuter marriage too facile. Although it is surely a response to the tensions of conventional marriage and to the tensions between that marriage and the modern economy, commuting spawns tensions of its own.

As we have shown, residential separation may heighten the romantic attachment between husbands and wives yet threaten the sense of order, rooted in daily exchanges, that sustains them. Residential separation may undermine the "taken-for-granted" quality of marriage, which is desired as well as disdained. Residential separation may equalize the division of labor between husband and wife, yet, at the same time threaten their sense of what marriage "should be." Residential separation may increase the time and energy each spouse has for other relationships, yet, for reasons both normative and structural, inhibit the formation and maintenance of relationships outside the marriage. Residential separation may provide the time for increased professional productivity, yet, especially for men, diminish the sense of security and order that makes continued productivity possible. Most generally, residential separation may open new opportunities for the career advancement of both spouses, but at the expense of shared space and time which are equally valued. Our analysis suggests that commuter marriage is a forced choice: Its benefits will outweigh its costs only in specific situations and its costs are never entirely absent.

As we have shown, commuters view their situation as temporary even without a tangible job offer to indicate its likely end. This paradox implies that compensatory psychic mechanisms are at work. Labeling oneself a temporary deviant may be a psychic adaptation to a problematic situation. In the language of labeling theory, it is a mechanism to undermine and forestall the possibility of becoming a self-acknowledged and publicly acknowledged deviant.

The fact that commuters resort to such temporizing is itself indication that they, too, do not regard theirs as the "best of all possible worlds." It is perhaps tolerable, but more as an adaptation to a difficult situation rather than a Utopian alternative to the conventional family. As researchers, we must respect the complexity of motivations and meanings, not pronounce advantages of a family structure without taking into account the considerable strains it may produce.

We have suggested then that commuter marriage is a rational response to endemic conditions of social life, in particular the tensions between culturally valued career advancement and a shared home. But this suggestion does not imply that it is an ideal family structure. Instead, couples face conflicting demands, values, and expectations. They want to live in one home, but they also want jobs and careers. As a result, they must sacrifice aspects of family life, especially in particular stages of the family or career. Let us now turn to an examination of these stages to provide a more general model of the relationship between family and work.

FAMILY AND CAREER: VARIATIONS
THROUGH THE LIFE COURSE

Commuter marriage is one of the most dramatic examples of work commitments intruding on family life. As we learned about the consequences of commuter marriage, we hoped our understanding would speak to our more general interest in the articulation of family and careers. We assumed that by specifying aspects of "work" and "family" we could begin to answer the question with which we began this study: What kinds of work obligations at what stage in each spouse's career fit best with what kind of family at what point in family development? As we shall see, although some kinds of work obligations fit with some kinds of family, at very few stages and for very few families is this fit altogether comfortable.

To begin to answer this question we look first at family and work stages simultaneously, specifying those combinations which minimize the strain deriving from relocation for the occupational group most relevant to commuters. That is, we begin by looking at only one type of employment pressure — the demand to relocate for career advancement — and its effect on family structure at different stages of development. Then we will be in a position to speak to more general issues of family and work articulation.

Our attempt to examine the relationship between the requirements of family and work at different stages hinges, of course, on the way in which the stages are conceptualized. There is a broad sociological consensus for dividing the family life span into the following stages, recognizing that the timing and spacing, and even occurrence of each of these stages, vary for different individuals and subgroups in our society[1]:

1. *Founding Stage*: the first few years of marriage (often referred to as the "honeymoon" stage).
2. *Transition Stage*: the years of marriage between the founding stage and the birth of children. For many American couples, this stage and the previous one can be collapsed because the average number of years between marriage and the first child is 2 to 3 years. However, increasing numbers of couples are delaying childbirth into their 30s. Especially, for those couples in which

---

1. A number of sociologists and historians now insist that more people are not going through these stages at all and, more generally, that the timing and sequence of the stages is increasingly flexible (i.e., parenthood appears before marriage, divorce stops the sequence of stages which may or may not begin again, people do not have children, etc.; see Aldous, 1978; Elder, 1977; Hirschorn, 1977; Neugarten, 1979; Rossi, 1980). While we recognize the importance of these changes (and will return to them later), we are first interested in presenting a "map" for analyzing those couples (still the majority) who do go through all of these stages. Furthermore, we will argue that because of the growing flexibility, individuals combine different career stages with any given family stage and these different combinations produce different family strategies and strains.

both spouses are professionally involved — or, more specifically, in which the wife has a postgraduate education — we can expect to find this "transition" stage (see Wilkie, 1981).

3. *Childrearing Stage*: the years when children are born and live in the parental home. Many sociologists divide this stage still further into several stages with each representing the age of the child, such as, less than six years, 6–12 years, 13–18 years. We have combined these stages for purposes of schematic presentation. But, even for our purposes, the divisions are not altogether irrelevant. (Again, for professional couples, this stage may be shorter than for the "average" American. Not only do they delay childbirth, but these professional spouses tend to have fewer children).

4. *Launching Stage*: the years beginning when children are leaving the parental home through the years when parents are living on their own. (Some authors — see Aldous, 1978; Duvall, 1971 — include in their typologies a final stage called the "retirement stage." Since this stage is defined in terms of employment and because we are interested in distinguishing career stages and family stages before considering them jointly, we have not included a "retirement stage.")

Just as the family unit tends to go through a series of such predictable stages, so, too, does participation in the labor market: Individual employees have "career lines" in which they pass through a series of occupational stages. And, of course, these stages will vary depending on particular occupations. Therefore, given our concern with dual-career couples, we need to consider not only family stages but also the occupations of *both* spouses as well as the career lines typical of these occupations.

The occupational group most likely to face the dilemmas of commuter marriage is salaried professionals. These professionals have relatively little personal control over the market for their labor and face standardized requirements for recruitment and promotion (Form & Huber, 1976). Moreover, they must maintain an ongoing involvement with work to obtain the rewards associated with it (Gross, 1958; Kanter, 1977). They may need at certain stages to become absorbed in their work and reduce involvement in their families.

Several specific characteristics of the labor market impose these requirements. First, salaried professionals tend to have a vertical career line. Withdrawal is costly and may, in fact, jeopardize later participation (Hall, 1975). Second, salaried professionals have a "late wage ceiling," the realization of which requires continual performance. Third, and most important, such salaried professionals often need to participate in a national labor market to maintain an ongoing career; they have the highest rates of geographic mobility of any occupational group (Ladinsky, 1967a, 1967b). Finally, many salaried professionals work in a highly specialized labor market; their skills can be utilized in only a limited number of jobs in restricted geographic locales.

In this study, almost all commuters were salaried professionals. Only 12 % were members of other occupational groups (typically that of independent professional) and almost all of these were married to salaried professionals. This occupational distribution was not, we would argue, a result of our nonrandom sampling; instead, it is the result of the special career contingencies operating on salaried professionals which we presented above.[2]

Let us consider, then, the typical career stages for salaried professionals. Adapting a typology developed by Miller and Form (1964), we can delineate the following typical career stages.

1. *Initial Stage*: the years when individuals are receiving their professional training and/or taking jobs which are explicitly temporary (e.g., professional school, postdoctoral fellowships, adjunct faculty positions, law clerkships, managerial traineeships).

2. *Trial Stage*: the years when individuals are in positions with the possibility of permanence contingent on performance (e.g., tenure track faculty, law firm associates, lower-level managers and administrators).

3. *Stability–Opportunity Stage*: the years when individuals are in positions which are guaranteed, but they also have the opportunity to improve their positions through inter- or intrainstitution mobility.

4. *Entrenchment–Disengagement Stage*: the last years of employment when individuals are entrenched in a final position and preparing to withdraw from the labor market.

---

2. Finer distinctions can, of course, be made even among these salaried professionals. As we discussed in Chapter 7, academics who have relatively flexible schedules requiring primarily individual (rather than cooperative) effort, have greater discretion over place and timing of work for some part of the year than do other salaried professionals (like lawyers, administrators, managers or editors). And if both spouses are academics, the flexibility is increased even further.

Having outlined both family and career stages, we begin to see the implications of their typical combination. Clearly, until very recently (if not still now), these combinations were quite different for married women and men, even if both had the credentials and aspirations to be salaried professionals. It was primarily married men who followed the orderly, predictable stages of the career line outlined above. For them, these career stages usually coincided with particular stages in the family. First, the initial stage of the career usually occurred during the same years as the founding stage of marriage. Second, the trial period of the career history coincided with the transition stage and often with the early childrearing years of the family. Third, the stability–opportunity stage of employment coincided with the latter years of childrearing and was likely to extend into the launching phase of the family. Finally, entrenchment in and disengagement from work generally overlapped with the latter years of the launching stage of the family.

In contrast, most married women (even salaried professionals) had (and many still do) a career that deviated from this male model. Particularly if their husbands moved for their jobs and when the couple had children, such women would withdraw from full employment (e.g., see Chapter 2 and Daniels & Weingarten, 1982; Poloma *et al.*, 1982; Yohalem, 1979). Such withdrawal might occur during the trial stage of their career or during its period of stability–opportunity. Typically it involved serious costs: Upon re-entering the labor force, their rewards (whether measured in status or income) did not measure up to those of their male or female counterparts with continuous employment histories.

Given these different patterns for husbands and wives, the nuclear family structure "fit" at all stages of the career, only if that "fit" was seen from the vantage point of the husband's career and family needs. Married men, with portable families, could become absorbed into their careers while meeting—indeed in order to meet—the demands placed on them as husbands and fathers. They could do so, because the primary demand as husband and father was breadwinning (Epstein, 1970) *and* because their wives shouldered the family responsibilities that allowed and sustained the husband's career involvement (Fowlkes, 1980; Hunt & Hunt, 1977; Papanek, 1973). But such intense career absorption, especially in its earlier stages, often came at the expense of men's early, intimate involvement with their families, which they might later come to regret (see Margolis, 1979; Valliant, 1977). This pattern is exactly the one which Parsons (1955) and Goode (1964) (see

Chapter 1) describe and prescribe when they suggest the nuclear family structure meets the demands of an industrial economy. That fit is predicated on a work absorbed husband and an un- or underemployed wife.

However, as more couples become dual-career or, more specifically, more married women aspire to become salaried professionals, that nuclear family structure no longer "fits" at all stages of the couple's work and family life. Instead, if both spouses are employed, both want to maintain steady career progress, and both agree that they should, couples may need to set up different family structures at different periods in their lives. In this book, we have focused on the commuter structure. As we shall now suggest, different structures — intact nuclear, commuter, modified extended — make work and family integration more manageable at different stages.

Most generally, at particular stages in the family's development, the demands that the *family* places on spouse's time, energies, and affections are likely to be particularly pressing, for example, during the founding and childrearing stages. But note that the source of the family's greater demands during these two periods is different: During the founding stage it is the couple's relationship that requires a great deal of attention, while it is children's needs which do so in the childrearing stage. Attending to differences inherent in either spousal or parental roles helps us specify what is at stake for the family at each career stage. With respect to careers, we might expect that at particular stages, the degree of pressure, involvement, and control from *employment* is likely to be particularly intense (e.g., during the initial or trial and the stability–opportunity stages). But, here too, the source of such pressure is different, for in the initial or trial stage the pressures of starting a career are problematic. During the stability–opportunity stage it is the possibility of solidifying advantages that creates pressure, in large part because this chance may be the last.

A joint consideration of family and career stages suggests that if a stage in which family demands are relatively high coincides with a career stage in which mobility demands are relatively low, the family can take priority without extreme career costs. And, if both spouses do accommodate family demands, neither spouse will suffer enormous or inequitable strains. Using the same logic, if a career stage in which pressures or options are relatively high coincides with a family stage in which demands are relatively low, spouses can establish a family structure that gives priority to their careers without suffering overwhelming costs to their families.

It is the shifting nature of demands from both family and career

which call for different family structures, such as intact nuclear, commuter, modified extended. These different and changing family structures, which are more or less responsive to mobility requirements of
both spouses' careers, will result in less stress for those who adopt them.
However, if we extend the logic of this argument still further, it becomes clear that if both members of a couple face great family and
career pressures simultaneously, any family structure will produce a
high level of strain. Such couples will have few options for establishing
a satisfying family structure.

FAMILY AND CAREER STAGE: EFFECTS ON FAMILY STRUCTURE

Let us consider, then, the specific combinations of family and career
stages of dual-career couples to locate the family structures most likely
to produce a favorable or unfavorable balance of costs and benefits.
We will begin with couples in which *both* spouses are salaried professionals in the same stage of their careers. Figure 9-1 presents an over-
view of likely combinations which our research highlights.

There are, of course, a number of situations not represented: individuals who have fast-paced careers, individuals with blocked careers, individuals who skip or move quickly through a family stage
(e.g., do not have children or have children very early). Thus, while
this chart represents common groupings and trajectories, it does not
present all possibilities or even all realities. Furthermore, and perhaps
most importantly, while the figure presents the stages of the career
and family as independent events, these two sets of stages can and do
affect one another. They are not independent but mutually contingent
events that interact in complex ways.

With these preliminary remarks in mind, we can discuss Figure
9-1 which presents the family structures likely to be most (and least)
manageable within the more common combinations of family and career stages.

As indicated in Figure 9-1, during the first family stage (the
"founding" stage), spouses are likely to be either in the initial or trial
period of their careers. During this family stage, spouses report the
highest levels of companionship, sex, and joint activity (Blood & Wolfe,
1960; Rausch, Goodrich, & Campbell, 1973;Rollins & Feldman,
1970). They must smooth conflict, establish joint habits, and develop
a base of intimacy, trust, and commitment. All of this lays heavy claim

FIG. 9-1. Family and career stages: Geographic mobility and consequent family structures of dual-career couples.

| FAMILY STAGES | CAREER STAGES | | | |
	Initial	Trial	Stability–opportunity	Entrenchment–disengagement
Founding	Intact nuclear or commuter*	Intact nuclear or commuter*	XXXXX[a]	XXXXX
Transition	Commuter	Commuter	XXXXX[b]	XXXXX
Childrearing	XXXXX[c]	Modified extended	Modified extended or commuter*	XXXXX
Launching	XXXXX	XXXXX	Commuter	Intact nuclear and modified extended**

Explanation of symbols:

* = *Both* family demands *and* career demands are particularly high. Either family structure is a compromise and each is likely to produce great stresses on either family or career.

** = *Neither* family demands *nor* career demands are as high as they have been earlier. Neither family structure will produce great strains in family or career.

XXXXX = Empirically rare combination.

a = While we have designated this a rare combination, it may occur increasingly because of the rising rate of remarriage. In our study, this combination occurred in three cases, all of which were second marriages (see Chapter 2).

b = We found no couples in this situation. However, it is not impossible, especially for those on the "fast track" of their careers.

c = While this combination may not be empirically rare among couples in which only one spouse has a career (i.e., this combination may not be rare for the husband), it is far less common among those couples in which both spouses are deeply involved in professional life, mainly because many of them delay having children.

on their energy and attention and, in so doing, requires a high level of face-to-face interaction. However, the ability to maintain that level of interaction depends on the career stage of both spouses.

If individuals are in the initial stage or just beginning the trial stage of the career line when they get married, the pressures of the career — especially geographic mobility — are also likely to be high (Long, 1974). Individuals have not yet established their reputations. Positions may be harder to find in a particular location during this stage than during later stages. Furthermore it is during the early years that individuals are most likely to need to focus a great deal of energy on their work to gain present as well as future rewards (Hennig & Jardim, 1977; Valliant & MacArthur, 1972). In this period, it may be particularly important to conduct a thorough job search for the best possible job, regardless of location, as good entry jobs often affect the possibility of good jobs during later stages (see Cole, 1979, for a discussion of such "accumulation of advantage").

Thus, couples in the founding stage of their families who are simultaneously in the initial or trial stage of their careers are likely to face strong cross pressures: High career demands coincide with high family demands. As a result, they may face a particularly difficult set of choices in attempting to set up a satisfactory family structure. For example, one spouse may be forced either to give up or reduce job involvement to remain in one home even though that choice might threaten career goals. Or the couple may be forced to set up two homes, even though that choice might threaten their not yet well-established marriage. As we found, those couples who did commute at this stage found it particularly trying; but as we are suggesting here, (and as the history of our older couples attests) if they had shared a home, that choice also would have been difficult, albeit for quite different reasons.

Turning to the second family stage, Figure 9-1 suggests that these couples are also likely to be in the initial or trial stages of their careers.[3] During this transition family stage preceding childbirth, spouses have already established some trust and commitment to one another. Their relationships will demand less than during the founding stage.

As for career line, we suggest that if spouses are still in the early (or even beginning the trial) stages of their careers, they may need to give priority to employment demands.[4] If both spouses want jobs, they may be unable to move together but instead may have to set up two homes. This situation includes many of the couples in our study.

3. In fact, it is among professional couples that we find the *creation* of this "transition" family stage. Here we see career stage influencing family stage. While many couples move directly from the founding stage to the childrearing stage, studies of married women professionals show that they often delay childbirth into their late 20s and 30s in order first to establish themselves in their careers (Daniels & Weingarten, 1982; Wilkie, 1981). Thus, only 4% of women with only high school degrees give birth to their first child between the ages of 30 and 34 compared to 20.3% of women with 16 or more years of schooling.

4. Though they do not specify career stages, McAuley and Nutty (1982) do suggest that it is during this family stage that couples are more likely to move for reasons related to employment. We suspect that is because they are also in the initial stages of their careers when mobility is most common (Leslie & Richardson, 1961; Long, 1974).

But for them, commuting was less stressful than for those in the founding stage of their families. We are predicting, then, that if the early stages of a career intersect with a transitional family stage, career demands are likely to be more pressing while demands of the couple's relationship are likely to be less pressing. At this point each spouse can focus on his or her career needs, even if that means limiting the amount of time they have together. Commuting is a further expression of this absorption. Under these conditions, then the commuter structure seems to "fit".

Returning to Figure 9-1 in the third family stage, childrearing, spouses are likely to be in the trial or stability–opportunity stage of their careers. During this family stage (especially its early years), spouses are expected to and often want to focus much attention and energy on their children. They experience heavy responsibilities and, often, deep involvement in family life. As we found, if one parent is away, he or she is likely to experience increased guilt and remorse while the one at home is likely to feel the increased burden which often breeds resentments toward the absent spouse. While these guilts and resentments vary according to the age and number of children, even parents with an older child will face greater demands than those without children in the home (see Chapters 4, 6, and 7).

In fact, in both career stages likely to coincide with childrearing, family needs may well outweigh those of employment. If both spouses are not assured of steady employment in a single locale (which is likelier at the beginning and end of the trial stage) they may have to "compromise" their careers to maintain a single home or "compromise" their family obligations and set up two homes (see Chapter 2). That is, living together or apart will create serious strains. Indeed, if the trial period does not develop into a more permanent position, the couple may continue to face stressful choices — none of which is fully satisfying. They cannot look forward to steady development in career lines or in family life. Given current labor market conditions, we expect that such a pattern and its associated stresses has become increasingly common. Finally, if couples are in the stability–opportunity stage, when they could receive an enticing job offer, they may also want to "compromise". In either career stage, separating when dependent children are still a focal point of parents' lives will produce difficulties, albeit different ones for the parent who leaves and the one who remains with the family.

Given the demands of the childrearing stage, the nuclear structure seems preferable to a commuter arrangement at any career point. Yet a closer look at demands on dual-career parents reveals the inadequacy of even the nuclear structure. In the usual intact nuclear residence, marital satisfaction is typically low when children are present (Campbell, Converse, & Rodgers, 1976; Glenn & Weaver, 1978; Miller, 1976) even if both spouses are professionally employed (Houseknecht & Macke, 1981) because children need such a high level of energy that even two participating parents may not be enough. Thus, at this stage, the most appropriate family structure may well be one that involves not only strong bonds between spouses, but also with other close primary groups. Adapting Litwak's (1960) usage of the term, we label this set of relationships a "modified extended family." While in the earlier stages of marriage, the couple may need to focus on the dyadic tie, they may now need a more open system with wider community ties. Many dual-career couples hire help whom they bring into their homes; many increase contact with kin, friends, and neighbors. When children are young, parents, especially mothers, do rely more on kin (Fischer, 1981; Fischer & Phillips, 1981). Also, parents, especially fathers, increasingly call upon neighbors and friends (Hess, 1976; Stueve & Gerson, 1977; Tamir & Antonucci, 1981).

Thus, commuting would be particularly costly at these times not only because it forces separation of parents but because it separates parents from others in the community (see Chapter 5). Moreover, these costs will be even greater when children are young, a time when spouses are more likely to be in the trial stage than in the stability–opportunity stage of their careers. Living apart is too difficult with very young children. Indeed we found very few cases in this category, forcing us to omit commuter marriage as even a feasible option during the trial stage. Instead, we are suggesting that the modified extended structure is preferable here as it is for the stability–opportunity stage. Since children are likely to be older by the time their parents have achieved some career recognition, the parents are more likely to be able to commute with less stress than at the trial stage. So as Figure 9-1 indicates, commuting is likely to be stressful whenever children are still in the home, and the modified extended family may well be the preferable form.

Finally, turning to the family's launching stage, spouses are most likely to be in the stability–opportunity or entrenchment–retirement stage of their careers. During the launching stage, children no longer live at home and spouses' marital commitment is more clearly established, as indicated by their low rate of divorce (U.S. Bureau of the Census, 1976). Though marital satisfaction is not as high as in the early stages of marriage, some studies suggest it is higher than during the previous family stage (Spanier, Lewis, & Cole, 1975). But as Swenson, Eskew, and Kolhepp (1981) found of couples in this stage: "Over the course of the lifetime together, both the amount of love expressed and the number of problems they have decline. That is, during this stage, there appears to be little happening between them" (p. 849). And, importantly, overall satisfaction during this stage may well depend on the establishment and/or maintenance of interests outside of the home (Powell, 1977; Rubin, 1979). Therefore, in this stage of family life demands both from the couple's relationship and daily parental obligations are likely to be low. At the same time, family expenses may increase as these salaried professionals send their children off to college. Both the decreased need for daily family involvement and increased expenses may lead spouses to focus on their careers without experiencing overwhelming costs to family life.

Again, the appropriate family structure is likely to depend upon the spouse's career stage. Many of the salaried professionals who have previously maintained an ongoing career involvement will be in the stability–opportunity stage of their careers. At this point, reputations are established. Men, recent research suggests, may well use this stage to engage in a "midlife review" and, as a result, want to switch jobs or even careers (Hirschorn, 1977). Like the spouses in our study, either the husband or wife may feel that this is the last chance to optimize career advancement, to realize life-long goals, and, as a result, feel a strong push to do so. This may require switching jobs. If either or both spouses are to take advantage of opportunities, they may be unable to get that "best job" in the same location.[5] Consequently, they may choose to establish a commuter structure which will impose few strains on their marriage because family demands are relatively low. Thus, again, commuter marriage "fits" to some extent. Indeed, judging from our comparison of "established" couples with either "adjusting" or "balancing" couples, commuter marriage fits better then than at any other life stage (see Chapter 7).[6]

5. Recent works seem to suggest that it is women, more than men, who at this point in life, want to turn outward to finally achieve while men begin to turn inward to finally involve themselves in their personal lives (for a discussion of this literature, see Rossi, 1980). If these differences should appear in a particular couple, who need to choose a particular family structure, they may be especially prone to conflict.

6. We are suggesting here that commuter marriage causes less strain for the "established" couples than the "adjusting" couples because of the relative demands of family and career. But we should also point out that the decision to commute at a later stage may also entail a higher commitment to careers than in the earlier stage. Older

But as we show in Figure 9-1, some couples in the family launching stage, especially its later years, are not in the stability–opportunity stage but the entrenchment–disengagement stage of their careers. Many couples do not launch their last child until they are in their late 50s or early 60s (see Rossi, 1980). Especially for those professionals who are now delaying childrearing into their mid-30s, this pattern will become increasingly common. If so, spouses are likely to be in the culminating and waning years of their careers. They will be established in a final secure position (perhaps having chosen it as a place to retire) and few job opportunities will appear. Or, they will have retired. At the same time, these older "launching" couples may become increasingly reliant on one another for physical help. For them, the commuter structure is likely to be less attractive and, if chosen, will produce a high level of stress. In fact, one of the oldest commuter women (aged 57; husband, 60) we interviewed spoke of such a fear, which was voiced by few others: increasing physical disability that threatened their life in two homes (see Chapter 4). But few commuters fell into this age group (see Appendix, Table A6). They did not, we suspect, because of the high family demands and low employment demands characteristic of the final family and career stages. This combination is unlikely to produce a commuter marriage. Instead, in the final stages of family and career, intact nuclear families are likely to produce relatively few problems. Indeed, here too, the most appropriate family structure may well be the modified extended family in which spouses maintain strong attachments to other primary groups.

In sum, we have suggested that an examination of the joint demands of family and career lines indicates that for dual-career couples, three different family structures — intact nuclear, commuter, modified extended — are likely to be more or less stressful or beneficial at particular family and career stages. Viewing different family structures as temporary adaptations introduces a more general approach for conceptualizing the family in contemporary society. Many social scientists have begun to discuss the family, and its future, in terms of a "pluralistic" system. In contrast to the functionalist model which assumes that only the nuclear family structure is "normal," they argue

---

couples, with two jobs in the same locale, could often remain in the shared home without complete withdrawal from work. But, for the younger couples, a single home often did mean a complete work withdrawal for one of the spouses. Thus, the lesser strain of commuting for the "established" couples may not be simply a result of the overall balance of work and family demands, but a result of the relative priority the older couples give to their careers.

that many different types of family structures may be useful and appropriate for different individuals (Ramez, 1978; Rapoport & Rapoport, 1976; Sussman, 1975). This notion of pluralism involves the coexistence of *various family structures at one point in time for different couples*. Other sociologists examine the life cycle of the "normal" nuclear family and suggest that *for any given couple, the family is not a static unit* (Aldous, 1978; Duvall, 1971; Rodgers, 1973). They write of the family stages we outlined and show the family changing regularly as members are added, age, and leave the home. Combining these two approaches, we have suggested another means for understanding family structure and its relationship to other societal institutions, particularly the economy: *a pluralism of family structures both across social groups and within the life course of those groups*. At the same time we have suggested that such "pluralism" should not be portrayed simply as a set of favorable options from which a couple may choose without constraint or cost. Instead, we argue that at any particular stage in a couple's history, that couple may adopt a family structure as a strategy for minimizing the costs to *both* family and careers.

FURTHER DIRECTIVES FOR STUDYING THE ARTICULATION OF FAMILY AND WORK FOR DUAL-CAREER COUPLES

Thus far we have discussed a scheme for analyzing the complex relationship between family and career demands. We have taken into account only one set of career demands and examined its implications only in terms of consequences for family structure. We have not outlined more specific directives for conceptualizing or studying this relationship, although what our scheme omits does alert us to some possible directives. We will discuss five of these.

1. We have developed a "map" only for those couples in which both spouses are in the same stage of their careers. Yet in many couples, spouses are in different career stages, typically with the husband more advanced. This situation represents many of the "balancing" and "established" couples in our study (see Chapters 2 and 7). The inconsistency between spouses' careers may well point to very different strategies for reconciling work and family lives. Here, the involvement level for each spouse's career will differ and the balance of employment demands relative to family responsibilities will also vary for each spouse. For example, if the husband is in a stable period of his career while the wife is in the trial period of hers, a childrearing couple may move together for her employment to benefit from both careers and to minimize stress on the family. But if such a couple is in the "launching" phase of the family, the husband may instead want to (and be able to) move ahead by finding the "best" job in a locale different from his wife's. In this case, neither the couple's relationship nor either spouses' career will face irreparable damage. We are suggesting, then, that dual-career research needs to make distinctions which jointly consider the husband's and wife's career stages (e.g., both early, one advanced, both advanced) if we are to understand the various strategies and stresses for dual-career couples.

2. We need to specify further how different occupations affect the relationship of family and work. We have considered only salaried professionals. But "salaried professionals" include a large number of occupations and too many studies of family and work make cruder distinctions among occupational groups. Yet family strategies and family structures may well depend on the particular occupation of each spouse and their attendant career lines.

3. We need to consider whether both spouses are in the same or different occupations. Couples in which both partners are in the same field are likely to face different issues than those in very different fields. Our research suggested that when both spouses are academics, the strains of commuting are reduced (see Chapter 7). Other research on academic couples suggests that a common profession can raise the professional output of both or block opportunities because of nepotism rules (Bryson & Bryson, 1980; Butler & Paisley, 1980; Heckman *et al.*, 1977). Or, to take another example, two self-employed professionals who work in the same office may find it easier to share work obligations and "trade off" responsibilities to the advantage of their families and careers. At the same time, the constant togetherness of such couples may increase tensions between them (Hunt & Hunt, 1982; Kanter, 1977).

4. We have presented a map for those couples in which both husband and wife engage in steady career and family progression. But an increasing number of individuals do not follow these conventional family stages: They have children before marriage; they do not have children at all; they divorce and remarry; they lose a spouse before the family stages are complete. These variants can influence individual strategies for reconciling family and work, as well as norms and reactions to the various combinations (Neugarten, 1979). So, too, many spouses do not follow career stages in the order we outlined. While

we have proposed that women's careers, in particular, often do not proceed in a lock-step pattern, men's careers may not either. In fact, some authors now suggest that increasing numbers of men, even salaried professionals, encounter or create greater flexibility in their careers (e.g., see Hirschorn, 1977). Whether these changes are a result of changing economic conditions, personal preferences, or blocked careers, they affect the strategies for establishing a satisfying family structure.

5. Any discussion of the articulation of family and work must recognize the particular historical period in which couples live and the particular groups of which they are members (see Elder, 1977, 1978, 1981, for a useful discussion of this idea). We have suggested that commuter marriage is a response to a particular set of contemporary conditions (see Chapter 2), but we have been less mindful of cohort differences and their possible effects: The "adjusting", "balancing" and "established" couples in our study are members of different cohorts. We have argued that they represent different stages of family and career development and, by implication, that "adjusting" couples will later face opportunities and constraints similar to those currently faced by the "balancing" or "established" couples. But because their lives will unfold under different societal conditions, and because they are likely to respond to these conditions in different ways, their strategies to reconcile family and work may well take different forms.

In sum, we are suggesting that a coherent and systematic map of the reconciliation between careers and family must consider the occupation of each spouse, the individual career stage of each spouse, and their family stage as well as the conditions under which these couples were born and now live. Clearly, simultaneous consideration of the many factors that do distinguish dual-career couples increases the complexity of research about the relationship of family and work. But only by grappling with the concatenations of multiple factors can we achieve a more sophisticated analysis of the articulation of family and work.

IN CONCLUSION: SOME REFLECTIONS ON WORK AND FAMILY LIFE

By considering family and career stages together, we have suggested that commuting is a family structure that poses the least costs under certain, limited conditions. But, even under these conditions, commuting is, at best, an adaptation to a bad situation. Commuters face a dilemma shared by many dual-career couples: both husbands and wives can work at fulfilling jobs or live in one home. They do not face an unusual dilemma; they make an unusual choice. The dilemma they face and the choice they make speak to general values and tensions in American society and in its family system.

The decision to commute speaks, first, to the weakness of the American family. Most individuals believe the occupational system is given and fixed. For many Americans, whether salaried professionals in a commuter marriage, employees who do shift work, managers who travel, or Merchant Marines who live apart, the family is far more subject than work to individual manipulation. Consequently, when there is a conflict between work and family demands, adaptations are made more often in the family. While sociologists and historians increasingly write of the family as an active agent of change, we find adaptations attesting to its weakness and passivity.

Among the commuters themselves, we find few expectations that might point to rearranging the work world's current dominance. They regret having to separate to meet career demands. They sometimes wonder if they are "freaks" for having made the decision to set up two homes. But they accept that the standard of career success requires them to do so. They tend to criticize themselves while accepting the social system.

Such acceptance, and the more general trends we suspect it represents, does not simply address the weakness of the family but the imperviousness of economic institutions and the insensitivity of employers to personal concerns. Today, many social analysts write of ways to adapt the economic system to family life because the employment of women makes the friction between family and work all the more evident. They write of the need for "flextime," for corporate child care, for employer's cooperation in meeting the career needs of relocated spouses, and for policies to hire couples as a team for one job. But few employers respond. Recent surveys find that employers rarely assist the spouses of relocated workers to find jobs, rarely offer child care, rarely provide flextime, and rarely hire couples as a team (Catalyst, 1982; General Mills, 1981; Stoper, 1982). The male model of careers, with its indifference to family demands, remains very much with us.

But the insensitivity is not limited to employers who maintain long-standing traditions. Professionals themselves are caught in a logic of careers and a culture that demands the dominance of work. This culture is too often supported by mainstream feminists whose calls for equality in the upper employment echelons urge women to become part of the established system. Thus, the prevalence of commuting — and the even greater prevalence of the tensions that produce it — speak both to the strength of feminism and to its darker side.

The women in our study felt that feminism had helped them stand up more for their rights, that it helped them to achieve on their own, to live apart from their husbands, and to be equals through the development of careers. The version of feminism they praised is a movement which values work outside of the home but, as a result, finds itself underplaying the work and emotion that go on inside of the home. Thus, feminists as social analysts and commuters as feminists must continue to ask what factors restrict the employment of women. But, in doing so, they must avoid devaluing the work women do and avoid accepting the conventional male model of what it is to be fully human.

The feminism of the last few years has tended to concentrate on how family obligations undermine the careers of women. Of course, they do. That is one of the major points we have tried to elaborate in our discussion of the lives of commuters before they set up two homes. But this inequality exists only when women have more home responsibilities than their mates, when the world of employment is structured around the lack of familial involvement and attachment, and when career obligations are regularly taken as more important than family responsibilities. The fact that women do continue to have more responsibility for home maintenance does not mean that they should. And the stubborn devaluation of family life need not persist. Rather than viewing family demands as obstacles to success, men and women might be better off recognizing the cushioning, rejuvenating functions such responsibilities can offer to their too intense work lives.

As we suggested in the first chapter, commuting can be understood as an extension of historical trends in American society. It is an extension of the ideology of individualism that has a long history of application to husbands, but is now applied to wives. Commuting represents an extension of the separation of work and family. And commuting extends the male model of careers to women who aspire to professional positions. However, we are questioning such deeply rooted values and behaviors in American society. Thus, the issue we are raising addresses not so much the question "Can commuting work?" but "Should it?" Our answer must be circumspect. Commuting is a necessary arrangement: Today's realities make it far easier for the family to change (even necessitate that it does) permitting the full utilization of women's and men's talents and resources. But we, like commuters themselves, would rather see a world where career demands cost less, and responded more, to the family life of women and men.

Methods of Research and Characteristics of the Sample

This book began as two separate studies — one by each of the authors. While collecting data, neither of us knew the other's research was under way. Then, in 1978, each of us gave a paper discussing our research at the annual American Sociological Association meeting. Over one of the many lunches at such academic meetings, we talked about our findings not yet knowing we were beginning a collaboration and friendship.

Our personal circumstances were quite different. Naomi, living on the East Coast, was in the early stage of her career, just having completed a dissertation on commuter marriage. Harriet, living in the Midwest, was already a full professor and had done much other research. Naomi was in the process of building a relationship, wondering if she would have to commute. Harriet had already been married for many years and was a mother of three, one already in college. Our intellectual training also differed. Harriet earned her PhD at the University of Chicago, where she had concentrated on the sociological analysis of deviance and become sensitive to different concepts of social reality. Naomi had just completed her PhD at Columbia, where she had concentrated on questions about social structure and its patterned effects on family life.

Despite these differences, the first meeting evolved into many more, leading to a series of coauthored articles and presented papers and, eventually, to this book. It had become quite clear that we had used similar techniques to collect our data and had come to similar conclusions. We decided that combining our studies would make for a better book than either of us could produce alone. The collaboration began in earnest, with chapters flying back and forth through the mail.

Collaboration at a distance had its drawbacks. We found ourselves in a commuter relationship of sorts with both the costs and benefits that such a relationship entails. Expensive phone calls, periodic trips, hectic schedules, and different demands sustained our relationship and made it more difficult. While avoiding divorce is the most extreme test of the viability of a commuter marriage, the most extreme test of a commuter colleagueship is the production of a manuscript. In this sense, we can say it worked.

The main focus of our research and of this book is the lives of couples who set up two homes so that both spouses can pursue a career. However, to specify the effects of separation, Harriet also interviewed a group of Merchant Marine couples who live apart but are quite different from commuters in other ways. In this Appendix we describe our samples and the techniques used to collect our data, as well as some selected characteristics of each group of respondents. Because we used similar sample sources as well as similar interviewing techniques, this Appendix combines descriptions of the two studies, except where we indicate otherwise.

THE COMMUTER SAMPLE

Both of us developed a list of potential respondents from several sources. Harriet placed an ad about her research in a local paper and the few couples who responded are included in the study. Naomi called journalists who had written articles about commuters and they provided some names and addresses. However, we both relied primarily on a system of referrals. Some commuters were identified by friends and acquaintances who learned about our research. Finally, commuters themselves identified other couples who commuted.

Obviously our respondents can in no way be called a random sample. Because the population parameters of commuters are unknown, we have no way of knowing how representative they are. As a result, any generalizations based on this research must be tentative. Yet, because we did have two separate studies with two separate data sets, but produced such similar results, we do have some confidence that our results have validity beyond these specific cases.

After generating a pool of commuters, we contacted potential subjects by phone, described our studies, asking if they were willing to participate. A total of 121 individuals agreed; they make up the final sample on which this book is based. The sample is divided into two groups. The large majority ($n = 114$) were commuting at the time of the research. A second, small group ($n = 7$) consists of those who had divorced while commuting. We included these divorced commuters to understand more fully the ways in which commuting may strain a marriage and the extent to which these spouses believed commuting contributed to divorce.

We were interested in examining the responses of both women and men as well as in comparing the responses of spouses. All too many studies of marriage include only wives, even though we now know that spouses typically have quite different values for, responses to, and perceptions of their marriage (see Chapters 1 and 6). Consequently, we attempted to interview both members of a couple. Table A1 shows the final composition of our two studies combined. Thus, while we only interviewed both spouses in 50 couples, we have some information on a total of 71 couples (50 full couples + 16 wives only + 5 husbands only).

The number of respondents included in the sample is very close to the number we contacted. Only two married commuters refused to participate. In one case, a man said: "I simply don't have the time." He went on to support his claim with a

TABLE A1. Commuter Sample Composition

| | RESPONDENTS | | | |
STATUS	BOTH SPOUSES	WIFE ONLY[a]	HUSBAND ONLY[b]	TOTAL
Married commuters	96 (48 couples)	14	4	114
Divorced commuters	4 (2 couples)	2	1	7
Total	100 (50 couples)	16	5	121

[a]"Wife only" includes cases in which we interviewed wives but not their husbands.
[b]"Husband only" includes cases in which we interviewed husbands but not their wives.

detailed description of his hectic schedule, and concluded by saying: "This lack of time is one of the real problems of commuting." As we found out in the course of the study, he shared at least this experience with most of the other commuters. The second refusal was a woman who said she was willing to participate but wanted first to see if her husband would as well. A few days later she called back, reporting that not only had he refused, but had attempted to dissuade her. Presumably wanting to prevent any marital discord, she declined the interview. In addition, two divorced commuters said they did not want to be in the study: In one case, the reason stated was lack of time and in the other, a desire not to review the unpleasantness associated with divorce.

Overall, then, the number of refusals was quite small. We attribute this low refusal rate to a number of factors. Many of these commuters, all highly educated professionals, expressed interest in research and even stated they felt obliged to contribute to it. So, too, many seemed to think theirs was a story worth telling. And, finally, because we generated the sample through referrals, we had the advantage of approaching potential interviewees through a mutual acquaintance.

The Commuter Interview

We conducted most of the interviews in the respondent's homes.[1] However, a few interviews took place in offices — often in the evening because respondents felt their work settings provided more privacy.

We both interviewed each spouse separately, assured them of complete confidentiality, and asked respondents not to talk to their spouses about the interview until they had also been interviewed. Several commented that this promise of secrecy would require considerable restraint, but all agreed to it. Because of our desire to interview spouses separately (and whenever possible to see their separate homes), Naomi trav-

1. Lynn Strauss, Harriet's graduate assistant, did some of these interviews.

eled extensively, visiting 17 states in all. Harriet also traveled to complete interviews with both spouses, but confined her research to driving distance (400 miles) of her Chicago base.

At the beginning of each interview, we asked if our discussions could be taped. Although we were warned that some respondents might refuse this request (given the intimate character of some of the topics), only two did so. During these two interviews, we took extensive notes.

The interviews themselves consisted of open-ended questions and intensive probes. Both authors used this open-ended technique and both covered the same topics with only one exception: Only one of us asked about extramarital sex. Consequently, the data reported on extramarital affairs come from only one study while the majority of information is based on both samples combined. Although the same general topics were covered in all interviews, the sequence of topics and the time spent on each topic varied considerably. This variation depended not on the interviewer, but on the respondents.

The interviews ranged in length from one to five hours, with most lasting two and one-half to three hours. In several cases, we were invited to remain after the interviews, often continuing discussions that had begun in them.

In general, most of the commuters showed a considerable degree of openness and willingness to discuss our full list of topics. Despite our initial fear that the interviewees would balk at responding to personal questions, they did not. Only two respondents refused to talk about their marital sex lives; only two declined to discuss extramarital sex; and one couple (neither husband nor wife), without children, would discuss their attitudes toward having children.

Most of the interviewees were cooperative beyond our expectations. Many commented on their own responses, expressing surprise that they were being so open. One man said:

I've never told my friends these things. They are just private matters. Of course, some of that is self-preservation.

And a woman said:

I can't tell by your face whether you've heard something you think is good or bad. I don't know you well enough. That's good. I can say how I feel and it's ok. I can't even believe myself that I am telling you all this.

Several commented that the chance to talk to a stranger was therapeutic. As one woman put it:

This is like free therapy. It's wonderful. Who else would sit and listen to all my problems for so many hours? Will you come back next week?

Then she laughed and went on:

No, maybe it's better that I won't see you again.

TABLE A2. Occupation of Women and Men: Commuters

| | WOMEN | | MEN | |
OCCUPATION	%	(n)	%	(n)
University faculty and graduate students	50	(33)	49	(27)
Administrators and researchers	18	(12)	9	(5)
Editors and journalists	10	(7)	4	(2)
Medical doctors and therapists	3	(2)	5	(3)
Lawyers	2	(1)	13	(7)
Business executives/managers	3	(2)	5	(3)
Other[a]	14	(9)	15	(8)
Total	100	(66)	100	(55)

[a]Includes architect, veterinarian, teacher not in university, engineer.

Social Characteristics of the Commuters

Though we make no pretense about the representativeness of the sample, it is useful to consider the demographic profiles of our respondents.[2] As Table A2 reveals, most were professionals. Half of the female commuters and almost half (49%) of the male commuters were academics. This skewed occupational distribution may be due in part to our sampling method, relying as it did so heavily on referrals. However, the high number of academics may also represent the actual commuting population. The flexibility of the academic work schedule, the greater discretion many academics have over schedules and work place, and their often solitary work conditions may ease the establishment of a commuter marriage. At the same time, the tight labor market currently characterizing much of the academic system forces these couples to set up two homes.

Most commuters were highly educated. As Table A3 shows, all had completed college degrees — more than four-fifths of the women had gone on to complete graduate degrees. Among the men, about two-thirds (62%) had PhDs or the equivalent (MDs or JDs) while most of the remaining (27%) had a Master's degree.

Most of these dual-career spouses also had high incomes. Table A4 shows, however, that more of the men (56%) than women (35%) earned above $20,000. The range of income of the commuter men was from $10,000 to $90,000, and the range for the women was $7,000 to $42,000. The range of joint family incomes was from $17,000 to $120,000.

Although the commuters were relatively similar in occupation and education, we purposefully chose respondents who varied in other family and life cycle charac-

2. We have combined both authors' samples for these demographic profiles. In addition, we have combined the divorced commuters with the married commuters because the divorced "subsample" is so small and, in any case, quite similar to the married commuters on the demographic characteristics reported here.

TABLE A3. Education of Women and Men: Commuters and Merchant Marines

	COMMUTERS				MERCHANT MARINES			
	WOMEN		MEN		WOMEN		MEN	
EDUCATION	%	(n)	%	(n)	%	(n)	%	(n)
Less than high school	0		0		28	(14)	17	(5)
High school degree	0		0		20	(10)	50	(15)
Some college	0		0		42	(21)	27	(8)
BA or equivalent[a]	17	(11)	11	(6)	10	(5)	6	(2)
MA or equivalent[b]	47	(31)	27	(15)	0		0	
PhD, JD, or MD	36	(24)	62	(34)	0		0	
Total	100	(66)	100	(55)	100	(50)	100	(30)

[a]Includes some graduate school but no advanced degree.

[b]Includes those working on PhD who already have MA or equivalent.

teristics. In particular, as Table A5 shows, we chose a sample in which about half did not have children at home (46% of the couples had no children; 13% had grown children) and about half did have children still living with them (24% had children less than 12 and 17% had children between the ages of 12 and 18 still in the home). We could locate only one commuter couple with an infant child and included them in the sample. Because of the norms promoting the presence of both parents and the time required for care, particularly during infancy, it seems likely that there are, in fact, very few couples who choose to live apart while their children are still so young.

As is typical for the American married population as a whole, the women in this study were somewhat younger than their husbands. Table A6 shows the mean age of the women was 39 years, and ranged from 26 to 58. The mean age of the men was 40 years and ranged from 27 to 60.

TABLE A4. Individual Income of Women and Men: Commuters

	WOMEN		MEN	
INDIVIDUAL INCOME	%	(n)	%	(n)
Below $10,000	21	(14)	5	(3)
$10,000–$14,999	29	(19)	13	(7)
$15,000–$19,999	14	(9)	22	(12)
$20,000–$29,999	27	(18)	36	(20)
$30,000 or above	8	(5)	20	(11)
Total[a]	100	(65)	100	(53)

[a]Total n reflects the fact that we did not obtain information on income from one woman and two men.

TABLE A5. Presence of Children: Commuters and Merchant Marines

NUMBER OF CHILDREN	COMMUTERS %	(n)	MERCHANT MARINES %	(n)
None	46	(33)	12	(7)
Children under 12 years	24	(17)	28	(16)
Children between 12 and 18 years	17	(12)	29	(17)
Grown children no longer at home	13	(9)	31	(18)
Total	100	(71)	100	(58)

With this wide range of ages, there was also quite a bit of variation in the number of years married: from one to 26 years. As Table A7 shows, most of these couples were certainly not newlyweds: Only 20% had been married five years or less. In fact, the mean number of years married was 13.

Commuters were also selected to insure variation on characteristics of the commute. First, the distance that they had to travel between their two homes varied greatly. It ranged from 50 miles to 2700 miles and, as shown in Table A8, the largest group (35%) clustered around 150 to 500 miles apart. Furthermore, couples varied in the amount of time they spent in a single shared residence. As Table A9 shows, the majority (55%) of commuters reunited on weekends. However, another 11% only saw one another every other weekend, and an equal proportion only came together once a month, usually for a few days. And finally, 23% of the couples were not even able to be reunited every month, though most of these did stay together for four or five days when they finally met.

The distance between the spouses was the major factor affecting the frequency of reunions. Table A10 shows that nearly all (95%) of those who lived less than 500

TABLE A6. Age of Women and Men: Commuters and Merchant Marines

AGE	COMMUTERS				MERCHANT MARINES			
	WOMEN %	(n)	MEN %	(n)	WOMEN %	(n)	MEN %	(n)
26–30	26	(17)	16	(9)	14	(7)	7	(2)
31–40	39	(26)	37	(20)	44	(22)	33	(10)
41–50	23	(15)	31	(17)	12	(6)	30	(9)
51–60	12	(8)	16	(9)	18	(9)	20	(6)
61–70	0		0		12	(6)	10	(3)
$\overline{X}$	39		40		42		45	
Total	100	(66)	100	(55)	100	(50)	100	(30)

TABLE A7. Number of Years Married: Commuters and Merchant Marines

NUMBER OF YEARS	COMMUTERS		MERCHANT MARINES	
	%	(n)	%	(n)
1–5 years	20	(14)	17	(10)
6–10 years	30	(21)	19	(11)
11–15 years	13	(9)	12	(7)
16–20 years	15	(11)	19	(11)
21 years or more	22	(16)	33	(19)
$\overline{X}$	13		15	
Total	100	(71)	100	(58)

TABLE A8. Distance between Primary and Secondary Residence: Commuters

DISTANCE	%	(n)
<150 miles	20	(14)
150–499 miles	35	(25)
500–1000 miles	21	(15)
>1000 miles	24	(17)
Total	100	(71)

TABLE A9. Time Spent Together in a Single Residence: Commuters

TIME TOGETHER	%	(n)
Every weekend or more	55	(39)
Two weekends per month	11	(8)
Once a month	11	(8)
Less than once a month	23	(16)
Total	100	(71)

TABLE A10. Distance between Spouses by Time Spouses Together in a Single Residence: Commuters

| | DISTANCE BETWEEN SPOUSES | | | |
| | < 500 MILES | | ≥ 500 MILES | |
TIME TOGETHER	%	(n)	%	(n)
Every weekend	95	(37)	6	(2)
Less than every weekend	5	(2)	94	(30)
Total	100	(39)	100	(32)

miles apart were able to see one another every weekend while nearly all (94%) of those who lived 500 or more miles apart were unable to reunite every weekend.

THE MERCHANT MARINE SAMPLE

In the years following our initial meeting we decided to compare commuters with another group of couples who lived apart to see if such a comparison would help us specify the effects of separation per se. Access to a comparison group became possible when Harriet learned that a new student of hers was the wife of a Merchant Marine, an engineer working on vessels that sail the Great Lakes. Through this student, Marie Van Gemert, we were able to enlist the cooperation of wives of seamen who lived in the Chicago and Sturgeon Bay, Wisconsin, areas. Marie and another graduate assistant, Christine Thomas, were trained to do in-depth interviewing.

Starting in the late fall of 1980, Harriet, Marie, and Christine began to interview wives — adding husbands in late 1981. Then in early 1982, we asked for and received permission to attend the annual meeting of the International Shipmaster's Association which was held in Duluth, Minnesota. During the three days of these meetings, a team of four (Harriet; her two graduate assistants; and a faculty colleague at Governors State University, Suzanne Prescott) interviewed husbands and wives who had come to Duluth to attend the convention. The couples who came to the convention live in Great Lakes port cities in Illinois, Indiana, Michigan, Minnesota, and Ohio. About half of the interviews in the sample come from this convention group.

Most of the husbands in the Merchant Marine sample are officers in one of the two main departments on commercial ships: the deck department, which includes (in rank order) captains, mates, and deckhands; the engineering department which includes (in rank order) chief engineers, assistant engineers, and oilers.

Only one wife, who was contacted before we went to Duluth, declined to participate. She felt she would not have anything "interesting" to say. In Duluth, those attending the convention received information about our study (an investigation of "Merchant Marine Family Life") in their registration materials. Those willing to be interviewed signed their names to scheduling sheets made available to them at the convention registration desk. Many more were willing to be interviewed than we could accommodate in the time available. Both wives and husbands were quite open and responded freely to our questions. Like the commuters, many even suggested that the interviews had been useful to them personally and expressed appreciation for the opportunity to think about and describe their family lives.

Although acquiring respondents from a population of convention participants creates the possibility of a selection bias, we know of no way to distinguish those willing to be interviewed from those who attended the convention but did not sign up to be interviewed. Judging from the large number of willing people, whom we could not accommodate, we feel the influence of this factor to be negligible. However, convention expenses might have biased attendance toward an older, economically better-off group. Yet, a large population of younger couples who live in the Duluth area also attended the convention and we did interview many of them. Their presence probably counteracted any age selectivity among those who traveled from out of town.

Social Characteristics of Merchant Marines

Three types of characteristics distinguish commuters as a group from Merchant Marines. First, these two groups have a very different sociodemographic profile. While for commuters both spouses are highly educated, only 6% of Merchant Marine husbands and only 10% of the Merchant Marine wives were college graduates. Further evidence of the educational disparity can be seen in the large proportion of both spouses in the Merchant Marine sample who had only completed high school or less: 48% of the women and 67% of the men (see Table A3).

Interestingly, these educational differences do not translate into comparable income differences despite the fact that commuters are two-income, and sailing, one-income, families. Table A11 shows that almost half (47%) of Merchant Marine families enjoy annual incomes above $41,000, whereas only one-third of the commuters attain that income level. (The lower family income of commuters may be ex-

TABLE A11. Joint Family Income: Commuters and Merchant Marines

JOINT INCOME	COMMUTERS %	(n)	MERCHANT MARINES %	(n)
$15,000–$20,999	12	(8)	0	
$21,000–$30,999	25	(17)	22	(13)
$31,000–$40,999	32	(22)	31	(18)
$41,000–$50,999	9	(6)	31	(18)
$51,000 or above	22	(15)	16	(9)
Total	100	(68)	100	(58)

plained in part by the fact that a substantial proportion of commuter spouses were still in early career stages.)

The second significant difference between commuters and Merchant Marines stems from the fact that all commuter wives work in professional positions or, more rarely, are in graduate programs preparing to do so. In contrast, only one-fifth of the sailing wives were employed outside of the home and only two of these 12 wives worked full time. One was a teacher; the other, a nurse. Moreover, these were the only two jobs held by sailing wives that carried formal educational requirements and none of these wives were pursuing graduate degrees.

The third characteristic distinguishing the commuters and Merchant Marines is the presence of children. Only 17% of the Merchant Marines were childless (and since these were the youngest in the sample, they probably will not remain so). In contrast, almost half (46%) of the commuters had no children (see Table A5). This difference, we suspect, is a result of the fact that Merchant Marines work in jobs that require they live apart throughout their marital lives. Commuters are more likely to live in two homes only temporarily and are far less likely to choose to do so when children, especially young children, are still in the home (see Chapter 9).

While commuters and Merchant Marines differ in their socioeconomic profiles and whether or not they have children, they are similar in age and in the length of their marriages. The mean age for commuter husbands was 40; for sailing husbands, 45; for commuter wives, 39; and for sailing wives, 42 (see Table A6). So, too, more than half (52%) of sailing spouses had been married for 16 years or longer as were 37% of commuters. Neither group was made up primarily of newlyweds: the mean number of years married for commuters was 13 years; for sailing couples, 15 (see Table A7).

The final important distinction between commuters and Merchant Marines concerns their patterns of separation and reunion. Not only have most sailing couples lived apart longer than most commuters, when they do reunite during the sailing season, most of them have less time together. To understand the Merchant Marines separation pattern, it is necessary to review briefly the history of sailing schedules and recent changes in these schedules.

As recently as from five to eight years ago, before unions negotiated vacation time, sailors worked the whole sailing season, from the end of March to the end of December. This meant that husbands lived away from their families for at least nine months. Except for the occasional time off that happened to come in ports near their homes, most returned to their homes only for the winter lay-off when the lakes were not navigable. In the last few years, the establishment of "family leaves" has changed this pattern somewhat. In principle, these leaves allow men to work a set period (e.g., 60 to 70 days, depending on the company and the union) followed by a vacation period (20 to 30 days). However, in practice, many men still do not take the vacations allowed them and all but the youngest in our sample (who came in under the new plans) worked a substantial part of their careers under the more restrictive conditions. They are not paid for vacation time and, as a result, are often reluctant to use their allotments.

Because of the differences in how the men actually take their vacations, there is great variability in their patterns. Seventeen percent of these men took the vacations allowed them (working a set pattern "on" and "off"); 28% could take alternate vacations but only took one—usually 30 days—during the summer; 29% had sporadic schedules with vacation time as little as one week during the sailing season to as much as one week off for every two weeks of work. For most in this category, the pattern was 30 "on" and 14 "off"; 26% did not take any extended vacation during the season.

Overall then, even today, most of the men do not live at home for much of the nine-month sailing season. However, while at sea, most (69%) do sail into the ports near their homes at least every two weeks. But since they are still working when the boat is in port, and are only off duty for a matter of hours, only a few have the chance to go home. Usually their wives meet them at the docks. In addition, some wives (and sometimes older children) spend time on board ship. Officers' wives (depending on the company) join their husbands on board for one or two short trips (three or four days) during the sailing season. And, of course, they are in phone contact throughout the sailing season. (Husbands call wives when they are in port. Wives can, but rarely do, call their husbands ship-to-shore because this line is an open one which precludes private conversation.)

What these conditions mean is that most Merchant Marine spouses have lived apart for much longer than is true of commuters (only recently have they had the option to do otherwise) and most do not spend much time with their families during the sailing season. But, at the same time, compared to commuters, these women and men spend longer unbroken periods of time together in a single home during the winter months. Or, to use the words of these sailing spouses themselves, their marital life alternates between "feast and famine."

References

Acker, J. (1980). Women and stratification: A review of recent literature. *Contemporary Sociology, 9,* 25–34.

Adams, B. N. (1966). *Kinship in an urban setting.* Chicago: Markham.

Adams, B. N., & Butler, J. E. (1968). Occupational status and husband–wife social participation. *Social Forces, 45,* 501–507.

Aldous, J. (1978). *Family careers: Developmental changes in families.* New York: Wiley.

Aldous, J., Osmond, M., & Hicks, M. (1979). Men's work and men's families. In W. Burr, R. Hill, F. I. Nye, & I. Reiss (Eds.), *Contemporary theories and the family* (pp. 227–256). New York: Free Press.

Allen, S. (1982). Gender inequality and class formalism. In A. Giddens & G. MacKenzie (Eds.), *Social class and the division of labor* (pp. 137–147). Cambridge: Cambridge University Press.

Arling, G. (1976). The elderly widow and her family, neighbors, and friends. *Journal of Marriage and the Family, 38,* 757–768.

Athanasiou, R., Shaver, R., & Tavris, C. (1976). Sex (a report to *Psychology Today* readers). *Psychology Today, 4,* 39–53.

Babchuk, N. (1965). Primary friends and kin: A study of the associations of middle-class couples. *Social Forces, 43,* 483–493.

Babchuk, N., & Bates, A. (1963). The primary relations of middle-class couples: A study of male dominance. *American Sociological Review, 28,* 377–384.

Ball, D. (1968). Toward a sociology of telephones and telephoners. In M. Truzzi (Ed.), *Sociology of everyday life* (pp. 59–75). Englewood Cliffs, NJ: Prentice-Hall.

Barrett, M. (1980). *Women's oppression today.* London: Verso.

Becker, H. (1960). Notes on the concept of commitment. *American Journal of Sociology, 66,* 32–40.

Bell, R. (1981). *Worlds of friendship.* Beverly Hills, CA: Sage.

Bell, R., Turner, S., & Rosen, L. (1975). A multivariate analysis of extramarital coitus. *Journal of Marriage and the Family, 37,* 375–384.

Bender, D. (1967). A refinement of the concept of household: Families, co-residence, and domestic functions. *American Anthropologist, 69,* 493–504.

Benston, M. (1969). The political economy of women's liberation. *Monthly Review, 21,* 13–27.

Berelson, B., & Steiner, G. A. (1964). *Human behavior.* New York: Harcourt, Brace & World.

Berger, P., & Kellner, M. (1974). Marriage and the construction of reality. In R. L. Coser (Ed.), *The family: Its structure and function* (pp. 157–174). New York: St. Martin's Press.

Berheide, K. W., & Chow, E. (1983). *The interdependence of family and work: Some models and proposals.* Paper presented at the annual meeting of the American Sociological Association, Detroit, August.

Berk, R., & Berk, S. F. (1979). *Labor and leisure at home*. Beverly Hills, CA: Sage.

Bernard, J. (1972). *The future of marriage*. New York: Bantam.

Bernard, J. (1973). *The sex game*. New York: Atheneum.

Bird, C. (1979). *The two paycheck family*. New York: Rawson, Wade.

Birnbaum, J. A. (1975). Life patterns and self-esteem in gifted family-oriented and committed career women. In M. Mednick, S. Tangri, & L. W. Hoffman (Eds.), *Women and motivation* (pp. 369–419). New York: Wiley.

Blood, R. (1962). *Marriage*. NY: Free Press.

Blood, R., & Wolf, D. M. (1960). *Husbands and wives: The dynamics of married living*. New York: Macmillan.

Bohannan, P. (1968). An alternate residence classification. In P. Bohannan & J. Middleton (Eds.), *Marriage, family and residence* (pp. 317–323). New York: Natural History Press.

Boss, P., McCubbin, H. & Lester, G. (1979). The corporate executive wife's coping in response to routine husband–father absence: Implications for family stress theory. *Family Process, 18*, 79–86.

Brown, P. (1979). Sex differences in divorce. In E. S. Gomberg & V. Franks (Eds.), *Gender and disordered behavior* (pp. 101–123). New York: Brunner/Mazel.

Bryson, J. B., & Bryson, R. (1980). Salary and job performance differences in dual-career couples. In F. Pepitone-Rockwell (Ed.), *Dual-career couples* (pp. 241–260). Beverly Hills, CA: Sage.

Butler, M., & Paisley, W. (1980). Coordinated career couples: Convergence and divergence. In F. Pepitone-Rockwell (Ed.), *Dual-career couples* (pp. 207–228). Beverly Hills, CA: Sage.

Campbell, A., Converse, P., & Rodgers, W. (1976). *The quality of American life*. New York: Russell Sage.

Castles, S., & Kosack, G. (1973). *Immigrant workers and class structure in western Europe*. London: Oxford University Press.

Catalyst. (1982). *Corporations and two-career families: Directions for the future*. New York: Catalyst.

Clausen, J. A. (1976). The life course of individuals. In M. W. Riley & A. Foner (Eds.), *Aging and society: A sociology of age stratification* (Vol. 3, pp. 457–513). New York: Russell Sage.

Cleveland, M. (1976). Sex in marriage: At 40 and beyond. *The Family Coordinator, 25*, 233–240.

Cohen, G. (1977). Absentee husbands in spiralist families. *Journal of Marriage and the Family, 39*, 595–604.

Cole, J. R. (1979). *Fair science*. New York: Free Press.

Cooley, C. H. (1909). *Social organization*. New York: Charles Scribner Sons.

Cuber, J., & Harroff, P. (1966). *Sex and the significant American*. Baltimore, MD: Penguin.

Daniels, P., & Weingarten, K. (1982). *Sooner or later*. New York: Norton.

David, D., & Brannon, R. (1976). *The forty nine percent majority*. Boston: Addison-Wesley.

Degler, C. (1980). *At odds*. New York: Oxford University Press.

Deitch, C., & Sanderson, S. W. (1983). *The geographic coordinates of marriage and career*. Paper presented at the annual meeting of the American Sociological Association, Detroit, August.

Dobash, R. E., & Dobash, R. (1979). *Violence against wives*. New York: Free Press.

Douvan, E., & Pleck, J. (1978). Separation as support. In R. Rapoport & R. Rapoport (Eds.), *Working couples* (pp. 138–146). New York: Harper & Row.

Duberman, L. (1974). *Marriage and its alternatives*. New York: Praeger.

Duncan, O. D., Schuman, H., & Duncan, B. (1973). *Social change in metropolitan Detroit*. New York: Russell Sage.

Duncan, R. P., & Perucci, C. C. (1976). Dual occupation families and migration. *American Sociological Review, 41*, 252-261.

Duvall, E. M. (1971). *Family development*. Philadelphia: Lippincott.

Dworkin, A. (1974). *Woman hating*. New York: Dutton.

Easton, B. (1979). Feminism and the contemporary family. In N. Cott & E. Pleck (Eds.), *A heritage of her own* (pp. 558-578). New York: Simon & Schuster.

Elder, G. H. (1977). Family history in the life course. *Journal of Family History, 2*, 279-304.

Elder, G. H. (1978). Family history and the life course. In T. K. Hareven (Ed.), *Transitions: The family and the life course in historical perspective* (pp. 17-64). New York: Academic Press.

Elder, G. H. (1981). History and the family: The discovery of complexity. *Journal of Marriage and the Family, 43*, 489-520.

Epstein, B. (1982). Family politics and the new left. *Socialist Review, 12*, 141-162.

Epstein, C. (1970). *Woman's place*. Berkeley: University of California Press.

Ferber, M. (1982). Woman and work: Issues of the 1980s. *Signs, 8*, 273-296.

Ferber, M., & Huber, J. (1979). Husbands, wives and careers. *Journal of Marriage and the Family, 41*, 315-325.

Finlayson, A. (1976). Social networks as coping resources. *Social Science and Medicine, 10*, 97-103.

Fischer, C. (1982). *To dwell among friends*. Chicago: University of Chicago Press.

Fischer, C., & Phillips, S. (1981). Who is alone: Social characteristics of respondents with small social networks. In L. A. Peplau & D. Perlman (Eds.), *Loneliness: A sourcebook of current theory, research and therapy* (pp. 21-39). New York: Wiley.

Fischer, L. (1981). Transitions in the mother–daughter relationship. *Journal of Marriage and the Family, 43*, 613-622.

Friedan, B. (1963). *The feminine mystique*. New York: Norton.

Form, W. H., & Huber, J. (1976). Occupational power. In R. Dubin (Ed.), *Handbook of work, organization, and society*. (pp. 750-806). Chicago: Rand McNally.

Fowlkes, M. (1980). *Behind every successful man*. New York: Columbia University Press.

Gardiner, J. (1975). Women's domestic labor. *New Left Review, 89*, 47-58.

General Mills. (1981). *The General Mills American family report 1980-1981*. Minneapolis, MN: General Mills, Inc.

Gerber, I. (1977). The widower and the family. In P. Stein, J. Richman, & N. Hannon (Eds.), *The family: Functions, conflicts and symbols* (pp. 335-337). Boston: Addison-Wesley.

Gillard, N. C. (1979). The problem of geographic mobility for dual career couples. *Journal of Comparative Family Studies, 10*, 345-357.

Glenn, N. (1975). The contribution of marriage to the psychological well-being of males and females. *Journal of Marriage and the Family, 37*, 594-600.

Glenn, N., & Weaver, C. N. (1978). A multivariate, multisurvey study of marital happiness. *Journal of Marriage and the Family, 40*, 269-282.

Glick, P. C. (1977). A demographer looks at American families. In A. Skolnick & J. Skolnick (Eds.), *Family in transition* (2nd ed., pp 90-108). Boston: Little, Brown.

Goode, W. J. (1964). *The family*. Englewood Cliffs, NJ: Prentice-Hall.

Goode, W. J. (1970). *World revolution and family patterns*. New York: Free Press.

Grieco, M. S. (1982). Family structure and industrial employment: The role of information and migration. *Journal of Marriage and the Family, 45*, 701-707.

Gross, E. (1958). *Work and society*. New York: Thomas H. Crowell.

Hall, R. T. (1975). *Occupations and the social structure*. New York: McGraw-Hill.

Harding, S. (1981). Family reform movements: Recent feminism and its opposition. *Feminist Studies, 7*, 57-75.

Hardy, K. R. (1964). An appetitional theory of sexual motivation. *Psychological Review,* *71,* 1–9.

Hartmann, H. (1981). The family as the locus of gender, class and political struggle: The example of housework. *Signs, 6,* 366–394.

Heckman, N., Bryson, R., & Bryson, J. (1977). Problems of professional couples: A content analysis. *Journal of Marriage and the Family, 39,* 323–330.

Hennig, M., & Jardim, A. (1977). *The managerial women.* New York: Doubleday.

Hess, B. (1976). Friendship. In M. Riley, M. Johnson, & A. Foner (Eds.), *Aging and society.* (pp. 357–393). New York: Russell Sage.

Hetherington, E. M., Cox, M., & Cox, R. (1976). Divorced fathers. *Family Coordinator, 25,* 417–428.

Hill, R. (1949). *Families under stress.* Westport, CT: Greenwood Press.

Hirschorn, L. (1977). Social policy and the life cycle: A developmental perspective. *Social Service Review, 51,* 434–450.

Holmstrom, L. (1973). *The two-career family.* Cambridge, MA: Schenkman.

Houseknecht, S. K., & Macke, A. S. (1981). Combining marriage and career: The marital adjustment of professional women. *Journal of Marriage and the Family, 43,* 651–662.

Hunt, M. (1974). *Sexual behavior in the 1970s.* Chicago: Playboy Press.

Hunt, J. G., & Hunt, L. L. (1977). Dilemmas and contradictions of status: The case of the dual-career family. *Social Problems, 24,* 407–416.

Hunt, J. G., & Hunt, L. L. (1982). Dual-career families: Vanguard of the future or residue of the past? In J. Aldous (Ed.), *Two paychecks* (pp. 41–59). Beverly Hills, CA: Sage.

Kahn, R. (1981). Work, stress and social support. In D. G. McGuigan (Ed.), *Changing family, changing workplace: New research* (pp. 67–76). Ann Arbor, MI: University of Michigan Center for Continuing Education of Women.

Kammeyer, K. C. W. (1977). *Confronting the issues.* Boston: Allyn & Bacon.

Kanter, R. M. (1977). *Work and family in the United States: A critical review and agenda for research and policy.* New York: Russell Sage.

Keller, S. (1982). *Love and the family: Past and future.* Paper presented at the University of Hartford colloquia, "New Images of Love," June.

Kirschner, B., & Walum, L. (1978). Two location families: Married singles. *Alternative Lifestyles, 1,* 513–525.

Kohen, J., & Feldberg, R. (1977). Isolation and invasion: The conditions of marriage and divorce. In P. Stein, J. Richman, & N. Hannon (Eds.), *The family: Functions, conflicts, and symbols* (pp. 314–324). Boston: Addison-Wesley.

Ladinsky, J. (1967a). The geographic mobility of technical and professional manpower. *Journal of Human Resources, 4,* 475–494.

Ladinsky, J. (1967b). Occupational determinants of geographic mobility among professional workers. *American Sociological Review, 32,* 257–264.

Laslett, B. (1979). *Production, reproduction and social change: A theory of family in history.* Paper delivered at the annual meeting of the American Sociological Association, Boston, August.

Laslett, P. (1974). *Household and family in past time.* London: Cambridge University Press.

Laws, J. L. (1976). *Patriarchy as paradigm: The challenge for feminist scholarship.* Paper presented at the annual meeting of the American Sociological Association, New York, March.

Lee, G. R. (1980). Kinship in the seventies: A decade review of research and theory. *Journal of Marriage and the Family, 42,* 923–934.

Leslie, G. R., & Richardson, R. H. (1961). Life cycle, career pattern and the decision to move. *American Sociological Review, 26,* 894–902.

Lewis, R. A. (1981). *Men in difficult times.* Englewood Cliffs, NJ: Prentice-Hall.

Lewis, L. S., & Brisset, D. (1967). Sex as work. *Social Problems, 15,* 8–17.

Lichter, D. (1982). The migration of dual-worker families: Does the wife's job matter? *Social Science Quarterly, 63,* 48–56.

Linn, E. L. (1971). Women dentists: Career and family. *Social Problems, 18,* 393–403.

Litwak, E. (1960). Geographic mobility and extended family cohesion. *American Sociological Review, 25,* 385–394.

Litwak, E., & Figueira, J. (1970). Technological innovation and ideal forms of family structure in an industrial democratic society. In R. Hill & R. Fox (Eds.), *Families in east and west* (pp. 348–396). Paris: Mouton & Co.

Litwak, E., & Meyer, H. (1966). A balance theory of coordination between bureaucratic organization and community primary groups. *Administrative Science Quarterly, 11,* 31–58.

Litwak, E., & Szelenyi, I. (1969). Primary group structures and their functions: Kin, neighbors, and friends. *American Sociological Review, 34,* 465–481.

Locksley, A. (1980). On the effects of wives' employment on marital adjustment and companionship. *Journal of Marriage and the Family, 42,* 337–346.

Long, L. (1974). Women's labour force participation and the residential mobility of families. *Social Forces, 52,* 342–348.

Lopata, H. (1979). *Women as widows.* New York: Elsevier.

Lopata, H. (1980). Spouses' contributions to each others' roles. In F. Pepitone-Rockwell (Ed.), *Dual-career couples* (pp. 111–141). Beverly Hills, CA: Sage.

Macke, A., Bohrnstedt, G., & Bernstein, I. (1979). Housewives' self-esteem and their husbands' success: The myth of vicarious involvement. *Journal of Marriage and the Family, 41,* 51–57.

Margolis, D. R. (1979). *The managers: Corporate life in America.* New York: William Morrow.

Martin, D. (1976). *Battered wives.* San Francisco: Glide.

Masters, W. H., & Johnson, V. (1970). *Human sexual inadequacy.* Boston: Little, Brown.

Mauss, M. (1954). *The gift.* Glencoe, IL: Free Press.

Maykovich, M. K. (1976). Attitude vs. behavior in extra-marital sexual relations. *Journal of Marriage and the Family, 38,* 693–699.

McAuley, W. J., & Nutty, C. L. (1982). Residential preferences and moving behavior: A family life cycle analysis. *Journal of Marriage and the Family, 44,* 301–310.

McCubbin, H. (1979). Integrating coping behavior and family stress. *Journal of Marriage and the Family, 41,* 237–244.

McCubbin, H., Dahl, B., & Ross, B. A. (1974). The returned prisoner of war: Factors in family reintegration. *Journal of Marriage and the Family, 37,* 471–478.

McCubbin, H., Dahl, B., Lester, G., Benson, D., & Robertson, M. (1976). Coping repertoires of families: Adapting to prolonged war-induced separation. *Journal of Marriage and the Family, 38,* 461–471.

McCubbin, H., Hunter, E. J., & Dahl, B. (1975). Residuals of war: Families of prisoners of war and servicemen missing in action. *Journal of Social Issues, 31,* 95–109.

McLanahan, S. S., Wedemeyer, N. V., & Adelberg, T. (1981). Network structure, social support, and psychological well-being in the single parent family. *Journal of Marriage and the Family, 43,* 601–612.

McLuhan, M. (1964). *Understanding media.* New York: Signet.

Merton, R. (1957). *Social theory and social structure.* Glencoe, IL: Free Press.

Miller, B. C. (1976). A multivariate developmental model of marital satisfaction. *Journal of Marriage and the Family, 38,* 643–658.

Miller, D., & Form, W. (1964). *Industrial sociology*. New York: Harper & Row.

Miller, S., Corrales, R., & Wackman, D. (1975). Recent progress in understanding and facilitating marital communication. *Family Coordinator, 24*, 143-152.

Mincer, J. (1977). *Family migration decisions*. Labor Workshop, mimeo.

Modell, J., & Hareven, T. (1978). Urbanization and the malleable household: An examination of boarding and lodging in American families. In M. Gordon (Ed.), *The American family in social historical perspective* (2nd ed., pp. 51-68). New York: St. Martin's Press.

Montgomery, B. (1981). The form and function of quality communication in marriage. *Family Relations, 30*, 21-30.

Morris, P. (1965). *Prisoners and their families*. London: Allen & Unwin.

Mott, P., (1965). *Shift work: The social, psychological and physical consequences*. Ann Arbor: University of Michigan Press.

Murdock, G. P. (1949). *Social structure*. New York: Free Press.

Murray, C. (1981). *Families divided: The impact of migrant labor in Lesotho*. Cambridge: Cambridge University Press.

Navran, L. (1967). Communication and adjustment in marriage. *Family Process, 6*, 173-184.

Neimi, B. (1975). Geographic immobility and labor force mobility: A study of female unemployment. In C. B. Lloyd (Ed.), *Sex, discrimination and the division of labor* (pp. 66-87). New York: Columbia University Press.

Neubeck, G. (1969). *Extramarital relations*. Englewood Cliffs, NJ: Prentice-Hall.

Neugarten, B. (1979). Time, age and the life cycle. *American Journal of Psychiatry, 136*, 887-894.

Oakley, A. (1981). *Subject women*. New York: Pantheon.

O'Neil, N., & O'Neil, G. (1975). *Open marriage*. New York: Avon.

Oppenheimer, V. K. (1970). *The female labor force in the United States*. Westport, CT: Greenwood Press.

Oppenheimer, V. K. (1977). The sociology of women's economic role in the family. *American Sociological Review, 42*, 381-405.

Oppenheimer, V. K. (1982). *Work and family: A study in social demography*. New York: Academic Press.

Orthner, J., Sullivan, J., & Crossman, S. (1980). *Long distance marriage*. Unpublished paper.

Otto, H. (1970). *The family in search of a future*. New York: Appleton-Century-Crofts.

Papanek, H. (1973). Men, women, and work: Reflections on the two person career. *American Journal of Sociology, 78*, 852-872.

Parsons, T. (1955). *Family, society, and interaction process*. Glencoe, IL: Free Press.

Parsons, T. (1965). The normal American family. In S. M. Farber, P. Mustacchi, & R. H. L. Wilson (Eds.), *Man and civilization* (pp. 31-50). New York: McGraw-Hill.

Paykel, E. S., Emms, E. M., Fletcher, J., & Rassaby, E. S. (1980). Life events and social support in depression. *British Journal of Psychiatry, 136*, 339-346.

Pietropinto, A. P. (1980). Frequency of coitus after twenty years of marriage. *Medical Aspects of Human Sexuality, 10*, 5.

Piotrkowski, C. S. (1979). *Work and family system*. New York: Macmillan.

Pleck, J. (1982). *The myth of masculinity*. Cambridge, MA: MIT Press.

Pleck, J., Staines, G. L., & Long, L. (1980). Conflicts between work and family life. *Monthly Labor Review, 103*, 29-32.

Poloma, M. M., Pendleton, B. F., & Garland, T. N. (1982). Reconsidering the dual-career marriage. In J. Aldous (Ed.), *Two paychecks* (pp. 173-192). Beverly Hills, CA: Sage.

Powell, B. (1977). The empty nest, employment and psychiatric symptoms in college-educated women. *Psychology of Women Quarterly, 2*, 35-43.

Price-Bonham, S. (1972). Missing in action men: A study of their wives. *International Journal of Sociology of the Family, 2*, 202–211.

Ramey, J. W. (1977). Alternative life styles. *Society, 14*, 43–47.

Ramez, J. (1978). Experimental familial forms: The family of the future. *Marriage and Family Review, 1*, 1–9.

Rapoport, R., & Rapoport, R. N. (1976). *Dual-career families re-examined*. New York: Harper & Row.

Rausch, H., Goodrich, W., & Campbell, J. D. (1973). Adaptation to the first years of marriage. *Psychiatry, 26*, 368–380.

Renshaw, J. R. (1976). An exploration of the dynamics of the overlapping worlds of work and family life. *Family Process, 15*, 143–165.

Robinson, J. N. (1980). Household technology and household work. In S. Berk (Ed.), *Women and household labor* (pp. 53–68). Beverly Hills, CA: Sage.

Rodgers, R. H. (1973). *Family, interaction, and transaction: The developmental approach.* Englewood Cliffs, NJ: Prentice-Hall.

Rollins, B., & Cannon, K. (1974). Marital satisfaction over the family life cycle: A re-evaluation. *Journal of Marriage and the Family, 36*, 271–282.

Rollins, B., & Feldman, H. (1970). Marital satisfaction over the family life cycle. *Journal of Marriage and the Family, 32*, 20–28.

Rossi, A. (1980). Life span theories and women's lives. *Signs, 6*, 4–32.

Rossi, P. (1979). *Why families move* (2nd ed.). Beverly Hills, CA: Sage.

Rubin, L. (1976). *Worlds of pain*. New York: Basic Books.

Rubin, L. (1979). *Women of a certain age*. New York: Harper Colophon.

Schafer, R. & Keith, P. M. (1981). Equity in marital roles across the family life cycle. *Journal of Marriage and the Family, 43*, 359–368.

Schlafly, P. (1977). *The power of the positive woman*. New York: Jove.

Schneider, D. (1968). *American kinship: A cultural account*. Englewood Cliffs, NJ: Prentice-Hall.

Seecombe, W. (1973). The housewife and her labor under capitalism. *New Left Review, 83*, 3–24.

Seidenberg, R. (1975). *Corporate wives — Corporate casualties?* New York: Anchor.

Shorter, E. (1975). *The making of the modern family*. New York: Basic Books.

Simmel, G. (1950). *The sociology of Georg Simmel* (K. H. Wolff, Trans.). New York: Free Press.

Singh, B. K., Walton, B. L., & Williams, J. S. (1976). Extramarital sexual permissiveness: Conditions and contingencies. *Journal of Marriage and the Family, 38*, 701–712.

Skolnick, A (1978). *The intimate environment* (2nd ed.). Toronto: Little, Brown.

Smith, P. (1978). Domestic labor and Marxist theory of value. In A. Kuhn & A. Wolpe (Eds.), *Feminism and materialism* (pp. 198–219). London: Routledge & Kegan Paul.

Spanier, G., Lewis, R. A., & Cole, C. L. (1975). Marital adjustment over the family life cycle: The issue of curvilinearity. *Journal of Marriage and the Family, 37*, 263–275.

Stein, P. (1976). *Single*. Englewood Cliffs, NJ: Prentice-Hall.

Stein, P. (Ed.). (1981). *Single life*. New York: St. Martin's Press.

Stolz, L. M. (1954). *Father relations of war born children*. Palo Alto, CA: Stanford University Press.

Stone, L. (1977). *The family, sex, and marriage in England: 1500*–1800. New York: Harper Colophon.

Stoper, E. (1982). Alternative work patterns and the double life. In E. Bonaparth (Ed.), *Women, power, and policy* (pp. 90–108). New York: Pergamon.

Straus, M., Gelles, R. J., & Steinmetz, S. K. (1981). *Behind closed doors*. New York: Anchor.

Stueve, C. A., & Gerson, K. (1977). Personal relations across the life-cycle. In C. Fischer, R. Jackson, C. A. Stueve, K. Gerson, L. M. Jones, with M. Baldassare (Eds.), *Networks and places: Social relations in an urban setting* (pp. 79–99). New York: Free Press.

Sussman, M. (1965). Relationships of adult children with their parents in the United States. In E. Shanas & G. F. Streib (Eds.), *Social structure and family generational relations* (pp. 62–92). Englewood Cliffs, NJ: Prentice-Hall.

Sussman, M. (1975). The four F's of variant family forms and marriage styles. *Family Coordinator, 24*, 557–576.

Swenson, C., Eskew, R. W., & Kohlhepp, K. A. (1981). Stage of family life cycle, ego development, and the marriage relationship. *Journal of Marriage and the Family, 43*, 841–854.

Tamir, L. M., & Antonucci, T. C. (1981). Self-perception, motivation and social support through the family life course. *Journal of Marriage and the Family, 43*, 151–160.

Thomson, E., & Williams, R. (1982). Beyond wives' sociology: A method for analyzing couple data. *Journal of Marriage and the Family, 44*, 999–1008.

Toennies, F. (1887). *Community and society* (C. P. Loomis, Trans.). New York: Harper & Row, 1957.

U. S. Bureau of the Census. (1976). Number, timing, and duration of marriages and divorces in the United States: 1975. *Current Population Reports*, Series P-20, No. 297. Washington, DC: GPO.

U.S. Bureau of the Census. (1980). *Statistical Abstracts of the United States*. Washington, DC: GPO.

Valliant, G. (1977). *Adaptations to life*. Boston: Little, Brown.

Valliant, G., & MacArthur, C. (1972). Natural history of male psychologic health: I. The adult cycle from 18–50. *Seminars in Psychiatry, 4*, 4.

Vanek, J. (1980). Household work, wage work and sexual equality. In S. Berk (Ed.), *Women and household labor* (pp. 275–291). Beverly Hills, CA: Sage.

Van Mering, F. (1971). Professional and nonprofessional women as mothers. In A. Theodore (Ed.), *The professional woman* (pp. 556–583). Cambridge, MA: Schenkman.

Verdon, M. (1980). Shaking off the domestic yoke or the sociological significance of residence. *Comparative Studies in Society and History, 22*, 109–132.

Waller, W., & Hill, R. (1965). Habit systems in married life. In H. Rodman (Ed.), *Marriage, family and society: A reader* (pp. 85–91). New York: Random House.

Weil, M. (1971). An analysis of the factors influencing married women's actual or planned work participation. In A. Theodore (Ed.), *The professional woman* (pp. 453–464). Cambridge, MA: Schenkman.

Weinbaum, B., & Bridges, A. (1979). The other side of the paycheck: Monopoly capital and the structure of consumption. *Monthly Review, 28*, 88–103.

Weiss, R. (1979). *Going it alone*. New York: Basic Books.

Weitzman, L. (1981). *The marital contract*. New York: Free Press.

Wilkie, J. R. (1981). The trend toward delayed parenthood. *Journal of Marriage and the Family, 43*, 583–592.

Wirth, L. (1938). Urbanism as a way of life. *American Journal of Sociology, 44*, 1–24.

Wolfe, T. (1976). The "me" decade. *New York, 9* (August 23), 26–40.

Yogev, S. (1981). Do professional women have egalitarian marital relationships? *Journal of Marriage and the Family, 43*, 865–872.

Yohalem, A. (1979). *The careers of professional women*. Montclair, NJ: Allanheld Osmun.

Young, M., & Willmott, P. (1973). *The symmetrical family*. New York: Pantheon.

Zaretsky, E. (1976). *Capitalism, the family, and personal life*. New York: Harper & Row.

Author Index

Subject Index